POLITICAL ECONOMY
RESEARCH FOCUS

POLITICAL ECONOMY RESEARCH FOCUS

WALTER R. LEVIN
EDITOR

Nova Science Publishers, Inc.
New York

For permission to use material from this book please contact us:
Telephone 631-231-7269; Fax 631-231-8175
Web Site: http://www.novapublishers.com

NOTICE TO THE READER

The Publisher has taken reasonable care in the preparation of this book, but makes no expressed or implied warranty of any kind and assumes no responsibility for any errors or omissions. No liability is assumed for incidental or consequential damages in connection with or arising out of information contained in this book. The Publisher shall not be liable for any special, consequential, or exemplary damages resulting, in whole or in part, from the readers' use of, or reliance upon, this material.

Independent verification should be sought for any data, advice or recommendations contained in this book. In addition, no responsibility is assumed by the publisher for any injury and/or damage to persons or property arising from any methods, products, instructions, ideas or otherwise contained in this publication.

This publication is designed to provide accurate and authoritative information with regard to the subject matter covered herein. It is sold with the clear understanding that the Publisher is not engaged in rendering legal or any other professional services. If legal or any other expert assistance is required, the services of a competent person should be sought. FROM A DECLARATION OF PARTICIPANTS JOINTLY ADOPTED BY A COMMITTEE OF THE AMERICAN BAR ASSOCIATION AND A COMMITTEE OF PUBLISHERS.

LIBRARY OF CONGRESS CATALOGING-IN-PUBLICATION DATA

Political economy research focus / Walter R. Levin (editor).
   p. cm.
  Includes bibliographical references.
  ISBN 978-1-60456-154-8 (hardcover)
  1. Economics--Political aspects--Research. 2. Economics--Political aspects--Case studies. I. Levin, Walter R.
  HB74.P65P658   2008
  330.072--dc22   2008007295

Published by Nova Science Publishers, Inc. New York

CONTENTS

PREFACE

Contemporarily, political economy refers to different, but related, approaches to studying economic and political behaviours, ranging from the combining of economics with other fields, to the using of different, fundamental assumptions that challenge orthodox economic assumptions. Political economy most commonly refers to interdisciplinary studies drawing upon economics, law, and political science in explaining how political institutions, the political environment, and the economic system - capitalist, socialist, mixed - influence each other. When narrowly construed, it refers to applied topics in economics implicating public policy, such as monopoly, market protection, government fiscal policy, and rent seeking.This book presents the newest research in the field.

Chapter 1 - There exists a large volume of literature on Korean success in economic development. However, Korea has experienced several economic crises in the development process. While the financial crisis in 1997 has received substantial amount of attention in the mass media and in the academic as well, Korea had not been immune to economic crisis prior to the 1997 financial crisis. This chapter reviews the experiences of economic crises and their resolutions in Korea since 1960s. The chapter examines each crisis and finds out that the factors that caused one previous crisis later brought about another crisis repeatedly. This indicates that the measures to resolve the previous crises were ultimately ineffective in the sense that the fundamental causes for the economic crisis had remained unresolved and, as a result, recurrence of the crisis has not been prevented. Most of the past crisis resolution measures were focused on disposing of the losses incurred by firms and banks through such instruments as bail-out loans. Stabilization measures were adopted just when the economy had begun to stagnate after a long period of boom, and seldom contributed to preventing recurrence of crisis; they rather amplified the intensity of the crisis. These results contain lessons for the current and future structural adjustment policy, to be adopted as a means to prevent recurrence of economic crisis. First, it should be designed in such a way as to encourage private agents to take initiative, with the government abstaining from direct intervention such as bail-out loans. This would eventually strengthen private sector capacities to overcome adverse shocks. Second, stabilization policies should be implemented in such a preemptive manner that they can prevent an exceptional boom or wide-spread speculation.

Chapter 2 - As George De Martino argues in *Global Economy, Global Justice,* neo-classical economics smuggles in a host of dubious normative premises beneath its veneer of scientific objectivity. In response, De Martino calls for an explicitly normative political economy oriented by the question: what constitutes a just economic outcome' My paper will focus on developing an answer to this question rooted in the idea, systematised in the work of John McMurtry, of the 'life-ground of value.' The paper will begin with an account of human social-organic nature. The goal of the first part of the paper is to demonstrate (against neo-classical orthodoxy) that human beings are defined by a set of objective organic, socio-cultural, and temporal needs. Because human beings must satisfy these needs through cooperative productive systems (economies), every such system contains an in-built 'life-grounded' principle of evaluation. Thus the basic normative question to be asked of every socio-economic system is: how well is it able to satisfy the defining needs of its members? In the second section the paper will evaluate the global economic system from this perspective. I will argue that the current global economic system fails to meet the objective needs of its members because its ruling value system is disconnected from the life-ground of value. The ruling value system assumes that whatever investment produces profitable returns is a good (just) economic outcome. The final section of the paper presents an interpretation of Pat Devine's 'negotiated coordination' economy as a life-grounded alternative to the present global system.

Chapter 3 - This paper argues that religion confers survival benefits on societies and individuals because it allows a general lowering of time preference. Time preference is one of the most basic economic concepts and a fundamental category of human action. Theories of interest, term structure, and opportunity cost all depend on time preference, which is also the basis for capital budgeting in modern finance. This paper establishes how and why the emergence of religious belief supported a reduction of time preference, allowing for employment of capital in time-consuming roundabout means of production.

The economic concept of time preference explains why belief in God conferred survival value as we evolved, and why it no longer does so. Time preference is the desire to enjoy immediate gratification. Though considered a universal determinant of human action, it has been observed to vary greatly in intensity across individuals. For example, time preference is especially high in children who lack experience and maturity, and in individuals with low life expectancy. Time preference is also high for criminals, and the general lowering of time preference both facilitates and is facilitated by the development of civilization and the increase in complexity of social relationships. The essence of low time preference is planning for the future, a willingness to delay gratification, and patience to wait for future benefits.

Once religious belief emerged among our distant ancestors, to be transmitted as a successful adaptation, it must have contributed to the reproductive success of the believers. Primitive humans experienced an appalling life expectancy. Homo sapiens evolved in an environment where infant mortality approached 100% and life expectancy *for those surviving infancy* was certainly below 20 years. Our remote ancestors had little reason not to consume all their seed corn at once, and deistic belief mitigated their natural tendency to enjoy whatever gratification they could immediately control. Religious belief enhanced the survival prospects of both individuals and communities by conditioning them to engage in longer-range planning through such beliefs as life-after-death, spirit survival, and reincarnation.

The survival benefit of religious belief is mostly lost once life expectancy lengthens to the point where, in and of itself, it results in lowered time preference and more responsible, more forward-looking behavior from the majority of agents in the community.

Chapter 4 - This paper analyses some issues related to the design and potential asymmetric effects of the monetary policy in the Eurozone. The authors analysis of monthly data from January 1999 to November 2005 by cointegration techniques suggests that the design of the monetary policy by the European Central Bank (ECB) can be characterized by a model that comprises a Taylor rule, in which a higher weight is given to the goal of price stability than to the expansion of output. Next, the authors try to assess whether the single monetary policy has similarly suited all the members of the European Monetary Union (EMU) to the same extent. They conclude that the costs associated to the single monetary policy are not the same for all of them. In particular, the higher the inflation rate in a particular country, the larger the costs entailed by the loss of monetary independence.

Chapter 5 - In this research, the authors explain that, in Spain, a relatively minor reform in unemployment benefits regulation has introduced a system to dismiss at will. Therefore, the fairness of the dismissal is not important in practice, although the whole legal system requiring a fair cause for dismissals remains. They present different empirical evidence supporting such statement.

Chapter 6 - Using a balanced-growth model with physical and human capital accumulation where the equilibrium allocation of skills between alternative uses (production of goods and education) is endogenously determined, this article analyzes quantitatively the long run effects of changes in the saving rate and in income distribution (i.e., in the shares of physical and human capital in income) on investment in human capital, growth of income, and the ratio of human to physical capital (all these variables being measured in efficiency units). It is assumed that in the long run the ratio of physical to human capital is constant, so that these two production factors can grow at the same rate. This rate is a function of the economy's exogenous technological and preference parameters and depends positively on the share of skills invested in human capital formation. In equilibrium, the authors also find that population growth is neither necessary nor conducive to economic growth and that the level of real income in efficiency units depends linearly on the level of human capital in efficiency units and is independent of population size.

Chapter 7 - This chapter considers the political economy of rent-seeking under the circumstances of concentrated markets. In concentrated markets there exist an "economic elite" whose members control the major companies of the market. The major companies, accompanied by their shareholders, participate in several rent-seeking contests, and as a result, one shareholder may co-operate with player A against player B in one contest, while the same shareholder may co-operate with player B against player A in a different contest. The authors consider the implications of this concentrated situation over the rent dissipation and the expenditures of the different participants in the contests and compare these results to those established in the traditional rent-seeking literature. They find that mutual interests among shareholders reduce the rent dissipation in the concentrated market. They also examine the behaviors of participants when the value of the rent changes in their model compared to the traditional model presented in the literature.

Chapter 8 – The authors goal in this paper is not so much to present a case for the right answer for Canada or the UK as to try to lay out the beginnings of a framework for analyzing both the normative economic issue of what countries should do and the positive political issue of what they are likely to do. A key theme is that the simple choices involving monetary integration involve a complex range of issues, some of which are still only dimly understood. Fortunately, however, we do have considerable analysis, both political and economic, on which we can draw.

In: Political Economy Research Focus
Editor: Walter R. Levin, pp. 1-45
ISBN: 978-1-60456-154-8
© 2008 Nova Science Publishers, Inc.

Chapter 1

WHY HAS KOREA EXPERIENCED SO MANY ECONOMIC CRISES? THE POLITICAL ECONOMY OF RECURRING ECONOMIC CRISIS IN KOREA

Jong Kyu Lee[1,] and Sanghack Lee[2,†]*

[1]Institute for Monetary and Economic Research, The Bank of Korea
[2]School of Economics, Kookmin University

ABSTRACT

There exists a large volume of literature on Korean success in economic development. However, Korea has experienced several economic crises in the development process. While the financial crisis in 1997 has received substantial amount of attention in the mass media and in the academic as well, Korea had not been immune to economic crisis prior to the 1997 financial crisis. This chapter reviews the experiences of economic crises and their resolutions in Korea since 1960s. The chapter examines each crisis and finds out that the factors that caused one previous crisis later brought about another crisis repeatedly. This indicates that the measures to resolve the previous crises were ultimately ineffective in the sense that the fundamental causes for the economic crisis had remained unresolved and, as a result, recurrence of the crisis has not been prevented. Most of the past crisis resolution measures were focused on disposing of the losses incurred by firms and banks through such instruments as bail-out loans. Stabilization measures were adopted just when the economy had begun to stagnate after a long period of boom, and seldom contributed to preventing recurrence of crisis; they rather amplified the intensity of the crisis. These results contain lessons for the current and future structural adjustment policy, to be adopted as a means to prevent recurrence of economic crisis. First, it should be designed in such a way as to encourage private agents to take initiative, with the government abstaining from direct intervention such as bail-out

---

[*] Tel: +82-2-759-5412, Fax: +82-2-759-5410, e-mail: jonglee@bok.or.kr
[†] Corresponding author. Address: School of Economics, Kookmin University, Seoul 136-702, South Korea. Tel.: +82-2-910-4546, Fax: +82-2-910-4519, e-mail: slee@kookmin.ac.kr

loans. This would eventually strengthen private sector capacities to overcome adverse shocks. Second, stabilization policies should be implemented in such a preemptive manner that they can prevent an exceptional boom or wide-spread speculation.

Keywords: Korea, Economic Crisis, Crisis Resolution, Structural Adjustment, Macroeconomic Policy, Economic History of Korea

I. INTRODUCTION

There exists a large volume of literature on Korean[1] success in economic development. However, it should be noted that Korea has also experienced several economic crises in the development process. While the financial crisis in 1997 has received huge amount of attention in the mass media and in the academic as well, Korea was not immune to economic crisis prior to 1997 financial crisis. This neglect of past economic crisis of Korea is partly attributable to spectacular performance of the Korean economy. It should, however, be noted that Korean economy had also experienced several economic crises before the 1997 crisis.

The Korean government adopted various policies or institutional devices to prevent recurrence of economic crisis since 1997. Commonly known as 'restructuring policy' or 'structural adjustment policy,' these policies aimed at preventing crisis by improving the structural efficiency of the Korean economy.

Whether such restructuring policies are on the right track, however, has been heavily disputed[2]. In light of a wide variety of criticism from various points of view, this chapter tries to reinterpret Korean experiences of economic crises in the past from a new viewpoint, and also tries to extract lessons for structural adjustment policies.

Most of the discussions and research on structural adjustment, now being extensively studied around the world, draw their arguments from experiences in the process of economic development, rather than from a general theoretical framework. The concept of structural adjustment was introduced by the World Bank; the World Bank came to use the term structural adjustment as it recognized, after many trials and errors, the importance of improving the efficiency of an economic system as a whole in achieving sustained growth. Since, it is practically impossible to design an ideal economic system *a priori*, any country that wants to improve the efficiency of its economic system will need to learn from its own experience, or from other countries' experiences in similar situations.

Foreign experience has only limited usefulness as a reference, however, because there are many factors specific to a country that make its experience difficult to apply to another country's structural adjustment process. In this respect, deriving lessons for a country from its own experience of structural adjustment would be more useful. Perhaps this is why, in the U.S.A., the Great Depression of 1929 is still a popular topic of research. Also, it is quite

---

[1] Korea refers to South Korea.
[2] The set of methods for assessing the effectiveness of restructuring policy includes: 1) comparing performances before and after reforms are introduced, 2) comparing actual performance with reform objectives, 3) comparing the economic performance of the reforming country with those of non-reforming countries, 4) comparing the economic performances of cases of reforming and cases of not reforming through counterfactual simulation (Schandler et al., 1995).

natural for one who wants to resolve a present problem to seek lessons from the past successes and failures.

Despite all the past restructuring, Korea is not immune to future economic crisis. The purpose of this research is to find out ways to enhance the effectiveness of measures for possible future economic crisis in Korea, by making use of the lessons extracted from the past economic crises Korea experienced since the launch of industrialization policy in the 1960s, and their resolutions. Even though Korea's history of economic development is relatively short, it contains several episodes of crisis worthy of thorough analysis. In particular, the experience of overcoming several crises in the past can be a valuable source of lessons useful in resolving the future crisis. Korean experience in crisis resolution as well as economic development can be a valuable asset to other countries seeking to emulate Korean economic success.

This chapter will look into the specifics and backgrounds of, and the policy measures undertaken to deal with four crises in Korea, and analyze the effectiveness of those policy measures. Besides the period since 1997, Korea has had several occasions of severe economic difficulties – including the period from the late 1960s to the early 1970s, that around 1980, and that from the late 1980s to the early 1990s. By comparing the specifics of each crisis, we are able to better understand the nature of the economic crises in Korea. Further, by assessing the effects of policies to resolve the former crises, we may be better able to derive some important policy agenda for overcoming-the future crisis.

The discussion will proceed keeping an eye on the causal aspects of each economic crisis: formation of bubbles, deterioration of profitability in the corporate sector, weaknesses in financial structure, maturity mismatches, and policy mistakes. This will provide a basis for comparing crises whose actual causes differed from each other in kind and in specifics.

It should also be mentioned that this chapter reviews critically the past experience in coping with crises. This criticism stems from the observation that the same factors that had caused a previous crisis later brought about another crisis repeatedly. For example, the factors behind the 1997 crisis were similar to those behind the past crises. This implies that the measures taken to resolve the previous crises were ultimately limited and/or ineffective.

The remainder of this paper is organized as follows. Section II starts with general discussion on the definition and causes of economic crisis. Section II then describes and analyzes the details, backgrounds, and policy responses by government to the four Korean episodes of economic crises[3]. In Section III the crisis resolution measures are assessed in terms of their effectiveness. On the basis of this, derivation of effective crisis resolution measures will be considered. In Section IV, the characteristics of the 1997 economic crisis are summarized, and the structural adjustment policy implemented afterwards is compared with those implemented in past cases. Finally, in the Concluding Remarks, the usefulness and limitations of this research are discussed and new research directions are suggested.

---

[3] The main contents of Section II and Section III are excerpted from Lee (2000). Those who are interested in details are advised to refer to Lee (2000).

II. KOREAN EXPERIENCE IN RESOLVING ECONOMIC CRISES

1. Four Economic Crises of Korea

An economic crisis is a situation of extreme economic difficulties, such as firms and banks going out of business one after another, the prices of goods, exchange rates, or interest rates fluctuating very rapidly, or production decreasing sharply with the unemployment rate increasing. Thus, it is sometimes treated as being equivalent to a severe recession.

This concept, however, does not give any information about the economic crisis, and is not so much helpful to theoretically grasping its systematic aspects. It is thus preferable to define an economic crisis as a situation in which exceptional responses of economic agents to unexpected economic events hamper the proper functioning of major parts of the economic system, and in extreme cases cause the whole system to collapse. In short, an economic crisis refers to a situation in which part or all of the economic system does not function normally, causing economic difficulties.

An economic system comprises various components. When all of the components combine organically and harmoniously, it works properly. When the various components do not combine harmoniously, it malfunctions. In this sense, an economic crisis is a kind of coordination failure – one especially severe in nature.

Table 1. Factors Behind Economic Crises

Theory		Causes
Business Cycles		– ·macroeconomic disequilibrium: over-investment, under-consumption – ·discrepancy between monetary and natural(real) interest rates – ·misperception or incorrect forecast – ·changes in profit rate
Monetarist		– ·banking panic
Financial Instability Hypothesis		– ·bubbles: speculative mania
Micro-finance Theory	Intrinsic Factors	– ·imperfect information – ·information asymmetry – ·nature of debt contracts – ·asset specificity – ·herd behavior – ·"me-first" tendency
	Immediate Causes	– ·deterioration of profitability – ·financial fragility – ·maturity mismatches – ·bubbles
Others		– ·policy failures – ·failures in internal risk control

The term "economic crisis" carries a strong negative connotation since the phenomenon itself brings economic suffering to many people. It also has a positive aspect, however, because economic problems which need to be addressed reveal themselves in a crisis. For instance, economic crisis tends to occur when an economy suffers from difficulties in adapting itself to a changed environment; once it occurs, the part of the economic system which has been unable to adapt is revealed. Therefore, an economic crisis also plays the positive role of informing policy makers and the general public of what the fundamental weaknesses of the system are, thus providing an opportunity for an economy to correct them and prosper again.

In the course of economic development, an economy faces significant changes in its economic environment. Sometimes, it adapts itself to them successfully. Sometimes, it fails. In the latter case, a crisis or a crisis-like situation takes place. In this sense, economic crisis represents the adaptive failure of an economy. Finally, an economic crisis, though it is exceptional and unique, is a universal phenomenon that can happen to any economy in any phase of development.

The factors leading to economic crises, as identified in the literature, are summarized in Table 1. This list is not intended to be exhaustive; there are many unknown causes, as is revealed by the fact that a crisis usually comes by surprise.

There are two kinds of theories for explaining the factors behind an economic crisis[4]. One pertains to the causes for an economic crisis and the other to the propagation mechanism of an economic crisis. Business cycle theories, monetarists' views, the financial instability hypothesis, and microeconomic finance theories are examples of the former. The views that attribute an economic crisis to policy failures, or to failure in internal risk control, also belong to this type of theory. On the other hand, contagion effects among sectors and countries, the effect of rumor, and the crisis-hit economy's loss of ability to restore equilibrium are the main building blocks of the latter type of theory. Therefore, it would be reasonable to mention two different sets of causes of economic crisis, in accordance with the two theories. Nevertheless, Table 1 lists the causes of economic crisis drawn from the first type of theory alone, since these causes seem to be applicable in case of economic crisis propagation as well.

Table 1 does not include shocks external to an economy as a cause of economic crises. The reason is mainly because this chapter aims at *deriving lessons* from the experience discussed; in other words, recognition of external shocks as the cause of a crisis does not lead to a meaningful answer to the question: what should we do to prevent another crisis? Therefore, it is preferred here to recognize internal vulnerabilities as the main cause of crisis. On the basis of this approach, the table focuses on causes of economic fragility[5].

Among various factors listed, the table refers to intrinsic factors behind an economic crisis, including imperfect information, herd behavior, and so on. These are hard to eliminate since they are intrinsic to human nature or the capitalist economic system. Thus, in cases where these factors are the main cause of a crisis, it would be hard to cure that crisis fundamentally. This is why herd behavior, though frequently blamed as the culprit, is seldom studied in depth. Unlike the case with external shocks, research on intrinsic factors can

---

[4] One of the reasons why there are few studies of economic crisis is that the mainstream economics have considered it too exceptional or abnormal a phenomenon to fit into their equilibrium model framework.

[5] In what follows are arguments that attribute the past economic crises in Korea to worsening world economic environments. However, this is not so much to identify the external shocks as the causes of the crisis as to represent the economic recession or deterioration of profits indirectly by it.

provide significant clues to understanding the process of economic development since the history of economic development can be said to have been a process of overcoming the limits imposed by these factors. Thus, a systematic study of an economic crisis will show the ways to long-term economic development as well as crisis resolution. This theme, however, is beyond the scope of this paper. This chapter will focus on the immediate causes of economic crisis, such as deterioration of profitability, financial fragility, maturity mismatches, and bubbles.

Based on the general understanding of the causes for an economic crisis and the measures for coping with it, we can identify four economic crises in Korea. There have been four crises[6], or similar situations, since the year 1962, when the first five-year economic development plan began. The first economic crisis took place during the period from the late 1960s to the early 1970s; it was characterized by high inflation, large and expanding current account deficits in the wake of the late 1960s economic boom, snowballing foreign debts, decreasing business profits, deteriorating financial soundness of firms, and impending large scale business failures in the early 1970s. The second crisis, around 1980, came about in the wake of the second global oil shock, soaring international interest rates, political unrest, and a bad harvest. Production literally decreased, and the foreign debt situation was so bad that the country could not repay some of them. The third crisis, during the period from the late 1980s to the early 1990s, was called a "critical situation on the whole." It followed deterioration in the international competitiveness of domestic firms, over-consumption and speculative bubbles on assets such as real estate. The fourth crisis, finally, happened in 1997. It was accompanied by serial bankruptcy of large business firms and increases in non-performing loans at financial institutions. Figure 1 depicts the growth rates of GDP since the 1960s and the economic crises in Korea.

2. The 1972 Economic Crisis

A. Unfolding of the Crisis[7]

The Korean economy faced a crisis in the early 1970s after an investment boom in the late 1960s, corresponding to the first half period of the second 5-year economic development plan. Investment stagnated three years in a row, from 1970 on (refer to table 2). Apparently, economic growth rates were not so bad. However, capital formation plummeted, casting doubt on future growth potential. Current account also deteriorated. It seems that not only the government's economic stabilization policy, which began around the end of 1969, but also the worsening of the firms' debt-servicing burdens contributed to the stagnation of business investment; firms could not expand their production capacity since they were under strong pressure to repay debts that had accumulated to very risky levels during the previous boom period. The stagnation of investment was a critical obstacle to the government's ambitious economic development plan to develop the heavy and chemical industries.

---

[6] Here, an economic crisis is seen simply as a severe economic difficulty or economically critical situation.
[7] This explanation of the 1972 economic crisis is largely based on Kim (1990).

(%)

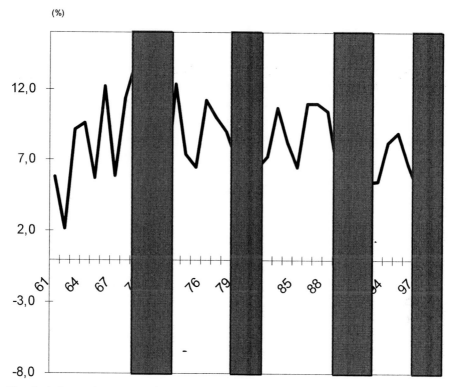

Note: The shaded areas indicate the periods of economic crises.
Source: The Bank of Korea, *Economic Statistics Yearbook*, various issues.

Figure 1. Growth Rates of GDP: Four Crisis Periods.

Table 2. Trends of Major Economic Indicators up to 1972

	1967	1968	1969	1970	1971	1972
Economic Growth[1](%)	5.9	11.3	13.8	8.8	8.6	4.9
(manufacturing)	21.6	27.2	21.6	19.9	18.5	14.3
Consumption	8.3	9.6	9.4	9.5	8.2	4.6
Capital formation	22.6	37.4	24.8	1.0	3.0	1.2
Exports	32.7	39.5	36.1	19.6	21.5	37.5
Imports	30.8	43.6	26.6	8.0	19.2	0.7
Current Account (100mil.USD)	-1.9	-4.4	-5.5	-6.2	-8.5	-3.7
WPI(rate of change, %)	6.5	8.1	6.9	9.4	8.6	13.8
CPI(rate of change, %)	10.9	10.8	12.8	15.5	13.5	11.7
M_2(end of year, rate of change, %)	61.7	72.0	61.4	27.4	20.8	33.8
Budget Balance[2]/GDP(%)	-2.57	-1.83	-3.10	-1.88	-1.70	-5.01

[1] Growth rates of GDP are on the basis of 1975 prices up to 1970 and thereafter on the basis of 1995 prices.

[2] Only the budget of central government is included.

Source: The Bank of Korea, *Economic Statistics Yearbook*, various issues.

Moreover, the number of delinquent firms had increased since the economic recession that began around 1969; many firms could not repay their foreign loans, which were guaranteed by domestic banks. The third-party banks' repayments of the foreign debt amounted to 0.5 billion Won in March 1970, and increased to 2.3 billion Won in August 1971[8]. The increase in business delinquencies might have been affected by the worsening profitability of firms due to the downturn of the business cycle. But the most important factor was the huge debt-servicing burden. The foreign loans that had been raised in large amounts in the late 1960s were reaching maturity. The burden had been further exacerbated by the Won depreciation, from 271.20 Won to 304.35 Won per US dollar in November 1969, and again to 370.80 won in June 1971.

By 1969, the government had recognized the seriousness of the situation and launched an operation to liquidate insolvent firms, by establishing an insolvent-firm liquidation unit under direct control of the president. In May 1969, this unit designated 30 foreign debt laden firms and 56 firms under bank control as insolvent[9].

The government was eventually forced to resort to an emergency decree on August 3rd, 1972, in consideration of the several factors as follows. First, the government perceived it difficult to let many delinquent firms go bankrupt because they were too big to fail and they were also greatly indebted to foreign banks, and their bankruptcies would have triggered a rush by international lenders to collect loans, and at the same time made them unwilling to provide new loans. Once this happened, the Korean economy would have faced severe difficulties in financing its economic development plan for the heavy and chemical industries since domestic savings were very limited in those days.

Second, policy makers began to worry that the firms' weak financial positions might bring about a disaster for firms and banks; the increase in the number of delinquent firms posed a potential threat to the banking system due to the increase in non-performing loans. Moreover, since the government had just started its campaign for heavy and chemical industrialization, the weak financial structures of the major firms were also perceived as a threat to the government's vision of economic development through active investment in those industries.

Finally, the booming curb money market was suspected as one of the main culprits behind the increasing number of corporate insolvency. Curb market lenders collected their loans whenever the borrowers were known to have difficulties in debt-servicing, ignoring the implicit maturities of the loans. The curb markets were thought to have other adverse effects on the economy as well, such as providing tax loopholes and disturbing the orderly operation of the financial system. On these grounds, the government issued the August 3rd Decree, aiming at improving corporate financial structure.

Thus, the early 1970s economic crisis was a corporate crisis in nature; that is, the primary source of the crisis was corporate insolvencies. Such factors as foreign debts, a slowdown in economic growth, and inflation were only secondary.

---

[8] The size of M_1 was about 300 billion won, and that of M_2 was about 900 billion won at the end of 1970.
[9] The unit was later succeeded by the corporation rationalization commission which took over the job of liquidation of troubled firms.

B. Background of the Crisis

(1) A Boom Financed by High Leverage – Rent Seeking through Financial Regulation

In the background of the worsening corporate financial positions lay the investment boom in the late 1960s, which was financed by ever-increasing leverage. Following the interest rate liberalization measures in September 30, 1965, monetary aggregates expanded rapidly (refer to Table 2). Together with this, the economy began to grow at more than 10 percent a year, with business investment growth averaging 28.3 percent a year during the period from 1967 to 1969. Lacking internal funds, however, domestic firms had to rely on external funds, especially bank loans. This implied that the faster the economy grew, the larger the borrowings of the firms, and the more vulnerable the firms would be to external shocks. This was what happened to Korean firms in the late 1960s. The debt-equity ratio of Korean manufacturing increased from 93.7 percent in 1965 to 394.2 percent in 1971. The financial expenses-to-sales ratio increased, accordingly, from 3.91 to 9.86 percent during the same period.

The high rate of return on investment in real assets, along with rapid economic growth, augmented corporations' ever-increasing demand for borrowing. A development boom raised the prices of real estate in several regions, and speculative investments boosted them further to extremely high levels. This produced a situation in which the gap between the rate of return in the real sector and that in the financial sector never narrowed. Even though the sum of the growth rates of GDP and the consumer price index, which was 22.3 percent on average during the period from 1967 to 1971, was lower than the lending rate for general funds, at 24.2 percent a year, the rate of return in the real sector is believed to have exceeded that in the financial sector because the levels of prices of many products were under strong government control. Moreover, considering the lending rates for policy loans such as equipment funds, the borrowing costs of firms seem to have been no more than half of their rates of return on investment.

(2) Underdevelopment of the Financial System

As a further background cause of the crisis, it can be pointed out that the financial system then was so backward that bank loans were almost the only source of external funds for most firms. The financial markets were segmented into a formal one and an informal one. Securities markets were in such an inactive state that they could be said to have been almost non-existent. There were several reasons for this. Firstly, the stock market was sluggish after a scandalous boom and bust in the early 1960s; secondly, expectation of inflation remained at a high level, which discouraged long-term investments in securities. Also, with most firms in their early stages of development and thus not proven to be creditworthy, fund raising through new issues of equity in the capital market was an unrealistic option. Thus, the increased demand for funds was mostly met by bank loans, and the excess demand for bank loans was spilled over to the curb markets.

Table 3. Financial Indicators of Korean Manufacturing Industry (%)

	1965	1966	1967	1968	1969	1970	1971	1972
Debt-equity ratio	93.7	117.7	151.2	201.3	270.0	328.4	394.2	313.4
Financial expenses-sales ratio	3.91	5.65	5.19	5.90	7.81	9.15	9.86	7.08
Net income-assets ratio	7.9	7.8	6.7	5.4	3.6	0.9	0.9	3.8

Source: The Bank of Korea, *Financial Statements Analysis,* various issues.

Table 4. Interest Rates and Related Indices (%)

	1965	1966	1967	1968	1969	1970	1971	1972
Interest rate on commercial bill discounts[1]	24.0	24.0	24.0	26.0	24.6	24.0	22.0	15.5
Interest rate on equipment funds[2]	11.5	11.5	11.5	11.5	12.0	12.0	12.0	10.0
Economic growth rate(A)	5.7	12.2	5.9	11.3	13.8	8.8	8.6	4.9
Rate of change in CPI [3](B)	13.5	11.2	10.9	10.8	12.8	15.5	13.5	11.7
A+B	19.2	23.4	16.7	21.7	26.7	24.4	22.1	16.4

[1] Offered by deposit monetary banks as of the end of year.

[2] Offered by the Industrial Bank of Korea as of the end of year.

[3] The figure in 1965 is for the Seoul district, and figures in 1966 and thereafter for all cities.

Source: The Bank of Korea, *Economic Statistics Yearbook*, various issues.

The distortion in financial parameters, a side-effect of the measures liberalizing interest rates in 1965, encouraged firms to borrow excessively and thus led them to suffer from excessive debt service burdens. As a result of the policy of keeping interest rates on policy loans at lower-than-the-market level, the loan-deposit interest rate spread became negative. This created excessive speculative demand for funds, thus distorting orderly operation of the financial system, and eventually resulting in the underdevelopment of the Korean financial system.[10]

(3) Adverse Effects of Economic Stabilization Policy

In the latter half of the 1960s, various signs of an overheating economy such as widening current account deficits and soaring prices emerged. The government, therefore, executed a comprehensive stabilization policy in November 1969[11]. However, this aggravated the difficulties of most firms, which had weakness in their financial structure. The main contents of the stabilization policy were regulation of private borrowing from abroad, tightening of government expenditures, control of the money supply, and so on (The Bank of Korea 2000, pp. 166). In particular, the Bank of Korea changed the monetary policy regime, from indirect monetary targeting to direct control of the domestic credits of financial institutions from 1970 on. In the meantime, as the economy cooled down, the Bank of Korea lowered the interest rates, which had been at excessively high levels since the interest rate rationalization in 1965.

---

[10] Lee and Cheong (2007) offer an empirical and theoretical analysis for the political economy of financial structure of Korean firms. They argue that financial markets are repressed to create rent, which were shared by politicians and business sectors. Kang (2002) also provides a related research on this issue.

[11] This measure was encouraged in part by the IMF.

The firms over-laden with large debts and their debt-servicing costs went to the curb market for funds when their access to financial institutions and foreign loans were limited. Because the interest rate in the curb market then climbed to and maintained levels higher than 3~4 percent a month (over 40 percent a year), the firms' financial burdens increased all the more. Furthermore, the risks of bankruptcy of firms increased as the economy marched into recession.

(4) Worsened World Economic Situation

Economic stagnation in advanced countries, in the wake of the breakdown of the old international monetary system (the Bretton-Woods system), also aggravated the difficulties of Korean firms, along with the domestic business slowdown. The United States found it difficult to maintain a fixed exchange rate for the dollar with its increasing current account and fiscal deficits. Thus, the U.S. suspended the convertibility of the dollar to gold and devalued it in 1971. As major industrial economies also adopted floating exchange rate systems, international financial markets became more volatile and the world economy subsequently began to stagnate. Influenced by this, the growth rate of Korean exports slowed down and, accordingly, profitability of the firms decreased. As a result, the firms' burdens of debt servicing worsened.

C. Crisis Resolution Measures   -

As the economy began to stagnate in early 1971, the government adopted a loose monetary policy stance, reversing the 1969 stabilization policy by lowering the interest rate and devaluing the Won on June 28th, 1971. In addition, a series of policy measures to boost the economy were adopted in February 1972. In spite of these policy measures, the firms continued to suffer, and the government finally promulgated the 'Emergency Decree for Economic Stability and Growth' on August 2nd, 1972, to come into effect on the following day.

The substance of the August 3rd Emergency Decree included above all rescheduling of the loans borrowed from the curb market as well as the banks (including the conversion of debts into capital) and promotion of policies boosting the economy. With a view to alleviating the debt-servicing burdens of firms, all reported curb-market borrowings were mandated to be converted to a new debt contract, with a three-year grace period followed by repayment in five annual installments at the interest rate of 1.35 percent a month or 16.2 percent a year. In addition, 30 percent of the outstanding short-term bank loans were rescheduled as long-term loans. A portion of the losses to financial institutions incurred by this was compensated for by support from the Bank of Korea. At the same time, the Bank of Korea lowered banks' lending and deposit rates to levels similar to those as before the interest rate liberalization in 1965. Meanwhile, the government provided tax benefits by allowing a higher depreciation ratio for fixed assets and larger corporate income tax deductions, with the purpose of stimulating investment. After the August 3rd Emergency Decree, the government promulgated three acts to attract curb-market funds into formal financial markets - the 'Short-term Financing and Banking Act,' 'the Mutual Savings and Finance Company Act,' and the 'Credit Union Act.'

3. The 1980 Economic Crisis

A. *Unfolding of the Crisis*

In the period around 1980, economic difficulties arose which were more severe than other difficulties a few years earlier, such as the 1972 recession and the first oil shock in 1973~1974. After a boom period from 1976 to 1978, the gross domestic product decreased, while inflation pressure emerged, in 1980, for the first time since the beginning of the 5-year economic development plans (refer to Table 5). The principal reasons for the decline of GDP were mainly external shocks such as the soaring oil price, political and social unrest, and a bad harvest. The probability of defaults on foreign debt increased as the current account deficit widened, mainly due to the increase in expenses for oil imports. Over-investment in the heavy and chemical industries, meanwhile, was another factor driving firms and banks to become insolvent.

The 1980 crisis unfolded in the following manner. Entering the year 1979, structural problems of the Korean economy began to surface. For example, exports decreased in volume terms in 1979. This decrease in exports reflected the surge in inflation in the latter half of the 1970s, which resulted in deterioration of the export competitiveness and profitability of domestic products (The Bank of Korea, *The 1979 Annual Report*). In addition, the direct control over the exports of some products, which was intended to stabilize domestic prices, also contributed to the decrease in exports. Thus, the decrease in export volume at that time may have resulted from the structural problems of the economy, even though it was affected as well by the world recession, the second oil shock, and neo-protectionism of advanced countries.

In particular, inflation began to soar in 1979. This was mainly due to the adjustment of controlled prices to more realistic levels as well as to the increases in import prices, e.g., of crude oil. The government had been setting the maximum prices of major products since it enacted the 'Act on Price Stability' on March 12th, 1973. During the late-1970s boom, however, numerous ways to circumvent the price controls were devised, such as setting dual prices, underground transactions, refusing to sell, cornering the markets for agricultural products, and so on. As a result, the price controls became ineffective and provoked such adverse effects as distortion of resource allocation and disruption of economic order. In light of this, the government rationalized or liberalized the prices of products and fees for public utilities.

In addition to soaring inflation, the economy suffered from a severe recession in 1980 as a result of a series of external shocks such as the sudden rise in oil prices and domestic political unrest. Private investment in equipment decreased rapidly as economic uncertainty increased in the midst of low capacity utilization following excessive investment in the 1970s. Domestic demand shrank as real income decreased due to inflation and a contraction of consumer confidence. In addition, production shrank because of a poor rice harvest. As a result of this, the economic growth rate became negative and unemployment rate increased, from 3.8% in 1979 to 5.2% in 1980. The ratio of dishonored bills also increased from 0.10% in 1979 to 0.18% in 1980.

Table 5. Trends of Major Economic Indicators circa 1980

	1975	1976	1977	1978	1979	1980	1981
Economic growth[1](%)	6.5	11.2	10.0	9.0	7.1	-2.1	6.5
(manufacturing)	12.9	23.1	14.4	20.8	9.5	-0.9	9.5
Consumption	5.6	6.8	5.2	8.1	6.3	1.1	4.7
Capital formation	7.7	21.0	28.6	34.4	9.7	-10.7	-3.7
Exports	19.3	39.1	20.9	13.8	1.0	8.6	15.7
Imports	1.9	24.7	20.9	28.0	11.8	-5.3	6.6
Current account (100mil.USD)	-18.9	-3.1	0.1	-10.9	-41.5	-53.2	-45.5
WPI(rate of change, %)	26.5	12.1	9.0	11.7	18.8	33.9	20.4
CPI(rate of change, %)	25.3	15.3	10.2	14.4	18.3	28.7	21.3
M_2(end of year, rate of change, %)	27.0	29.2	37.0	39.3	26.8	25.8	27.4
Budget balance[2]/GDP(%)	-3.29	-1.13	-0.83	-0.21	0.38	-1.55	-2.22

[1] Growth rates of GDP at 1995 prices
[2] Only the central government budget is included.
Source: The Bank of Korea, *Economic Statistics Yearbook*, various issues.

Table 6. International Oil Prices, Interest Rates, and Total Foreign Debt

	1978	79	80	81	82
Oil Prices [a]	12.95	29.22	36.68	35.27	32.45
Interest Rate[b]	8.85	12.09	14.19	16.87	13.29
Total Foreign Debt[c]	148.2	202.9	271.7	324.3	370.8
(Net Foreign Debt)[c]	(99.0)	(139.9)	(196.3)	(244.7)	(283.0)

[a] Average crude price (USD/Barrel): U.K. Brent (light), Dubai (medium), and Alaska North Slope (heavy), equally weighted.
[b] Libor 3-month, %.
[c] In 100 million US Dollars.
Sources: IMF, *International Financial Statistics Yearbook* (1997).
National Statistics Office, *Major Statistics of Korean Economy*, various issues.

The current account, which had been in balance and once showed a surplus in 1977, turned into a large deficit in 1979 (refer to Table 6). The deficit reflected, to some degree, the structural problems in energy consumption as well as the increase in oil imports after the oil price hike.

Demand for foreign exchange began far exceeding supply as the current account was in increasingly large deficit. Meanwhile, foreign confidence in the Korean economy deteriorated as a result of the political and social unrest and the economic recession. Foreign debt turned out to be about 15 billion dollars at the end of 1978, and interest payments on this debt amounted to 0.9 billion dollars (Economic Planning Board 1985, p. 6); this was a substantial interest burden, considering the fact that the total exports of the nation were only 12 billion dollars then. Due to the large current account deficit since 1979, the country was in need of additional inflow of foreign funds. It faced difficulties in raising funds in international financial markets, however, because those markets were also in unstable situations with soaring interest rates. The country could hardly have avoided default on its foreign debt but for its drawings from the IMF funds[12]. Foreign debt continued to accumulate, however, up to 37 billion dollars at the end of 1982.

At the same time, adverse effects from the government's promotion of heavy and chemical industries began to appear. Ambitious investments in the heavy and chemical industries during the 1970s had led to duplication of investment in some industries. Domestic markets for heavy and chemical products were small, while the international competitiveness of those firms remained low. Thus, the firms that entered these industries performed poorly in terms of profitability, and it was worried that most of them would go bankrupt in the long run. Even those firms which were highly competitive could not perform well because of the world-wide economic stagnation. Moreover, it had become practically impossible to continue to channel funds to those industries, since their demand for funds was too large. For example, the demand for funds by about 40 firms in the heavy and chemical industries amounted to 80 percent of the increments in money supply that year (Economic Planning Board 1979, p. 1185). Similarly, the overseas construction companies and shipping companies, which also absorbed large investments in the latter half of the 1970s, were accumulating bad assets as well.

In short, the nature of the 1980 economic crisis was a combination of several kinds of crises. It was a macroeconomic crisis in the sense that it resulted from an external and internal disequilibrium. In particular, it was a balance of payments crisis or a foreign debt crisis since widening current account deficit and the subsequent shortage of foreign exchange supply was one of the main causes for the crisis. From the microeconomic point of view, it can be seen as a structural crisis, in the sense that it revealed the shortcomings of the economic system that had prevailed in Korea during the 1970s. It also had the characteristics of a corporate crisis and a banking crisis, because of the delinquencies of the heavy and chemical industry firms and the financial distress imposed thereby on banks.

B. Background of the Crisis

(1) Over-heating and Speculation

The direct causes for the deterioration in the domestic firms' competitiveness in the export markets were an over-heated economy, during the 1976~1978 period, and an accompanying speculative rally in asset markets. Thanks in part to the measures contained in the 1972 August 3rd Decree to stimulate business activities, and also in part to the stabilized oil prices since 1975, the Korean economy recorded high growth rates of around 10 percent on average during the 1976~1978 period. Exports expanded rapidly along with recovery of the world economy, and income from overseas construction increased due to the construction boom in the Middle East. However, the rapid growth of monetary aggregates – of around 40 percent a year – resulting especially from the inflow of liquidity from abroad, generated pressure for inflation. Speculative booms, meanwhile, occurred in the markets for real estate, stocks, and commodities in short supply[13]. These factors, i.e., over-heated economy,

---

[12] The government withdrew about 500 million SDR from the IMF based on the stand-by agreement, in which Korea's credits were increased from 20 million SDR to 649 million SDR.

[13] In those days, the prices of real assets rose so sharply that the period was called an "age of premium"; the price of human capital, i.e., wages, also increased rapidly due to a labor shortage (Korea Development Institute 1981, p. 5).

speculative boom in asset markets, inflation, wage increases, were what weakened the competitiveness of domestic firms in the international export markets.

(2) Duplicated and Excessive Investment in Heavy and Chemical Industries

The adverse effects of the policy of promoting heavy and chemical industries, and of the hasty and aggressive implementation thereof in the late 1970s, included the increases in the number of delinquent firms and distortions in industrial structure. These problems, among others, caused the 1980 economic crisis. Firms which had initially been skeptical of investing in the heavy and chemical industries till the early 1970s, rushed to participate in the investment projects after confirming the government's determination to foster these industries. The amount of investment was too large, however, compared to the sizes of the markets. The capacity utilization of firms investing in new projects was so low that they could not reach the break-even point. Stagnation of the domestic economy and the world economy alike lowered the profitability of firms further and drove the heavy and chemical industries into a state of potential delinquency. Moreover, concentration of resources on the heavy and chemical industries resulted in short supplies of necessities and other products of light industries, and eroded long-term growth potentials of those industries.

(3) Repressive Economic Policy

The Korean economy in the 1970s was a repressed economy[14], if not a completely planning economy, in the sense that there existed a large amount of government control and intervention in the operation of the economic system. Since the August 3rd Decree in 1972, the government controlled commodity prices, interest rates, and exchange rates and continually intensified its intervention in resource allocation.

Seen from a structural point of view, the crisis beginning in 1979 was a result of the vulnerability stemming from the structural weaknesses or inefficiencies of a repressed economy. The policy makers those days also shared this view. The Economic Planning Board, for example, in its Comprehensive Economic Stabilization Policy promulgated on April 17th, 1979, stressed that structural policy measures were in need for fostering the growth potential of Korean economy in the long run (Korea Development Institute 1981, p. 371). In a similar context, the Bank of Korea attributed the then crisis to structural problems (The Bank of Korea, *1980 Annual Report*, p. 1), and asserted that the managerial efficiency and financial structures of firms should be improved to enhance their competitiveness (p. 8).

Repressive policy measures might have been unavoidable in order to foster the nation's infant industries. It is also true, however, that they distorted and weakened the economic structure. For example, interest rate ceilings brought about such problems as excess demand for bank loans, prevalence of the curb money market, and decreased incentives to save. Policy loans and required approval of foreign borrowings led not only to economic problems such as over-borrowings by firms, but also to non-economic problems such as cronyism, i.e., 'intimate' relationships between firms and the government. Direct control by the government stifled the individual will to innovate and thus discouraged the spontaneity essential for a harmonious working of the market system. Due to the intensive government intervention in

---

[14] The term "repressed economy" refers to an economy in which the government severely intervenes in private sector's resource allocation via price and quantity controls. For details as to repression, see MacKinnon (1973), Krueger (1993), Fry (1995), and others.

the financial sector, financial institutions had little incentive to screen loan applicants and monitor borrowers, and also lacked initiative in developing new financial techniques. Firms tended to seek profit maximization not so much through managerial innovation as through lobbying the government. Consequently, it seems highly likely that the government's control weakened the private sector's adaptability to changing economic environment.

The government's control of the economy is also likely to have stalled growth in the sophistication of the economic system and to have made it fragile to external shocks. In order to increase the flexibility of an economy, it is necessary to allow for a variety of heterogeneous elements in the system. Strict control by the government, however, led to an unsophisticated or monotone economic structure, which was more fragile than a sophisticated one.

(4) Imbalances Between Real and Financial Sectors (Underdevelopment of Financial Sector)

From the beginning of its economic development, Korea chose an unbalanced growth strategy for economic development, and pursued it faithfully. This produced various inter-sectoral imbalances, among them imbalances between real and financial sectors, begotten by the policy of promoting industrialization through financial repression. These imbalances became one of the major background factors behind the 1980 economic crisis. The degree of imbalance had intensified all the more because of the August 3rd-Decree in 1972, which forced the financial sector to sacrifice for the sake of the real sector, especially the large firms, by means of a compulsive conversion of debt contracts and rescheduling, with a suppression of interest rates to below the market rates. Even though the decree contained some measures to encourage financial development, such as the establishment of non-banking financial institutions, it lacked respect for market principles in development of the financial sector. Behind this lay the developmentalist view that financial development was only supplementary to industrial development. Since the government controlled the commercial banks, investors did not find any incentive to buy bank stocks, and this of course hampered issuance of stocks by the banks[15]. In the late 1970s, there were cases where no single nation-wide commercial bank had even as much capital as the amount needed to finance a large investment project proposal by a big business firm. Among the most harmful effects of these imbalances between the real and financial sectors were retardation of the banks' capabilities to monitor and check firms' activities, and inability of the banks to restrain over-borrowings and inefficient use of them by firms.

C. Measures to Cope with the 1980 Crisis

The set of economic policies implemented from 1979 to the early 1980s to cope with the economic crisis consisted of a macroeconomic stabilization policy, an export promotion and foreign exchange policy, deregulation, measures to correct inefficient and duplicate investment projects, and others as microeconomic measures.

First, the government implemented a macroeconomic stabilization policy, beginning from 1979 when the domestic economy showed stagnation along with steeply increased international oil prices. The policy was promulgated as the Comprehensive Economic Stabilization Measures on April 17th, 1979. It consisted of measures to stabilize the prices of

---

[15] At that time, the government was the largest stockholder in four out of the five nation-wide commercial banks.

products and the supply of necessities, fiscal restriction, restructuring of heavy and chemical industries, and increases in the interest rates paid on bank deposits. The basis of the stabilization was maintained relatively consistently thereafter. The only exception was the expansionary monetary policy sought after June 1980 to boost the economy. To counter the destabilizing effects of this monetary expansion, stronger fiscal restriction was pursued. In order to control increases in expenditures, the government adopted a zero-base budget formula from 1981 on. In line with macroeconomic measures, stabilization was pursued through direct and microeconomic measures such as release of government-stock rice, strengthening direct controls on prices of major products, and anti-speculation policy in the real estate market.

Second, the government implemented a policy to promote exports and support firms' repayments of foreign debts, to alleviate the burden of foreign debt servicing by firms. The Won was devalued in January 1980. At the same time, the government increased its subsidies to exporting activities by increasing the loan for trade. In order to help public corporations and the heavy and chemical industries repay their foreign debts, the government introduced a special foreign-currency loan program on April 3rd, 1980. It also opened the stock market as part of an economic liberalization program, and tried to induce foreign capital by establishing an investment fund exclusively for foreigners, the first ever vehicle for foreigners' indirect investment in domestic securities.

- Third, the government pushed forward a liberalization policy, admitting that the economic difficulties at that time stemmed from structural inefficiencies formed by its own excessive economic intervention. In the financial sector, the government privatized the nation-wide commercial banks, attempted to allow for more autonomy for bank management, and reduced the extent of policy loans. On September 6th, 1979, it introduced a new system for setting interest rates at individual banks, utilizing spreads over prime rate replacing the previous system of government-set interest rate ceilings. Subsequently, the government introduced new financial instruments, whose rates of returns could supposedly be determined by market forces, such as commercial papers (CPs), cash management accounts (CMAs), and negotiable certificates of deposits (CDs). The Bank of Korea tried to shy away from direct control of the domestic credits of financial institutions and introduced an indirect mode of managing the money supply, utilizing the price function of the interest rate from January 7th, 1982. As for industrial policy, the government changed from a selective to a functional or across-the-board intervention mode. In 1986, it abolished the seven acts pertaining to promotion of seven individual industries and enacted the 'Industry Development Act,' which integrated and unified these former acts. The thrust of this move was to provide a means to support industries across-the-board. With this measure, it became possible for preferential loans to be provided to an unspecified number of firms in the way of supporting exports or purchases of domestically produced machines. The government also promoted trade liberalization in a trial attempt to outgrow the protective industrial policy. On behalf of securing the orderly operation of the market system, the Fair Trade Commission was established. In addition, the legal system was improved in such a way as to change the character of regulations from a positive system to a negative system.[16]

---

[16] Positive list system refers to the legal system in which activities allowed are listed. Those not listed are deemed to be not allowed. Negative list system refers to the legal system in which only those activities not allowed are listed and those not listed are deemed to be allowed. Thus, in general, the positive list system is a more strict and regulatory legal system than the negative list system.

Fourth, in response to worsening cash flows and excess capacity in the heavy and chemical industries, the government established measures to restructure these industries. On the basis of the Heavy and Chemical Industry Coordination Plan, drafted in May 1979, the government tried to coordinate business restructuring, so-called industry rationalization, in such industries as electrical generators, diesel engines, automobiles, electronic switchboards, and transformers. It also attempted to resolve excess-capacity problems in the overseas construction and shipping industries. For various reasons including excessive burdens to financial institutions and recession, however, the so-called industry rationalization policies were not fully implemented prior to the mid-1980s. Measures were also taken to make up for the losses sustained by banks, as these losses had resulted, by and large, from government intervention in the financial sector. On several occasions, the Bank of Korea paid interest on banks' reserve deposits held in accounts in the BOK. The government also allowed banks to enter into new businesses, such as the credit card business, with a view to improving their profitability.

Finally, the government implemented several measures to discourage speculation in real estate and reckless management of firms. For example, a measure to improve corporate financial soundness was announced in September 1980, which urged sales of land held for non-business purposes, disposal of affiliate firms and strengthening of external audits for joint-stock corporations. To stabilize the prices of real estate, the government also announced a long-term plan for construction of houses. It also expanded home financing for the lower-income classes.

Table 7. Trends of Major Economic Indicators around 1989

	1985	1986	1987	1988	1989	1990	1991	1992
Economic growth[1](%)	6.9	12.4	12.0	11.5	6.2	9.2	8.5	5.1
(manufacturing)	7.1	18.3	18.8	13.4	3.7	9.1	8.9	5.1
Consumption	6.3	8.4	8.1	9.7	10.7	10.1	9.3	6.8
Capital formation	4.7	12.0	16.5	13.4	16.9	24.0	11.8	-0.8
Exports	4.5	26.1	21.6	12.5	-3.8	18.4	12.8	11.0
Imports	-0.6	17.8	19.4	12.8	16.3	29.1	11.0	5.1
Current account (100mil.USD)	-8.9	46.2	98.5	141.6	50.5	-21.8	-87.3	-45.3
WPI[2](rate of change, %)	0.5	-2.6	2.7	2.3	1.2	7.2	1.9	1.6
CPI[2](rate of change, %)	3.1	1.4	6.1	7.2	5.0	9.4	9.3	4.5
M2(end of period, rate of change, %)	11.8	16.8	18.8	18.8	18.4	21.2	18.6	18.4
Consolidated budget balance/GDP(%)	-0.9	-0.1	2.3	1.2	0.0	-0.9	-1.9	-0.7

[1] Growth rate of GDP at 1995 prices.

[2] Compared with that of previous year.

Source: The Bank of Korea, *Economic Statistics Yearbook*, various issues.

The Ministry of Finance, *Government Finance Statistics of Korea*, various issues.

4. The Post-1989 "Grave Situation"

A. Unfolding of the Situation

The economic situation during the period from 1989 to 1992 worsened relatively compared to that in the 1986~1988 period, although not so bad as to constitute an actual economic "crisis." Government officials termed it a "totally grave situation" before others subsequently called it a crisis. Immediately after the high-performance in late 1980s, in which all three major macroeconomic targets – rapid growth, current account surplus, and price stability – had been achieved, things turned the other way; growth, the current account, and prices all worsened simultaneously. At this time, government authorities seemed to be at a loss, as changes in domestic and external conditions brought about many new difficulties for them in designing and implementing proper policies. The term 'grave situation' seems to have been used more to indicate the difficulties in policy implementation than to point to the economic difficulties themselves.

The main economic difficulties then can be described as a slowdown of economic growth, widening current account deficits, and inflation. The economy that had shown double digit growth rates during the 1986 ~1988 period suddenly slowed down in 1989, growing only 6 percent in that year. Owing to the grand government-promoted project of building 2 million houses, along with a rise in consumption, however, the economy recovered to a growth rate of 9 percent during the following period from 1990 to 1991. Meanwhile, the current account reversed to deficit in 1990 and recorded an even bigger deficit in 1991. The reversal from surplus to deficit reflected the loss of international competitiveness of Korean firms and a large increase in imports. Inflation rose because of excess demand resulting from increased expenditures by residents.

An unfavorable world economic situation at this time amplified the worries over stagnation. The dollar was weak in the international financial markets, while competition in the domestic and overseas markets had intensified. Domestically, Korea had to open its markets as promised in its liberalization plans[17], and the Won was on an appreciating trend reflecting the current account surpluses. International oil prices also increased substantially due to the Gulf War in 1990.

Despite the need to respond to this deteriorating economic situation, the government confronted many difficulties in doing so, as proper means were not readily available. Along with the political transition from an authoritarian regime to a democratic regime, public demand for wage increases and improvements in the quality of life became uncontrollable, so that the government could not find ways to constrain wages or consumption increases. Direct controls were unthinkable because of the economic liberalization trend. For example, after the government adopted a market average exchange rate system on March 2nd, 1990, its influence on exchange rates diminished to a great extent. Seen from this point of view, the economic crisis at that time was indeed actually more of a policy dilemma in nature, in that the government was unable to offer proper means to deal with the economic difficulties.

---

[17] After succeeding in opening the Japanese economy through the *Yen-Dollar Committee* in 1984, the US government pressed Korea for market opening.

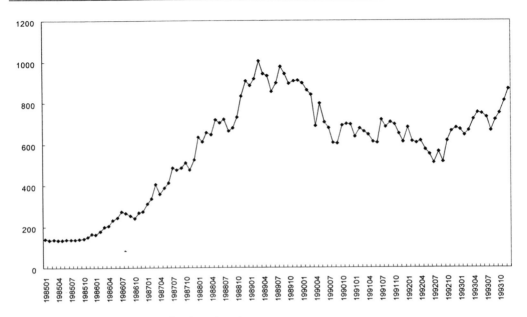

Source: Korea Stock Exchange, *Stock*, various issues.

Figure 2. Trends of Stock Price Index.

B. Background of the Situation

(1) Speculative Boom

Against the economic boom in the latter half of the 1980s, another round of speculative boom appeared in the stock and real estate markets. The stock price index, which had been 137 in October 1985, began to rise from around the end of 1985, and reached 1,003 in March 1989 (refer to Figure 2). This long-rising trend of stock prices was followed by jumps in the prices of land and houses from around 1988. The prices of land and houses increased 129 and 56 percent, respectively, during the period from the end of 1987 to the end of 1991 (refer to Figure 3).

These asset bubbles caused several disturbances to the economy as they spread, even though there were no cases of their sudden bursting. Speculative demand for credit increased rapidly as speculators financed their investments through bank loans. The resultant increases in interest rates eroded the international competitiveness of domestic firms. Due to the wealth effects of the asset appreciation, consumption and construction investment increased. The changes in the structure of aggregate demand from exports to domestic demand generated worries over erosion of the home base for export production. The proportion of GDP consumed by the private sector or invested in construction was 65.5 percent in 1988, but it increased to 76 percent by the early 1990s. Moreover, the firms sought capital gains from the real assets, while neglecting their needs to improve managerial efficiency, and this weakened their competitive edge even further.

Table 8. Demand Structure of GDP (Shares in GDP) (%)

	1980	1985	1988	1989	1990	1991	1992
Private Consumption(A)	63.4	57.5	50.0	52.0	52.3	52.3	52.9
Construction(B)	18.0	16.2	15.5	17.6	22.2	24.2	23.1
A+B	81.4	73.7	65.5	69.6	74.5	76.5	76.0

Source: The Bank of Korea, *National Account*, various issues.

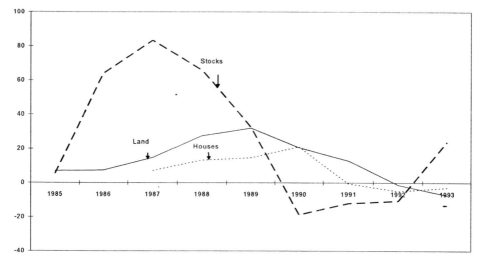

Source: Korea Stock Exchange, *Stock*, various issues. Ministry of Construction and Transportation, *Land Price Statistics*, various issues. Housing and Commercial Bank, *Survey of Urban Housing Price Trends*, various issues.

Figure 3. Changes in Prices of Stocks, Land, and Houses.

(2) Liberalization and Democratization Accompanied by Eruption of Demand for Basic Needs

While liberalization had been a basic theme since the early 1980s in the economic sphere, democratization had also progressed steadily in the political sphere. The June 29th Democratization Declaration in 1987 set the stage for a jump in the number of labor disputes. Rapid increases in wages[18], together with social unrest, caused a decline in the international competitiveness of Korean firms and lowered international confidence in the Korean economy. In this situation, an economic opening policy, including freed overseas travel and liberalization of luxury consumer goods imports[19], was also promoted in order to help manage the large current account surplus. Owing to income and wealth growth, and to the appreciation of the Won, these measures triggered increases in consumption, especially of

---

[18] It is highly probable that the wage rate would have increased, the democratization decree notwithstanding, since the unemployment rate in late 1980 stayed at the level of 2 percent, well below the projected natural unemployment rate of 3 percent.

[19] After travel abroad by elderly people was liberalized in January 1988, the policy was applied to all citizens. In addition, import of luxurious home electronic products, such as large refrigerators and large TVs, was liberalized in 1989.

luxuries. This in turn caused workers to ask for further wage increases and led to more labor disputes. The 1988 Olympics held in Seoul also brought about a laxity in social discipline.

(3) Changes in World Economic Environment

The worsening of the world economy and the Won appreciation together aggravated the difficulties of the government in conducting economic policies. By then, international pressure was growing for Korea to increase its role in the international community, commensurate with its improved economic status. Specifically, pressure from advanced countries mounted for the opening of Korean markets. This was a fundamental change in trade policy for these countries, which had previously preferred to stall rapid increases of imports from Korea. Moreover, as the WTO system was expected to come into effect before long, there arose worries about foreign firms' taking over domestic markets in agricultural products and financial services, as well as markets for manufactured goods.

(4) Lessened Effectiveness of Economic Policies

One of the background factors of the post-1989 grave situation was that the old-style economic policies could not respond effectively to the changes brought about by economic liberalization and movements in the domestic and world economic environments. The economic situation was nothing exceptionally severe, but the government nevertheless called the situation a grave one. The reason was that the policy makers felt ill-equipped to handle the situation. In fact, institutions, including an adequately working market mechanism, had not evolved sufficiently to incorporate the new economic order required under the liberalized system. The government had lost the use of its previous policy instruments and had not yet developed the capabilities needed to coordinate economic matters under drastically changed economic conditions.

In addition, it was hardly possible to come up with a solution to disentangle the combination of stagnant stock markets and over-heated real estate markets. An expansionary macroeconomic policy would help support stock prices, but it would hamper the efforts to stabilize real estate prices.

C. Measures to Cope with the Situation

The economic policies in this period comprised an industrial restructuring policy, a measure to stifle real estate speculation, and a policy to boost stock prices. A stabilization policy was also promoted, although not in the sense of managing macroeconomic demand, but rather in the sense of wage stabilizing, stock price stabilization, and asset prices stabilization, control of commodity prices, and stabilization of the living conditions of the common people. From the latter half of 1991, a traditional macroeconomic stabilization policy was pursued. Liberalization and opening were also among the main themes of the policy. During this period, the speed of promotion of liberalization went up.

The industrial restructuring policy aimed at addressing the issue of improving firms' profitability and competitiveness, which had deteriorated due to increasing wages, the Won appreciation, and inflation. As for the mode of policy implementation, the government advocated an indirect provision of support to firms; that is, it tried to remain basically a promoter of infrastructure, basic technology development, and an elastic supply of skilled labor, excepting that it might use direct measures to support the small and medium-sized firms. Despite the government's assertion, however, things were not done so differently from before, as the government provided support to targeted activities directly and frequently twisted the arms of banks to get them to supply the required funds for the preferred sectors. For example, to help firms invest in improving their equipment, the government created special equipment funds on November 14th, 1989 and April 4th, 1990, providing loans for this purpose on preferential terms. It also allowed a temporary investment tax deduction on July 4th, 1989, and requested that banks lend in foreign currency to firms which imported new equipment. The government also increased subsidies for exporting activities by increasing the Bank of Korea rediscount proportions applied to foreign trade bills. It also lowered interest rates. In addition, it promoted a policy inducing big business firms to specialize in their core business areas. In order to facilitate this policy, the credit control system was also modified.

One of the priority policy agenda items during this time was cooling the rampant real estate boom. This is well demonstrated by the fact that, during the three years from early 1989 to early 1992, almost twenty related policy measures were announced. This high level of concern was based on the government's judgment that an excessive boom in real estate markets would cause inefficient allocation of resources, trigger demands for wage increases, induce over-consumption, and bring about a sense of incongruity in society by destabilizing the lives of the common people. Thus, the government introduced four laws based on the concept of public ownership of land on December 30th, 1989, and this was meant above all to calm the real estate market[20]. In addition to this, regulations concerning the general land tax (June 16th, 1989), permission for land transactions (December 20th, 1989), and compulsory registration of real estate (April 13th, 1990) were introduced. A measure to encourage the sale of real estate held by big business firms and financial institutions, and one to prevent new acquisition were also introduced. Finally, there was the plan for construction of two million houses, promulgated on April 27th, 1989 with a view to increasing the supply of houses.

Varied measures to stop the steep decrease in stock prices were implemented as stock prices continued to fall after recording their peak in March 1989. On December 12th, 1989, the government announced a policy measure to boost the stock market, and this was followed by measures to control the volume of the stocks issued and to establish a stock market stabilization fund (September 18th, 1990) and a measure to open the stock market to foreign investors (November 30th, 1991). The government also arranged for commercial banks to provide 2.7 trillion Won to investment trust companies, so that these companies could buy stock in the market. On May 27th, 1992, the Bank of Korea supplied 2.9 trillion Won to the investment trust companies to help improve their profit earnings.

Meanwhile, a series of deregulatory measures was put in place with ever-increasing speed, in accordance with the long-term plan for financial liberalization and market opening. In December 1988, interest rates were fully liberalized. Although this policy soon underwent *de facto* repeal when the government's window guidance on determination of interest rates was resumed in response to the sudden economic recession in 1989, it reverted again to plan, when the first stage of the four-stage interest rate liberalization plan of August 1991 was implemented in November 1991. Capital market opening was only partly promoted until 1993, in the form of an increase in the amount of investment funds available exclusively for

---

[20] Included in the laws were the Ceiling on Housing Ownership Act, Restitution of Development Gains Act, Land Excess-Profits Tax, Special Account for Land Management and the Balanced Regional Development Act.

foreign investors. Then, however, the government announced a comprehensive blueprint for Korea's financial deregulation and capital market opening over the following five years.

Macroeconomic policy in those days was used so as to to boost economic activities, rather than as a tool to stabilize them. As for monetary policy, relatively tight money had been pursued through the introduction and operation of the so-called marginal reserve system until the first half of 1989, as a way of handling the large balance of payments surplus. From the second half of 1989, however, money began to be supplied to fuel an expansionary phase. The reason for this turn-around in monetary policy was a change in the basic goals of monetary policy to include that of providing sufficient funds to the private sector to activate corporate investment and stimulate the stock market. As the economy entered an over-heated phase under the influence of this expansionary policy from 1990 to 1991, the policy took a turn to contraction from the end of 1991. It turned around to expansion once again, however, when the New Economy 5-Year Plan was implemented in 1993.

5. The 1997 Economic Crisis

A. Details of the Crisis

The 1997 economic crisis took place through a complex process: beginning from recession and terms of trade deterioration, then moving to corporate bankruptcies, to banking crises, to contagion from foreign currency crises of South East Asian countries, and to a currency crisis. In addition, during the crisis resolution, a series of corporate bankruptcy and subsequent banking crises repeated itself. The 1997 crisis provided a window for looking at the problems innate in the Korean economic system. This is one of its distinct features.

Before going into the details of the 1997 crisis, this chapter first takes a look at the economic situation in 1996. Above all, it should be noted that the economy slowed down in 1996, after showing a high growth rate of over 8 percent a year on average in 1994 and 1995. At a first glance, the 1996 slowdown looked like a soft landing, since GDP grew almost 5 percent that year.

Looking at the details of economic growth in 1996, however, one can find problems in the Korean economy. The nearly 5% growth rate was mainly attributable to increases in inventories, which occurred as firms struggled to continue production under sluggish demand. The reason for this was that the cost of stopping factory operation was extremely high in processing industries such as the petrochemical, steel, and semiconductors, which are the major industries in the Korean economy. The volume of inventories began to weigh heavily on the corporate sector. The portion of inventory increases in GDP mounted up to 1 percent. Thus, if it had not been for the increase in inventories, the economic growth rate in 1996 would have ended up at the mere 3 percent level.

The current account deficit, which had been increasing from 1994 to 1995, amounted to 23 billion dollars, 5 percent of GDP in 1996. Decreases in the prices of major exports, such as semiconductors, and continuous increases in imports were main contributory factors to the widening deficit of the current account. Moreover, the decrease in the unit prices of exports, combined with increases in export volume, worsened the profitability of exporting activities.

Table 9. Trends of Inventories (in 1995 constant prices) (Billion Won, %)

	1990	1991	1992	1993	1994	1995	1996	1997	1998
Changes in Inventories	234.2	1,943.6	1,690.1	-1,767.5	2,170.9	1,825.7	3,914.4	-4,218.3	-27,983.1
(Ratios to GDP)	(0.1)	(0.7)	(0.6)	(-0.6)	(0.6)	(0.5)	(1.0)	(-1.0)	(-7.0)

Source: The Bank of Korea, "Recent Trends of Inventories," *Press Release* 2000-1-17.

Table 10. Decomposition of Exports

	Amount of Exports[1]	Amount Index[2]	Unit Value Index[2]	Volume Index[2]
1990	650.2	52.0	94.2	55.2
1991	718.7	57.5	94.7	60.7
1992	766.3	61.3	93.2	65.9
1993	822.4	65.7	93.6	70.2
1994	960.1	76.7	95.2	80.7
1995	1,250.6	100.0	100.0	100.0
1996	1,297.2	103.7	86.6	119.8
1997	1,361.6	108.9	72.8	149.6
1998	1,323.1	105.8	60.5	174.9

[1] In 100 million US dollars
[2] Indices express values relative to 100 in 1995.
Source: The Bank of Korea, *Economic Statistics Yearbook*, various issues.

Table 11. Trends of Major Economic Indicators Around 1997

	1993	1994	1995	1996	1997	1998
Economic growth[1](%)	5.7	8.4	8.2	4.8	2.4	-7.1
(manufacturing)	5.4	10.8	11.3	6.8	6.6	-7.2
Consumption	5.4	7.1	8.2	7.2	3.2	-8.2
Capital formation	6.3	10.7	11.9	7.3	-2.2	-21.1
Exports	11.3	16.1	24.6	11.2	21.4	13.3
Imports	6.2	21.6	22.4	14.2	3.2	-22.0
Current account (100mil.USD)	9.9	-38.7	-85.1	-230.0	-81.7	403.6
WPI(rate of change, %)	1.5	2.7	4.7	3.2	3.9	12.2
CPI(rate of change, %)	4.8	6.2	4.5	4.9	7.5	0.8
M_2(end of period, rate of change, %)	18.6	15.6	15.5	16.2	19.2	19.0
Budget balance[2]/GDP(%)	0.08	0.53	0.45	0.03	-0.02	-2.97

[1] Growth rate of GDP at 1995 prices
[2] On the basis of the central government budget
Source: The Bank of Korea, *Economic Statistics Yearbook*, various issues.

The total foreign debt of residents was climbing rapidly at that time, increasing from 120 billion U.S. dollars at the end of 1995 to 160 billion U.S. dollars at the end of 1996. This was mainly attributable to the widening current account deficit, but it was also influenced by increases in foreign borrowings by domestic firms and financial institutions following capital account liberalization.

Table 12. Trends of Foreign Debt (end of period, 100 mil. dollars)

	1992	1993	1994	1995	1996	1997	
						11p	12p
<IMF criterion>							
Long-term	260	267	303	410	575	729	860
	(..)	(2.9)	(13.5)	(35.5)	(40.3)	(26.7)	(49.5)
	<41.2>	<39.9>	<34.2>	<34.2>	<36.5>	<45.0>	<55.7>
Short-term	370	403	584	787	1,000	889	685
	(..)	(8.9)	(44.9)	(34.9)	(27.1)	(-11.1)	(-31.6)
	<58.8>	<60.1>	<65.8>	<65.8>	<63.5>	<55.0>	<44.3>
Total Foreign Debt	629	670	887	1,197	1,575	1,618	1,544
	(..)	(6.4)	(32.4)	(35.0)	·(31.6)	(2.7)	(-2.0)
<World Bank criterion>							
Total Foreign Debt	428	439	568	784	1,047	1,161	1,208
Long-term	243	247	265	331	437	545	696
Short-term	185	192	304	453	610	616	512

Numbers in ( ) denote rates of change and those in < > denote composition ratios.
Source: The Bank of Korea, *Statistical Yearbook of Foreign Exchange,* 1998.

Because of a recession with increased financial burdens of firms, entering 1997, cases of corporate insolvency began to propagate, and the banking sector's non-performing loans accumulated accordingly. Starting with the Hanbo Steel Company, which went bankrupt on January 23rd, 1997, the *chaebols* (Korean big business groups) began going under in a series consisting of Sammi, Jinro, Daenong, Hanshin-Gongyoung, and others. Accordingly, the portion of non-performing loans (classified as substandard, doubtful, and estimated loss credits) in total loans of banks rose from 4.1 percent at the end of 1996 to 6.0 percent at the end of 1997. These bankruptcies of big business groups revealed the evils of the Korean economy implied by cronyism or cozy relationships between political groups and businesses, and played a crucial role in the loss of Korea's economic credibility in the international community.

Under these circumstances, then, the Thailand Baht suddenly plummeted on July 2nd, 1997, signaling the beginning of currency crises in South East Asian countries. The Baht had been put under speculative attack as the Thai government attempted to maintain its value, while at the same time bailing out the troubled financial institutions in the wake of a bubble-like boom and bust, and collapse in the real estate market. Through contagion effects, the currencies of Malaysia, Indonesia and the Philippines, which were in similar situations or had close trade relationships with Thailand, also began steep depreciation. Afterwards, the speculative attacks on currencies spread to Taiwan and Hong Kong.

Immediately after the South East Asian currency crises, Kia Motors became insolvent, and foreign investors' confidence in the Korean economy was further undermined by the protracted resolution of the Kia Motors' problem. After the speculative attacks on the Taiwan and Hong Kong currencies took place, international credit rating agencies downgraded Korea's sovereign credit rating. From then on, international financial institutions would hardly agree to roll over their loans to Korean financial institutions. Korea's domestic financial institutions, no longer able to obtain finance abroad, were forced to purchase foreign currency on the domestic foreign exchange market for their daily settlements. The Bank of Korea accordingly provided them with foreign reserves, and the nation's stock of foreign reserves was rapidly depleted as the financial institutions failed to recover their credit-worthiness. In consequence, the Korean government asked the International Monetary Fund for emergency credits.

Immediately after the announcement of the IMF stand-by credit agreements and the associated IMF/IBRD economic reform program, the economic situation in Korea became genuinely critical due to break-down of financial intermediaries under the widening spread of business bankruptcies, to the point where normal operation of the economy was seriously threatened. Shortly thereafter, however, credits from international financial agencies flowed in, foreign debts began to be rolled over, and the balance of payments turned to surplus. In addition, the crisis began to be resolved, as Korean firms and financial institutions showed progress in restructuring. With these developments, the foreign exchange markets began to calm down, and Korea was able to emerge from the crisis situation.

The above discussions indicate that the 1997 economic crisis comprised a number of different characteristics – a corporate crisis, a banking (financial) crisis, a currency crisis, and a policy-driven crisis. It was nevertheless the typical type of economic crisis defined in Chapter 2, since the whole economic system was close to collapse.

B. Background of the 1997 Crisis

Since the nature of the 1997 crisis was so complicated, its causes may not be summarized by only one or two factors[21]. But for the sake of comparison with the other crises that happened in Korea, the following may be enumerated as important factors of the 1997 crisis:

(1) Over-investment

It is doubtful that the economy had been in an over-heated state in the period from 1994 to 1995, or that a speculative boom had occurred. The economic growth rates during the period were not as high as those in the past boom periods; investment showed no more than a mild increase. Thus, the economy at the time can hardly be viewed as having been in an over-heated state, let alone a speculative boom.

Table 13. Cases of Corporate Integration

	1991	1992	1993	1994	1995	1996	1997
Horizontal integration	43	39	36	40	58	73	78
Vertical integration	45	38	34	24	43	69	80
Conglomeration	66	72	53	131	224	252	260

Note: Horizontal integration brings together similar or related business types. Vertical integration occurs between businesses that have a supplier-customer relationship. A conglomeration integrates firms whose products are largely unrelated to each other with each other.

Source: Korea Fair Trade Commission, *White Book of Fair Trade*, various issues.

---

[21] In light of this, discussions in the Korean media after late November, when the currency crisis began to emerge, attributed the crisis to political, social, and cultural factors as well as economic ones.

From the viewpoint of industrial organization, however, the problem lay in the excessive-competition and over-investment in major industries, which resulted when many of the big business groups expanded their business areas by entering industries already full of competition. Heterogeneous business conglomeration, a type of business integration of companies whose products were largely unrelated to each other, increased rapidly from the mid-1990s. During this period, the firms seemed to have actively diversified their business areas in response to the trend toward globalization and domestic market opening. However, their strategy of entering new industries was ill-founded; the big business firms were seldom observed entering new and promising industries based on their own technological innovation. Rather, most of them entered industries in which other firms had already become established, and were known to be realizing high profit rates. The *chaebols* competed with each other in building petrochemical, electronic, and automobile factories, facilities for the distribution industry, and in the construction business. Such competition led to over- and duplicated capacity. Table 13 shows that heterogeneous business conglomeration, compared to other types of corporate integration, increased rapidly from the mid-1990s. Such over-investment resulted in over-production, and the profit prospects of the firms involved became dim. This over-investment underlined the inefficiency of the Korean economic system as a whole, and from time to time, triggered worries over the solvency of these firms.

(2) Over-borrowings and Maturity Mismatches   -

Deterioration in the financial structures of firms from the mid-1990s was one of the important factors behind the 1997 economic crisis. While firms expanded into new business areas, the economy began to stagnate, and corporate cash flows dried up. The firms thus attempted to meet their increased needs for funds through external financing. This practice was especially notable from 1996, when the economy entered a recession period. The debt-equity ratio in Korean manufacturing was 396 percent at the end of 1997[22], which was 110 percent points higher than that at the end of 1995.

Table 14 . Financial Indicators of Manufacturing in the 1990s (%)

	1990	91	92	93	94	95	96	97
Debt-equity ratio	282.5	306.7	318.7	294.9	302.5	286.8	317.1	396.3
Financial expenses-sales Ratio	5.12	5.69	6.31	5.93	5.64	5.57	5.84	6.39
Net income-total assets Ratio	1.48	1.41	0.89	1.04	1.90	2.83	0.50	-0.93
Current ratio	99.44	95.33	92.75	94.13	95.59	95.39	91.89	91.76

Source: The Bank of Korea, *Financial Statement Analysis*, various issues.

---

[22] The sharp rise in the debt-equity ratios of firms in 1997 was due partly to the steep depreciation of the Korean Won. But the *Financial Statement Analysis* of the Bank of Korea shows that the amount of debts denominated in foreign currencies owed by the manufacturing firms was about 10 trillion Won, which was not more than 3 percent of total debts. Even without the depreciation in 1997, the debt-equity ratio would have reached the level of 370~380 percent, considering that the loss from foreign exchange revaluation amounted to about 9 trillion Won and the capital stock was about 102 trillion Won.

Table 15. Foreign Debt by Borrowers (end of period, 100 mil. US dollars)

	1992	93	94	95	96	97
Public Sector	56	38	36	30	24	180
	<8.9>	<5.7>	<4.0>	<2.5>	<1.5>	<11.7>
Non-Bank Private Sector	137	156	200	261	356	423
	<21.8>	<23.4>	<22.6>	<21.8>	<22.6>	<27.4>
Financial Sector	436	475	651	905	1,195	941
	<69.3>	<70.9>	<73.4>	<75.6>	<75.9>	<60.9>
Total Foreign Debts	629	670	887	1,197	1,575	1,544

Numbers in < > denote composition ratio (%).

Source: The Bank of Korea, *Statistical Yearbook of Foreign Exchange,* 1998.

In the midst of globalization and capital account liberalization, corporations placed securities in the international financial markets on the strength of their own credits and increased their short-term borrowings of trade credits. Table 15 shows a big increase in the non-bank private sector's foreign borrowings.

Excessive maturity mismatches of debts were among the main factors that caused the 1997 economic crisis. Firms suffered from liquidity problem because their investments had not yielded normal profits yet, while a lot of their funds were fixed due to investments. For Korean manufacturing industry, the current ratio, i.e., the ratio of liquidity assets to liquidity liability, was a mere 92 percent at the end of 1996, the lowest recorded during the 1990s[23].

The same problems of the maturity mismatches occurred in the external sector as well. Firms and banks came to rely more and more on short-term foreign debt during this period. The ratio of short-term to total foreign debt at the end of 1996 was 63.5 percent by the IMF criterion, and 58.3 percent by the World Bank criterion as shown in Table 12. The short-term debt increased because current account deficits were financed mainly through short-term borrowings by financial institutions and through trade credits by business firms. The financial institutions used too much of the foreign exchange funds that they financed on short-term bases to make long-term investments. Moreover, the domestic financial institutions' investments were concentrated in the markets of the South East Asian countries and Russia, which went sour when those countries experienced currency crises at almost the same time as Korea did. Meanwhile, official foreign reserves were allocated in such a way that sufficient reserves could not be secured. Fairly large amount of Korea's foreign reserves were deposited with domestic banks and their overseas branches, and deposits could not be withdrawn in an emergency.

(3) Lack of Discipline

The lack of market discipline was another factor behind the 1997 crisis. Market discipline was at very disappointing level. Even though the country had already undergone such big changes as political democratization, economic liberalization, and market opening, Since government control or management had been able to deter economic agents from engaging in hazardous activities, the past government-led development system had at least been capable

---

[23] The current ratio decreased further to the level of below 90 percent in 1998 when corporate insolvencies increased steeply.

of sustaining itself, even if it could not attain the first best efficiency. With the results of economic liberalization and market opening, however, the government had been largely removed from such a role. Nevertheless, a new market discipline, the so-called market mechanism, had not been settled down.

Even after financial liberalization, for example, financial institutions remained too inactive to take on the role of checking and monitoring the behavior of customer firms. Nor were stockholders so active in monitoring managers as might have been expected, in light of the increased importance of the capital markets as the channel of financial resource allocation. Disclosure of information essential for checking management performance was also insufficient, while the role of credit evaluation agencies had not been established, either.

Regulation and supervision of financial institutions were still hardly developed. Prudential regulation was known to be essential in a liberalized environment, and some regulations had been established. In practice, however, they were neither sufficient nor effectively enforced. In fact, the playing field in the financial sector was tilted in favor of the non-bank financial institutions, leaving them with regulatory loopholes or loose supervision. Some of them, while lacking adequate capabilities to manage risk, nevertheless took extremely high risks in pursuit of high returns.

Failure to form a new disciplinary mechanism led to a situation in which individual actors' optimal choices conflicted with those of others or deviated from the social optimum. Making matters worse was the fact that there were no longer corrective actions which could be effectively taken. The government tendencies to gloss over the economic situation and practice excessive forbearance were never effectively corrected. Financial institutions took advantage of the implicit public guarantee of deposits, and engaged in gathering as much deposits as possible, while neglecting improvement of their profitability, or their capabilities to manage risk. Firms abused their increased ability to borrow, and engaged in high risk-high return strategies. The owner-managers of *chaebols* maximized their leverage and control, despite their small percentage shares of equity, by abusing mutual debt payment guarantees and cross-share holding. These owner-managers tended to manage a number of large firms dogmatically, or even despotically.

Such problems had been concealed by the brilliant growth performance of the Korean economy. Once revealed, however, they exposed Korean markets to sudden swings in investor confidence, i.e., to a crisis. The foreign – especially, short-term banking – capital that had previously flowed in, taking advantage of capital account liberalization and domestic market opening, abruptly withdrew from the Korean markets after confirming that the market's inefficiency stemmed from lack of discipline.

The lack of market discipline was certainly related to the continually accelerating promotion of liberalization before the crisis. One cannot say, however, that liberalization was the direct and fundamental cause for the absence of discipline. Even after liberalization, it takes time and effort – not only of the government but also of the market participants – to form market discipline. Thus, it is more to the point to say that a continuation of government control – different in form but similar in kind to that under the past authoritarian system – most impeded the formation of market discipline. To say it in another way, the liberalization was led by the government, and in the presence of government control or intervention in the financial sector, private sector initiative was not sufficiently exercised, especially in monitoring and checking the behavior of trade partners.

In this sense, it can be said that the predominance of government influence in the working of the financial sector was a cause for the sector's lack of discipline. The analysis here will not pursue this line any further, however, because termination of the so-called repression would not have automatically brought about market discipline. What is emphasized here is that lack of discipline and the resultant coordination failure exacerbated the adverse effects of the bounded rationality of economic actors, and thus provided a ground for the crisis.

(4) Loss of Confidence in Government's Policy

In some sense, inconsistency and ambiguity in the government's handling of the 1997 crisis exacerbated it. Proper action taken by the government in accordance with the circumstances would have prevented a critical situation from proceeding to a crisis or collapse. This had, in fact, always been the case in the past, when critical situations arose due to the government's pursuit of too rapid economic growth; through successful adaptations to the situations at such times, the government had always been able to preserve market confidence. In 1997, however, the government's policy response was unable to generate market participants' confidence. The government could not find its proper role in a market economy system. It failed to correctly diagnose the economic fundamentals, and to design the right prescription to cure what ailed them. It sometimes hid policy information that would have served the economy better if disclosed. It struggled to resist market forces even when it was obvious that accepting them was a better option. It failed to stop the propagation of the crisis; it did not heed the lessons of past experience, even after it had seen a few rounds of the crisis propagation process: corporate insolvencies leading to banking distress, and then to the near depletion of foreign reserves. In retrospect, there were several chances for the government to break the Korean economy's rolling in the vicious circle leading towards economic crisis in 1997. In this respect, the Korean government's policy mistakes during the years 1996 and 1997 can be listed as one of the factors behind the 1997 economic crisis

C. Policy Response

The government took varied measures to cope with the 1997 economic crisis, based on the recognition that the crisis resulted from accumulated structural imbalances in many areas. The main framework for crisis resolution, which was molded after the method of general IMF crisis resolution, was stated in the stand-by agreement, or letter of intent. It was composed of a macroeconomic stabilization policy and a microeconomic structural adjustment policy. The former was centered on restriction of domestic demand and expenditure-switching, to correct the balance of payments deficits. Exchange rates were thus allowed to depreciate freely and reflect market forces fully. At the same time, money market rates were raised sharply to control the inflationary impact of the Won depreciation. This extremely tight macroeconomic policy aimed at both restraining domestic expenditures and preventing capital outflows. The microeconomic structural adjustment policy, meanwhile, included measures to resolve structural problems in each market. Its fundamental theme was to establish the institutional setting for a well-functioning market mechanism.

Under the above framework, implementation of policies was practiced on the basis of a moving target approach, in which specific policy targets were changed according to circumstances. Right after the currency crisis, the primary target was to calm the foreign exchange markets through a sharp hike of money market rates, and to restore investors' confidence in the Korean economy through announcement of a restructuring plan, including the exit of troubled banks and the restructuring of industrial investments. From May 1998, when the foreign exchange market began to calm down and the Won stabilized, monetary policy was relaxed and the money market rates were lowered, in consideration of the by-then increased uncertainty in the domestic financial markets. The instability of domestic financial markets in mid-1998 reflected the credit crunch and wide-spread bankruptcy of firms at that time. The credit crunch resulted because all banks undergoing screening by the supervising authority, for possible market exits, refrained from lending. The widespread number of bankruptcy was due partly to this and partly to the high level of interest rates.

Table 16. IMF Reform Program

	Sector	Contents
Macro-Economic Policy	monetary and exchange rate policy	• tight money to contain inflation and limit downward pressure on the Won – large liquidity injection to be reversed, and money market rates raised – day-to-day conduct of monetary policy to be guided by movements in the exchange rates and short-term interest rates – targeting growth of M_3, reserve money, and net domestic assets of the BOK
	fiscal policy	• tightened to achieve a surplus – raising transportation tax, special excise tax, broadening the tax base – reducing current expenditures
Micro-economic Structural Adjustment Policy	financial sector	• comprehensive restructuring and strengthening of the financial system to make it sound, transparent, and more efficient – a clear and firm exit policy, strong market and supervisory discipline, increased competition
	trade and capital account liberalization	• streamlined import certification procedure and other trade-related regulations • acceleration of ongoing capital account liberalization program
	corporate governance and corporate financial structure	• improvement of corporate governance through financial reform and capital liberalization – easing restrictions on M&As, introduction of internationally accepted practices in accounting and consolidated balance sheets, revision of bankruptcy provisions, break from past policies of bail-outs
	labor market	• easing dismissal restrictions to improve labor market flexibility – facilitation of reemployment to ease the burden of layoffs

Source: IMF (1997).

Structural adjustment was largely divided into two stages. The first stage involved establishing basic institutions needed for smooth operation of a market economic system, and forcing insolvent firms and banks out of the market. For this purpose, varied policy measures were undertaken. The institutional capabilities for restructuring were enhanced by integrating the three extant financial supervisory agencies into one agency, the Financial Supervision Commission, and by expanding the function of Korea Deposit Insurance Corporation (KDIC), and establishing Korea Asset Management Corporation (KAMCO) to dispose of non-performing loans. Bankruptcy law provisions were amended and M&A restrictions eased. Disclosure requirements for accounting information were also strengthened, and measures to improve corporate governance introduced, to provide for better monitoring and supervision of corporate or bank managers by interested parties. The authorities also devised measures to restrain over-borrowing by firms, such as prohibition of mutual debt guarantees among firms in the same large business groups. The government forced extremely troubled banks to exit the market, and at the same time used public funds to buy non-performing loans from and recapitalize the viable ones. It let the main creditor banks lead the debt workout programs to liquidate delinquent firms.

The second stage structural adjustment plan aimed at improving the management and governance of firms and banks through their own initiatives. So far, however, firms and banks were not ready to enter this stage. This is mainly because the amounts of non-performing loans increased to an unexpectedly large extent, and because the first stage restructuring was delayed due to unexpected events such as the Daewoo Group's going into a workout program.

III. APPRAISAL OF POLICIES FOR RESOLVING THE CRISES IN THE PAST

1. The 1972 Crisis

The policies incorporated in the August 3rd Decree were evaluated by the authority as a success (The Bank of Korea 1973). The appraisal was based on economic performance, such as visible improvement in corporate financial structures and expansion of exports one year or so after the policies were implemented.

Seen from the present point of view, however, it can be said that the Decree was problematic in some ways; also, its effects were not so great in the long run. The nature of the economic crisis had been rightly identified as a corporate crisis, and the focus of policy appropriately put on improving the financial structure of firms and modernizing the financial system by introducing non-bank financial institutions. The problem lay in the methods used in pursuit of this policy. Especially, the write-offs of debts were obviously biased in favor of enterprises and against finance. The curb loan freeze and rescheduling did not leave room for autonomous financial transactions. It also violated the principle of private ownership and freedom of contracts. The root problem of worsening financial structure of corporations had been their strategies for unsustainably rapid expansion, despite their lack of internal funds. What was actually necessary to improve corporations' financial situations, therefore, was to slow down economic growth and restrain corporations from over-borrowing. Direct subsidies to firms, however, impeded the formation of a reasonable incentive mechanism, and deepened firms' prevalent tendencies to rely on external funds and government support.

The policy of fostering the establishment of non-bank financial institutions served to broaden the scope of the Korean financial system. However, the policy was ineffective in eradicating the curb market, which flourished again in the latter half of the 1970s and first half of the 1980s. Regulatory discrimination between banks and the newly established non-bank financial institutions brought about adverse side effects. The authority gave preferential treatment to the non-bank financial institutions, compared to the banks, in order to help these institutions grow out of their infancy. In this circumstance, the banks lost their market shares, which impeded their sound development. The fragility or weakness of the Korean financial system, a background factor of the 1997 economic crisis, seems to have originated from these policies in the 1970s.

At the time of the 1972 Crisis, the stabilization policy tended to rely on direct controls, rather than on orthodox macroeconomic tools. The government attempted to calm inflation by directly controlling the prices of products such as rice, construction materials, and living necessities. It managed the money supply through direct control of domestic credits from 1970. Unfortunately, this mode of policy implementation brought about adverse side effects afterwards, such as the spread of underground markets and dual prices, and supply shortages of important necessities. In particular, the direct control of domestic credits failed to prevent an excess supply of money in the late 1970s. It eroded the basis of the autonomous operations of banks as well. With regard to the basic stance of macroeconomic policy, in fact, it was expansionary. This was in some sense unavoidable, of course, as stimulating investment in the heavy and chemical industries was given a higher priority than resolving the problems associated with the over-heated economy in the late 1960s. However, the expansionary macroeconomic policy eventually caused over-heating and real estate speculation to spread widely in the late 1970s, and this was among the factors underlying the 1980 economic crisis.

Most of the 1972 crisis resolution measures shared characteristics of direct intervention and subsidies by government. For example, in relieving firms from financial distress, the government intervened directly by freezing their liabilities at the expense of breakdown of the curb market. Thus, the firms enjoyed a free lunch. In short, the crisis resolution measures in the early 1970s were effective to some extent in the short run, but in the long run deepened the structural anomalies of the Korean economy. These structural anomalies paved the way for both the 1980 crisis and the 1997 crisis.

2. The 1980 Crisis

The crisis resolution measures for the 1980 economic crisis contained a systematic blueprint based on a synthetic analysis of the various kinds of problems in the Korean economy. The government had at hand a stabilization plan prepared in 1979. The plan generally indicated the right direction for reforming the Korean economy, which was maintained even after the 1980s. Prices were visibly stabilized from 1982, and this contributed to the sustained surpluses in the current account in the latter half of the 1980s. Moreover, the liberalization policy after the crisis was quite consistently and gradually executed. Thus, it put in place a stepping stone for more aggressive liberalization policies in the 1990s.

The crisis resolution measures also laid the groundwork for financial development, both in quantity and in quality. Thanks to price stability, demand for financial assets increased, and correspondingly many new financial instruments were introduced. Especially, the stock and insurance markets, so underdeveloped previously, were able to grow substantially from the mid-1980s when inflation almost ceased. These developments in the financial sector in part reflected shift in emphasis in government's economic policy, from real to financial development, or its recognition of importance of both of them.

The public's perception of economic policy matters also changed as a result of the policy measures introduced in the early 1980s. In particular, the government campaign to deepen public understanding of stabilization policies succeeded, to some extent, in making the public to realize the importance of economic stability, among other objectives, and to accept the shift in policy focus from growth to stability. It seems that these consolidated efforts of the government and the public were rewarded by the country's excellent economic performance later.

Seen from the present point of view, however, the policy measures implemented following the 1980 economic crisis contained some problems as well. The trade-off between growth and stability was neglected, and both were pursued simultaneously. The policy tools for both were mixed together, causing considerable confusion. For example, in the latter half of 1980, about one year after implementation of the stabilization policy, expansionary monetary policy tools were used again. Once again, in the latter half of 1982, the government attempted, (through what were called the June 28th Measures) to activate the economy with a low interest rate policy similar to those in the 1970s. At the same time, the government sought economic stability through tight fiscal policy and direct control of prices. This combination of tight fiscal policy and expansionary monetary policy might be seen as an appropriate policy mix, in that the heavy and chemical industrialization plan required continuous investments by companies lacking internal funds. The fact that from the outset monetary contraction had been ruled out as a means of maintaining economic stability, however, implied that the policy means actually employed might not have been optimally suited to accomplish the policy goals. The fact that monetary policy tools remained only as a means for boosting the economy also indicates that the attitudes of the policy makers had not changed much; that is, they still put great importance to industrial development than to financial development.

The measures taken for liberalization also contained certain problematic aspects. It was then understood that liberalization was inevitable and necessary since the only way to cure the structural problems caused by repression or excessive government control was to liberalize. However, the actual liberalization measures included mostly deregulation of price controls, without serious consideration of need to provide the infrastructure for efficient markets. For example, interest rate liberalization, one of the major targets of liberalization policy, left much to be desired, in terms of stimulating innovation on the part of banks, because it was pursued in a narrow range with various forms of government intervention. It can also be pointed out that liberalization was a government-initiated process, rather than one initiated by private sectors. Thus, it was largely designed to meet the needs of the government, and not those of the private sector. Regarding the speed of the liberalization policy, it put too much importance to a gradual approach to bring about substantial effects. Moreover, it produced adverse side-effects, e.g., institutional disequilibrium such as the uneven playing field between banks and non-bank financial institutions.

In some senses, the nature of many of the economic policies remained largely similar to those in the past, in that such policy tools as controls and intervention were frequently used. Controls were applied to the management of prices, to restraining real estate speculation, and to improving corporate financial structures. In addition, selective industrial policies continued to be pursued through, for example, the Distribution Industry Modernization Plan, the Agricultural Machinery Import-substitution Plan, the Small- and Medium-sized Enterprises Promotion Plan, and the Electronic Industry Promotion Plan.

In short, even though the 1980 crisis resolution policy was rightly directed and performed well in the short run, it had only a limited effect in curing the fundamental problems of the Korean economy. This was verified in part by the similar crises recurred in the 1990s.

3. The Post-1989 "Grave Situation"

The government's attempt to overcome a policy-driven crisis by introducing the concept of industrial restructuring seems appropriate. It was also prudent for the government to have maintained consistency in its liberalization policy since the 1980s. There were problems, however. The policy goal was not clearly set, for one thing; and the same policy tools as in the past were applied.

The fact that the target of economic policy was not clear was, in part, due to the lack of a thorough analysis of the causes of the grave situation. The period was in the midst of revolutionary changes in political and social affairs; thus, a radical change in the goals, instruments, and mode of policy implementation was also required. Since the period had seen an eruption of desires that had previously been repressed, showing a stronger tendency for individual actors to pursue their own self-interests, a new policy paradigm, which would accord with these changes, was needed. Economic policy should have addressed such problems as the coordination of conflicting interests and the establishment of market infrastructure, rather than that of managing economic variables to optimal levels. It chose the latter, however; that is, policy makers addressed the short-term issues by making use of direct controls, as in the past. In order to sustain stock prices, for example, the government directly controlled the supply of and demand for stocks. In order to promote industrial restructuring, it provided preferential loans to borrowers importing equipment for factory automation and rationalization, through which many firms were induced to invest in equipment, the same kind pattern as observed in the past.

In another similarity to the past pattern, the government allotted macroeconomic policy to the objective of boosting the economy. Coming as it did after the long economic boom in the late 1980s, the period was characterized by big changes not only in political and social structures, but in consumption patterns as well. To facilitate the economy's adjustment, a dramatic change in policy tone was not desirable at the time, especially because uncertainty needed to be kept to a minimum. Macroeconomic policy, however, was operated in the manner of alternating, within a very short time period, between "stop(contraction)" and "go(expansion)." Furthermore, the economy was then confronted with contradicting trends, such as a slump in stock prices, a rally in real estate price, domestic recession, and a balance of payments deficit. Such a situation hardly yielded itself to a macroeconomic cure. Ideally, macroeconomic policy should have been kept neutral.

The nature of economic policy was not much different from the past, either. As mentioned above, the policy tools included direct controls, and were employed to temporarily address the problems revealed, rather than resolve them fundamentally. Preferential treatment of the real over the financial sector remained unchanged. Some policies were implemented in a manner that contradicted the trend of financial liberalization; for example, the policies for stabilization of stock prices, promotion of investment in manufacturing, and expansion of credits to small- and medium-sized enterprises were backed up mainly by using measures in the financial sector which might repress financial sector development.

In short, the substance of the policy responses to the grave situation in 1989 crisis was to employ direct control measures to resolve the problems which had surfaced. Policy makers neglected probing for a new policy paradigm appropriate for the new socio-economic structure and economic environment. Even worse, these problems innate in the economic system, rather than being fundamentally resolved, were covered over again after the New Economy 5-Year Plan was promoted in 1993.

4. Effectiveness of Crisis Resolutions in the Past

Crises of a similar type have repeatedly taken place under similar backgrounds, such as deterioration of the profitability of firms, over-investment and worsening financial structures, backwardness of the financial sector, and policy mistakes. The genetic processes of all the crises also resembled each other, since they all occurred after economic booms, or in over-heated economies. All in all, the economic crises in Korea may be regarded as having broken out as internal weaknesses – e.g., over-borrowings by firms – were exposed to external shocks – e.g., economic recession, worsening world economic environments, and so on. Similar policy measures were undertaken repeatedly to cope with the crises. In all cases, promotion of investment, through financial and fiscal incentives, was used immediately after the crisis outbreak, and macroeconomic policy was operated on an accommodating base. Moreover, direct controls on prices were frequently employed.

The mere observation that similar crises were being repeated implies that the past crisis resolution policies were not effective. In fact, the past crisis resolution measures consisted mostly of patching over the problems revealed, rather than addressing the root causes of the crises or trying to prevent crises beforehand. Instead, such measures tended more to deepen the structural problems. For example, most of the past crisis resolution measures focused on disposing of the losses incurred by firms and banks through such instruments as bail-outs. This might have lessened the difficulties facing firms and banks at those times; the effects were only temporary, however, and not of such kind as to help improve efficiency. Measures such as subsidies spoiled economic agents' independence and autonomy, eventually allowing them to stick to high leverage strategies or cronyism, distorting incentives and creating structural problems.

Delay of macroeconomic policy also tended to aggravate critical situations, rather than preventing further crisis. Before a crisis broke out, contractionary policy was introduced, but only after the adverse effect of the over-heated economy, or of the asset appreciation, had materialized. By the time the adverse effects are visible, the economy is already starting to slow down; thus, an expansionary, rather than a tight macroeconomic policy is needed. In Korea, however, a contractive policy has been adopted at this juncture, thus making the economy shrink rapidly. It has thus never been possible, however, for the contraction introduced to be promoted strongly enough or sustained long enough. This is because firms and banks have always asked for stimulus policies as production declined and profits decreased. Accordingly, immediately after the economic crises, governments had no choice but to relax macroeconomic policy. Pump-priming measures and favorable foreign economic conditions have then led to economic booms. This in turn sowed the seeds of a future crisis. Then, the story repeated itself.

IV. CHARACTERISTICS OF THE 1997 ECONOMIC CRISIS AND APPRAISAL OF ITS RESOLUTION

1. Main Characteristics of the 1997 Economic Crisis

The 1997 crisis differs from the previous ones in that the country could not resolve the critical situation with its own resources. There had been previous crises in which foreign debt had been the main problem, and in which the economy faced difficulty in inducing further capital inflow. At those times, however, the country had overcome the crises on the basis of its own creditworthiness. In 1997, in contrast, Korea could not borrow abroad any more. Thus, it had to depend on the liquidity facilities of international financial institutions and maturity rescheduling of foreign debts.

Another feature of the 1997 economic crisis is that even though the external shocks were weaker than those during the previous crises, e.g., the 1980 crisis, their effects were much stronger. As for the 1980 crisis, it was triggered by a number of large shocks. Externally, unstable international oil prices, turmoil in the international financial markets, and world-wide economic recession were all happening together. Internally, bad harvests were accompanied by political and social unrest. In 1997, however, the only shock was the instability in the international financial markets caused by the South East Asian currency crisis. The terms of trade had worsened in 1996, to a larger degree than expected, but they had then improved somewhat in 1997.

As for the impacts, that of the 1997 crisis seems to have been larger than that of the 1980 crisis, which was severe enough. The economic situations of 1980 and 1998 can be compared like this: in 1980, the growth rate was -2.1 percent and the unemployment rate 5.2 percent; in 1998, they were -6.7 percent and 6.8 percent, respectively. Moreover, the psychological impact seemed to be also larger in the 1997 crisis, because the crisis was a setback to Koreans who had taken such pride in the development of the Korean economy to join in the group of the advanced countries. The social impacts, such as damage to the middle and lower classes, were also huge.

The fact that the impact of the 1997 crisis was by far larger than those of other crises, even if the external shocks were relatively small, indicates that the main problem was weakness of the economic system as a whole. Of course, the extremely tight macroeconomic policy measures undertaken by the IMF program exacerbated the deep recession. However, the emergence of the crisis itself, even without any particularly large external shock, shows that the economic system was extremely fragile to shocks.

The extreme variety of types of crises involved in it may be another distinct feature of the 1997 crisis. Even though the 1980 crisis comprised many types of crisis factors, such as troubled firms, foreign debt-servicing problems, and inflation, it is analyzed as having been in essence a result of the simultaneous occurrence of external shocks. In the 1997 crisis, however, the sequence of events (firm insolvencies →non-performing loans of banks → loss of international confidence in the Korean economy) repeated itself twice or three times and generated corporate crisis, banking and/or financial crisis, and currency crisis in a series. To this list of crisis types might be added a balance of payments crisis, in that widening of current account deficits was one cause of those other types of crises. One trait of a policy-driven crisis may also be attached to the list, in that crisis resolution policy faltered over and again.

Considering the variety of features of the 1997 crisis, it seems to have resulted from all the problems remaining unresolved from past crises which all erupted at once by a relatively small shock from abroad. To put it another way, the innate problems of the Korean economic system finally came to greatly hinder the smooth operation of the economic system. The fact that a flaw in one sector could not be offset by the strength of another sector indicates that each part of the economic system was fragile. The variety of features of the 1997 economic crisis reflected these various weaknesses in almost all parts of the Korean economic system.

2. Comparison of the Structural Adjustment Policy since 1997 with the Past Economic Crisis Resolution

It appears too early to assess the policy responses to the 1997 crisis, since some of policy measures are in an ongoing process. In addition, its complexity would not allow an easy appraisal. One window to assess the recent crisis resolution measures may be provided, however, by comparison with the past crises. Compared with those adopted during past crises, the measures to cope with the 1997 crisis have some different aspects as well as some similar ones. Since most past crisis resolution measures were not effective, difference from them may be assessed as a positive feature, while similarity to past measures would be regarded as a negative feature of the recent structural adjustment policy. For example, the recent measures included an attempt to address the structural problems, something which was absent on past occasions. This can be evaluated as a positive feature.

A. Differences from the Previous Crisis Resolutions

The measures to resolve the 1997 crisis, unlike the previous ones, included attempts to provide indirect assistance to troubled firms and banks on the condition that they make their own efforts and take responsibility themselves to resolve their own problems. This differs from the unilateral provision of support in the previous crisis resolutions in that it has required the firms and banks being bailed-out to conduct restructuring. This is an improvement over the past crisis resolution measures, considering the fact that the past unilateral assistance tended to reduce the efficiency of the recipient firms and banks.

The recent crisis resolution policy also differs from the past ones in that the measures have spanned over a wide agenda and addressed fundamental issues. The measures included not only macroeconomic policy but also efforts to correct problems in the financial, corporate, labor, and public service sectors.

Another difference between the recent policy and earlier ones is that this time it addressed the issue of regulating the undesirable behavior of economic agent, for example, moral hazard, by adopting the global accounting standards and by strengthening the rule by law. This approach to curing the structural problems of the Korean economy should be highly evaluated.

The crisis resolution policy was so radical in a sense that it covered a wide-range agenda and touches the root causes of economic crisis. This was made possible by a social consensus, which was readily reached thanks to clear appearance of the structural problems as well as the wide-ranging impacts of the crisis.

The content of the policy was also different from those of previous ones in that it has included preemptive measures, to prevent recurrence of crisis, as well as *ex post* measures to cope with the troubled firms and banks. In the past, crisis resolution policy usually did not contain preventive measures. Nor was policy such as the clearance of non-performing loans of financial institutions promoted in a timely manner, right after the crisis breakout; rather, it tended to be implemented after the critical situation had somewhat calmed down. In contrast to this, the recent policy implemented the exits of insolvent banks and firms first, of all items on the agenda. Furthermore, policies taken at this time included changes in the laws and regulations, which was also *ex ante* in nature since it too aimed at preventing another crisis. Accordingly, the contents of the recent policy have also become different. In the past, the same policy tools as before were used again and again; in response to the 1997 crisis, however, new policy tools were adopted or old tools employed in different manners.

The mode of policy implementation this time changed to a radical reform or big-bang approach. This was because the government wanted to resolve the problems in many sectors within a short time span. Radical reform has the advantage of speeding up learning by all economic actors. It has the disadvantage, however, of requiring high adaptation costs. This contrasts to the gradual reform in the past, adopted mainly to reduce adaptation costs.

Another new feature in the recent crisis resolution is the improved variety and quality of policy instruments. In the past, financial instruments were almost the only measures used to cure any economic problem. In the 1997 crisis resolution, however, fiscal instruments and institutional rearrangements were added to the financial instruments, as new tools. Diversification of policy tools is meaningful; it has reminded policy makers that there are other policy tools than financial ones to achieve economic policy objectives.

In short, the 1997 crisis resolution policy can be highly evaluated in that it addressed the fundamental issues with various and wide-ranging policy tools.

Unlike the past ones, the recent structural adjustment policy has also attached more importance to the financial sector than to the real sector. Thus, the reform tends not to take the real sector's activities into account seriously. This is a cause for concern, because the source of long-run economic development in Korea has always been and still is in the real sector, and in the near future this situation does not seem likely to change dramatically; the Korean economy is still in the phase of economic development in which value is added mostly through industrial rather than financial competitiveness. In the increasingly competitive global environment, an economy is required to be very active in research and development in the real sector. Recently in Korea, however, investment has been extremely sluggish except in a few industries. This is partly because of the negligence of the structural adjustment programs in the real sectors.

B. Similarities to the Previous Crisis Resolutions

The *1997* crisis resolution policy also has some similarities with previous ones. Above all, it resembled past experience in that the government is playing a leading role in its design and implementation. The government first derived a consensus among workers and employers through the Tripartite Commission, and then promoted structural adjustment through the initiative of private actors. As time has gone by, however, the private sector agent's will to restructure has weakened, and in some cases the government has coercively pushed reforms to overrule disputes. Government initiation was certainly inevitable, because the reform was in its first stage (hardware reform) – a stage in which resolution of the troubled firms and banks was the focal issue[24]. However, the government has not been able to proceed to the second stage reform (software reform).

Since the reform was mainly led by the government, the effects were expected to be limited. For example, although firms have sharply reduced their debt-equity ratios, as the government forced them to do so, this did not necessarily mean that they had quit their old ways of doing business; in fact, they lowered their ratios largely through the revaluation of assets and issue of new stocks, rather than by redeeming debts or selling assets.

The operation of macroeconomic policy during the recent crisis resolution process resembled the past, too. Just as in the previous cases, the stabilization policy implemented in the early stage of the crisis exacerbated the situation further. It does seem, however, that while the switch of macroeconomic policy from a restrictive to an expansionary base from mid-1998 was similar to the past in its timing, it was different in its purpose. It was done not so much to boost the economy, as it had been in the past, as to stop the troubles in firms and banks from spilling over to others. The policy seemed to have amplified the intensity of the business cycle because it was so strong in magnitude and was introduced in an environment characterized by greater uncertainty. It also misdirected or lessened the effects of the restructuring efforts.

3. Implications for Structural Adjustment Policy

The main lesson from the above analysis of four crises in the Korean economy is that the problems intrinsic to the economic system should be cured fundamentally so that a crisis does not recur. The 1997 economic crisis was caused by over-borrowings by firms, financial sector weakness, inefficiency in the economic system, and policy mistakes. All of these factors are fundamental problems of the Korean economy; they had all been causes for past crises. Mishandling of the problems in the past might have contributed to the 1997 crisis. Measures to prevent future crises should focus on resolving these fundamental problems[25].

In order to prevent the same problems causing further crises, the methods used in crisis resolution should be different in nature from those employed in the past. In the past, similar

---

[24] The government's intention to distinguish between the first stage structural adjustment (hardware reform), which attempts at introduction and establishment of formal institutions such as laws and regulations, and the second stage structural adjustment (software reform), which aims at changing the behaviors of individual actors, may be interpreted as having resulted from neglect of the fact that institutions comprise not only rules, but also behavioral patterns.

[25] That an economic crisis may happen because of factors other than those so far discussed remains a possibility, of course.

policies were repeatedly used, such as subsidizing distressed firms and financial institutions. These policies were not effective, as is shown by the recurrence of similar crises afterwards. In other words, to protect, to support, and to foster firms and banks just because they are core components of the economic system, is not an appropriate way to go. On the contrary, such a policy aggravates the fragility of the economic system. Therefore, a crisis resolution policy should avoid using such bail-out measures, in order to prevent a crisis from coming back. The fact that structural adjustment policy following the 1997 crisis did not use unilateral subsidies to troubled firms and financial institutions should be highly evaluated.

It should also be noted that the measures initiated by the government, including the introduction of new laws and guidelines to improve the financial structures of firms and financial institutions, are not sufficient to prevent reoccurrence of a crisis. The measures so far were undertaken to establish the proper environment to enable firms and financial institutions to do business in a changed manner. The undertaking of such measures is one thing, and whether the firms and financial institutions will actually change their behavior is another. Firms and financial institutions should reinforce their business competence by themselves, lest they confront crisis again.

All economic agents, including firms and financial institutions, stakeholders, and the government, should make efforts together in order to complete the structural adjustment policy successfully. Above all, firms and banks must put their efforts into reducing their structural weaknesses. Moreover, the roles of stockholders, employees, creditors and customers, in checking and monitoring the behavior of firms or financial institutions, should also be strengthened. In addition, the government should enact regulations and laws ensuring that firms and financial institutions operate on their own initiative and exert their creativeness freely, and that they also assume responsibilities consonant with their new freedom to choose.

In this respect, introduction and implementation of the concept of the so-called second-generation reform is necessary for the success of the second stage structural adjustment policy. While the first-generation reform typically involves liberalization, stabilization, and selected structural reforms, the second-generation reform focuses on deeper and broader institutional reform, to enhance institutional capabilities (World Bank 1997). The first-generation reform can mostly be enacted through executive order, and thus the main actors are limited to the few elite technocrats. The second-generation reform, however, relates to all those affected by the institutional change. This implies that the government should refrain from initiating reforms, and ways should be opened for all interested parties to participate in the reform process, i.e., in identifying the problems, improving institutions, and creating a new economic order, all with the willingness for mutual understanding and compromise.

Macroeconomic policy, moreover, as a part of the crisis prevention measures, should be implemented in a manner different from the past. It is the timing of a stabilization policy that matters. In the past, poor timing of stabilization policy typically lessened the effects of stabilization policy. Stabilization measures were introduced just when the economy had begun to stagnate after a long period of boom, and seldom contributed to preventing recurrence of crisis. If a stabilization policy is to be used, it should be implemented in a preemptive manner so that it can prevent an exceptional boom or wide-spread speculation, which is one of the main macroeconomic causes of an economic crisis. Even in that case, of course, the authorities must remember that microeconomic means to reduce corporate over-borrowings and restrain banks' exposures are no less important in achieving the purpose than aggregate demand management

V. TENTATIVE CONCLUSION

This chapter employed an approach different from those lying behind the various common views of the recent structural adjustment policy in Korea. This chapter has first defined structural adjustment policy as a set of measures to prevent economic crisis from recurring, and then evaluated the effectiveness of the crisis resolution measures from this perspective. Utilization of this approach could probably do away with the confusions, which have arisen, among various reasons, from lack of a consistent analytic framework.

Another feature of this chapter is that it has attempted at finding some ways to enhance the effectiveness of the structural adjustment policy, based on analysis and comparison of past experiences. The successes or failures in past attempts at crisis resolution should be of great help in evaluating the recent one, considering the fact that there is no complete theory or experimentation on what constitutes an ideal restructuring program.

Finally, it should also be noted that historic facts are subject to different interpretations, depending upon what point of view they are seen from. The same is true of the interpretation of the ongoing Korean economic structural adjustment policy. A researcher may arrive at different conclusions or draw different policy implications from those contained in this chapter if he starts from a different point of view. Therefore, more effective assessment of the structural adjustment policy would entail analyses from many points of view, and then a synthesis of them.

Bearing all of these points in minds, this chapter can reach a tentative conclusion as follows: Korea has experienced four episodes of economic crisis since the 1960s. This chapter examined each crisis and found out that the same factors that caused one previous crisis later brought about another crisis repeatedly. This implies that the measures taken to resolve the previous crises were ultimately ineffective. Most of the past crisis resolution measures focused on disposing of the losses incurred by firms and banks through such instruments as bail-out loans. As far as macroeconomic policy is concerned, stabilization measures were introduced just when the economy had begun to stagnate after a long period of boom, and seldom contributed to preventing recurrence of crisis; rather, they amplified the crisis intensity.

These results suggest several lessons for the restructuring policy. First, it should be designed in such a way as to encourage private agents to take initiative, with the government abstaining from direct intervention such as bail-out loans. This would eventually strengthen private sector capacity to overcome adverse shocks. Second, if a stabilization policy is to be used, it should be implemented in a preemptive manner, so that it can prevent an excessive boom or wide-spread speculation.

ACKNOWLEDGEMENTS

The authors would like to thank their colleagues for their constructive comments and suggestions. This chapter is a substantially revised version of the working paper entitled "Korean Experiences of Economic Crisis Resolution" by the first author. The views contained in this paper are the authors' own, and do not necessarily represent the official views of the Bank of Korea.

REFERENCES

In Korean

The Bank of Korea, (1973). *A Comprehensive Report on The August 3rd Economic Emergency Decree,* Seoul: The Bank of Korea.

_____, *Economic Statistics Yearbook*, various issues.

_____, *National Account,* various issues.

_____, *Financial Statement Analysis,* various issues.

_____, (1998). *Statistical Yearbook of Foreign Exchange*, Seoul: The Bank of Korea.

_____, (2000). *The Bank of Korea: A History of Fifty Years, Seoul:* The Bank of Korea.

Economic Planning Board, (1980). *Economic Policy in the Periods of Liberalized and Open Economy: 30 Years of the Economic Planning Board* Ⅱ, Seoul: Economic Planning Board.

Fair Trade Commission, *Fair Trade White Book,* various issues.

Kim, Jung-Ryum, (1990). *30 Years of Economic Development Policy in Korea: Memoirs of Kim Jung-Ryum*, Seoul: Jungang Ilbo

Korea Development Institute, (1981). *Collections of Economic Stabilization Policy Measures* (Book I and Book II), Seoul: Korea Development Institute.

Lee, Jong Kyu, (2000). *Economic Crisis: Causes and Genetic Process, Economic Studies Series, No. 2*, Seoul: Economic Studies Office, The Bank of Korea.

In English

Fry, Maxwell J., (1995). *Money Interest, and Banking in Economic Development* (2nd Ed.), Baltimore and London: Johns Hopkins University Press.

Goldstein, Morris and Philip Turner, (1996). *Banking Crises in Emerging Economies: Origins and Policy Options,"* BIS Economic Papers, No. 46, Basle, Switzerland: Bank for International Settlements.

IMF, (1997). *Republic of Korea − Request for Stand-by Arrangement,* mimeograph.

Kang, David, (2002). Bad Loans to Good Friends: Money Politics and the Development State in South Korea, *International Organization* 56, 177-207.

Kindleberger, Charles P., (1996). *Manias, Panics and Crises: A History of Financial Crises,* 3rd edition, New York: John Wiley and Sons.

Krueger, Anne O., (1993). *Political Economy of Policy Reform in Developing Countries,* Cambridge: MIT Press.

Lee, S. and K. Cheong, (2007). The Political Economy of Financial Structure of Korean Firms, *Journal of Developing Areas,* forthcoming.

MacKinnon, Ronald I., (1973). *Money and Capital in Economic Development,* Washington D. C.: Brookings Institution.

Schandler, Susan et al., (1995). IMF Conditionality: Experience under Stand-by and Extended Arrangements, Part I: Key Issues and Findings, *IMF Occasional Paper,* No. 128, Washington D. C.: IMF.

World Bank, (1997). The State in a Changing World, *World Development Report* 1997, New York: Oxford University Press.

In: Political Economy Research Focus
Editor: Walter R. Levin, pp.47-68

ISBN 978-1-60456-154-8
© 2008 Nova Science Publishers, Inc.

Chapter 2

NORMATIVE POLITICAL ECONOMY

Jeff Noonan
University of Windsor, Windsor, Ontario, Canada

ABSTRACT

As George De Martino argues in *Global Economy, Global Justice,* neo-classical economics smuggles in a host of dubious normative premises beneath its veneer of scientific objectivity. In response, De Martino calls for an explicitly normative political economy oriented by the question: what constitutes a just economic outcome' My paper will focus on developing an answer to this question rooted in the idea, systematised in the work of John McMurtry, of the 'life-ground of value.' The paper will begin with an account of human social-organic nature. The goal of the first part of the paper is to demonstrate (against neo-classical orthodoxy) that human beings are defined by a set of objective organic, socio-cultural, and temporal needs. Because human beings must satisfy these needs through cooperative productive systems (economies), every such system contains an in-built 'life-grounded' principle of evaluation. Thus the basic normative question to be asked of every socio-economic system is: how well is it able to satisfy the defining needs of its members? In the second section the paper will evaluate the global economic system from this perspective. I will argue that the current global economic system fails to meet the objective needs of its members because its ruling value system is disconnected from the life-ground of value. The ruling value system assumes that whatever investment produces profitable returns is a good (just) economic outcome. The final section of the paper presents an interpretation of Pat Devine's 'negotiated coordination' economy as a life-grounded alternative to the present global system

In his *Global Economy, Global Justice,* George DeMartino contrasts the responses of neo-classical economics and his version of a human capabilities-based approach to economics to the question: what makes for a good economic outcome?(DeMartino, 2000). The aim of this contrast is to expose to criticism the ruling assumption of neo-classical theory: a good economic outcome is any outcome that maximally satisfies consumer preferences as determined by people's allocation of income through market transactions. In conditions of absolutely free markets, a good outcome would thus coincide with whatever outcome ensues. In less than ideal conditions, a good outcome is whatever best approximates the utopian optimality of self-governing markets. As DeMartino carefully demonstrates, the neo-classical answer, which purports to be descriptive, objective, and scientific, in fact rests upon unargued normative assumptions about value, human motivations and rationality, the role of choice, and the meaning and conditions of human freedom. Rather than describe a neutral economic reality, DeMartino argues that neo-classical conceptions of good economic outcomes both presuppose and serve to legitimate a definite set of historically specific values (norms). The serious and growing economic inequality in the world today, DeMartino believes, is strong evidence in favour of the necessity of an alternative answer to this question.[1]

The significance of DeMartino's question lies in its uncovering the normative core of political economy. That is, political economy is not a science like physics or chemistry which simply measures the states of energetic systems and processes that occur independently of conceptual structures of evaluation and decision. The so-called uncertainty principle notwithstanding, the objects of physical science are not arbitrary symbolic creations of scientists, and the properties, dynamics, and potentialities of those objects, while modifiable and manipulable, are the products of ten or so billion years of the evolution of energy in the universe and as such relatively indifferent to human symbolic and institutional organization. The objects of political economy are quite otherwise. While it is true, as we will see, that economics too has a material foundation in the life-supportive field of nature, how human productive activity interacts with and utilises that nature cannot be understood in a value neutral way. The half life of a radioactive isotope does not depend upon there being scientists who believe in half-life, radioactivity, or isotopes. Whether an economy reproduces itself through gifts, central authoritarian decisions, or market transactions, however, is not a norm-independent fact of nature, but a symbolic-institutional reality that depends as much on the beliefs and motivations of those whose actions reproduce it as on the more or less fixed external nature upon which productive activity draws.

My aim in this paper is to work from DeMartino's question to the deepest foundation upon which a sound answer can be based. That foundation I will call, following the pioneering work of John McMurtry, the "life-ground of value." (McMurtry, 1998, p. 23). Human societies, including their economic dimensions, will be understood as different systems of value. The goodness of any particular system of value, in turn, will be determined by how well or ill it advances this underlying life-ground. In the most general terms, the life-ground of value is the "connection of life to life's requirements" that must be maintained by all living things if they are to preserve their existence and unfold their defining life-capabilities in the widest and deepest ways that they are able. Although it is clear from this general definition that all life has some degree of life-value, my focus here will be exclusively on human life because it is, as I will explain below, the most valuable form of life that we

---

[1]Measuring economic inequality is a notoriously difficult empirical task. For a balanced overview of the difficulties and a convincing conclusion in favour of the reality of growing inequality, see Wade, 2003, pp. 18-46). For a more technical examination of the difficulties of determining inequality in the international arena, see Milanovic, 2006) Milanovic finds that contrary to the expectation that open markets would increase inequality in rich countries and lessen it in poor countries, this is not what has tended to happen. As in Wade, the evidence suggests that income inequality has been growing in poor, middle, and high income countries. (p. 11) For the reality of growing income inequality in the United States, see (Economist.com, Tuesday June 12th 2007- anonymous report).

know. I will argue that the value structure of the ruling Global Capitalist Market System (GCMS) is systematically blind to this underlying life-ground.

This systematic life-blindness does not mean, of course, that the GCMS never satisfies human life-requirements, but rather that its ruling value system judges life-value in terms of money-value, and this judgement rests on what I will argue is a systematic inversion of intrinsic and instrumental values. This inversion of values means, concretely, that the GCMS selects for forms of investment which are most likely to increase money-value and judge this increase as an increase in life-value full stop, even in cases where it becomes clear, from a life-grounded perspective, that gross failures of life-requirement satisfaction are occurring. While it is true that the GCMS has generated unprecedented social wealth, this wealth has only been utilised for collective life-supportive infrastructure under pain of social struggles operating from opposed systems of value. This on-going struggle over life-supportive resources, in the context of growing environmental threats to overall life-security, calls forth, I will argue, the need for an alternative understanding of economic systems and measures of value. Alternative economic systems cannot, of course, simply be stipulated by argument and then willed into being. Life-protective social institutions, historical experience teaches, must evolve and develop through very complex forms of coordinated human activity. The programmatic nature of my comments regarding an alternative set of economic institutions and practices is not meant to suggest that it is a ready made programme that can handle all contingencies. Abstracting from real-life complexity in this case is justified only by the need for clarity. Hard cases and unforseen eventualities cannot be pre-empted by theory.

The argument will be developed in three general parts. In the first part I will explain and justify the life-ground of value, the understanding of human nature that it implies, and its relationship to economic value generally construed. In the second part I will examine the ruling system of value in the GCMS and demonstrate how its expansion proceeds on the basis of a destructive moral inversion between its steering value (money-value) and life-value. In the third and final part I will explicate the basic outlines of an alternative set of economic institutions and practices consonant with the life-ground of value.

PART I: NATURE, LIFE-REQUIREMENTS, AND THE LIFE-FUNCTIONS OF ECONOMIES

It is a fact that might be denied in sceptical philosophy but never in reality, that all life depends upon a more or less fixed range of basic life-requirements. Judged from this perspective, nature is the most fundamental field of life-support. While the content of life-requirements differs for aerobic and anaerobic organisms, animals with gills and animals with lungs, and animals with simple nervous systems and animals with complex cerebral cortexes that produce consciousness and the ability to mediate their life-activity with symbolic meaning, the *value* of nature for all is the same: nature is the most fundamental and irreplaceable field of life-support that there is and can be. Even if artificial life and intelligence were someday created, it too would depend upon regular inputs of energy that would ultimately derive from a natural source. Hence nature, as the irreplaceable field of life-support, is the *given* (i.e. not consciously created) basis of life-value. It is the ultimate source of the life-requirements upon which all basic and higher life-activities depend. All individual life forms exist within and depend upon a natural-material field of life-support for their existence, their health, and their range of capability development.

While the sciences of physics, chemistry, biochemistry, biology, zoology, evolutionary genetics, and ecology study the natural life-field from the standpoint of its quantifiable energetic organization, their startling and magnificent insights over the past two hundred years cannot replace philosophy as a systematic and irreducible inquiry into this same field of energetic organization as a field (or, as we will see, fields) of *value.* Value I define as 'that in the *object* which makes it an object of care and concern for a *subject.*' Both objective and subjective poles are essential to understanding value. The objective pole is necessary so that there is a basis of value beyond the manipulable conscious beliefs and desires of subjects. The subjective pole is equally necessary because value is fully realized only in conscious enjoyment of it. For example, we might say that a painting has aesthetic value because of the formal organization of its content, but this value can only be fully realized if there are conscious subjects who appreciate it and grow in experience through seeing and thinking about it. Value is thus *grounded* in the object, and *realized* in the subject. The importance of the two-sided nature of value will become apparent when I turn to the question of the nature of economic value.

Of all the different forms of value (aesthetic, economic, sentimental, etc) the most basic, i.e., that which is presupposed by all the other forms, must be life-value. First, without life there are no subjects, and therefore the condition for the realization of any value whatsoever would be lacking. Second, all other forms of value are valuable in so far as they make different concrete contributions to the growth of the value of life for living subjects. Comprehended philosophically and not as simple metabolic and reproductive processes, life is essentially a dynamic of conscious valuation of better over worse states of being. In other words, living things, and human beings most of all, strive to maintain those connections with their life-requirements that enable them to live, to be healthy, and to more fully realize and enjoy their vital capabilities in society with others. This understanding of life-value entails what McMurtry calls the 'life-sequence of value' as the basic metric of value creation. In schematic form this sequence is stated as L— Ml— L' where L is life, Ml is means of life, and L' is more life. As he explains, "In this formula *life* , means organic movement, sentience and feeling, and thought. *Means of life* refers to whatever enables life to be preserved or to extend its vital ranges, ... to reproduce life-value is to hold these capacities at their established scope. To increase life value is to widen or deepen them to a more comprehensive range." (McMurtry, 1998, p. 298). The key point to note here is that life-value is realized by, but not reducible to, the appropriation of the means of life (life-requirements) by all who need them. Satisfying life-requirements is the necessary instrumental condition of realizing and enjoying the life value of feeling, moving, and thinking in their multiple dimensions.

Human historical development makes clear that humans have long since ceased to live directly on the bounty of the earth's fields and streams and oceans. As Marx rightly observed, that which distinguishes human beings from our fellow creatures is that we universally produce *out of the natural field of life-value*, the goods and products that our specific form of life requires. (Marx, 1975, p. 37). Production, distribution, and appropriation of goods is the domain of economics. We can see, therefore, that in essence economic (productive) activity is the basic form of life-activity for human beings. Judged from this life-grounded foundation, economic activity is the immediate connection of human beings to their basic life-resources. The 'goods' that a life-grounded economics concerns itself with must therefore be those resources without which human life cannot continue, cannot be healthy, and cannot develop and enjoy its full range of defining capabilities in society with others.

This understanding of economics clearly contrasts with the dominant understanding of economic activity in neo-classical thought. Neoclassical economics abstracts completely from the life-grounded foundation explained above and instead examines economic activity as a complex series of market exchanges without regard to whether or not those exchanges concerns goods that are life-valuable, life-indifferent, or life-destructive. This understanding of market exchnage is clearly expressed by one of its most insightful students, Friedrich von Hayek. "The decisive step which made ... peaceful coexistence possible in the absence of concrete common purposes was the adoption of barter and exchange. It was the simple recognition that different persons had different uses for the same things ... all that was required to bring this about was that rules be recognised which determined what belonged to each, and how such property could be transferred by consent."(Von Hayek, 1976, p. 109). This interpretation is sound as far as it goes, but note what it presupposes. It presupposes the most basic fact to be explained: how it is that there are any people to buy and sell in the market place. The very existence of market agents clearly presupposes that they have been born, fed, cared for, educated to the minimal extent of being able to speak a language, cured of fatal diseases, and so forth. Yet these most basic facts are left unaccounted for in the classical and neoclassical models. From Adam Smith onward, economic science simple assumes already highly developed market institutions populated by conscious adults. Whether Smith's " propensity to truck barter and exchange" is a fact of human nature or not, it is obvious from experience that it does not manifest itself at birth, but is the behaviour of humans who have attained a minimum of physical and cognitive maturity. (Smith, 1979, p. 117). But how do humans arrive at this point if not by satisfying their life-requirements via regular connection to the fields of life support? But neoclassical economics completely ignores the essential underlying condition of any human activity, including market activity: the regular satisfaction of human life-requirements, or needs.

As will become clear, neoclassical economics ignores the category of need for essential reasons. Before explaining those reasons, however, it is necessary to define clearly what is meant (and not meant) by 'need.' The life-grounded conception of need refers to any fundamental life-requirement of human beings, where "fundamental" indicates that deprivation of the object of the need regularly results in objective harm. Needs in this sense may be distinguished from the consumer demands central to neo-classical economics as well as from instrumental system needs by McMurtry's criterion: "n is a need, if and only if, and to the extent that, deprivation of n always results in a reduction of organic capability."(McMurtry, 1998, p. 164). Needs as fundamental life-requirements are distinct from consumer demands because the objects of consumer demand have no necessary connection to life, health, or active well-being (and often detract from all three). For example, it is a fundamental life-requirement that I regularly eat nutritious food. Having grown up in North America during the fast food age, I nevertheless sometimes want (i.e., demand) high-fat, high sodium hamburgers from fast food restaurants. Since being deprived of this demand results in no reduction of organic capability, (indeed, avoiding fast food improves my health), it is not a need, and no real harm ensues my being deprived of it, regardless of how I might feel. The subjective feeling of deprivation I might feel can be alleviated by changing my self interpretation. If I am malnourished, on the other hand, no change of self-interpretation can alter the harm that I will suffer.

Instrumental system needs are a more difficult case. An instrumental system need is an object that I require given the structure of the society that I live in, although if society were otherwise organized I would not need that object (or at least not to the same extent). For example, if someone lives in a suburb ill-served by public transit, they will have an instrumental system need for a private automobile. Real harm can ensue to someone deprived of such a system need, *but only to the extent that society is not reorganized to provide different alternatives.* If adequate public transit served the area where the person lived, or if zoning regulations changed to allow mixed use land development, the instrumental system need would be correspondingly altered.

The point of defining needs as fundamental life-requirements is not to determine from the outside, by authoritarian fiat, what everyone should want and how they should live. Rather, it is to establish a life-grounded base-line to which public policy can turn to establish productive priorities. Thus the question arises: what is the scope of needs as fundamental life-requirements, that is, what ought the priorities of production be in a well-functioning economy? Answering this question requires that we pause to reflect upon the social organic nature of human beings. It is only once we are clear about what human nature is that we can be clear about what our essential capabilities are, and thus what the fundamental requirements a well-functioning economy ought to prioritise are. Rather than list, in a more or less ad hoc fashion, a set of capabilities (as, for example, Martha Nussbaum does), the life-grounded approach searches for comprehensive minima that follow from uncontroversial capabilities people have. (See Nussbaum, 2006, pp. 76-78) The most obvious capability that human beings have is organic movement and sentience– the basic metabolic functions and sensory capabilities that define human beings in the organic dimension of their existence. Maintaining these basic metabolic and sensory functions requires basic material inputs throughout the course of life: water, vitamins, minerals, proteins, physical care while young, health care when sick, clothing and shelter from the elements, and so forth. Hence the first set of life-requirements a life-grounded economic system is obliged to prioritise are the basic material elements necessary for *life.*

It would be correct to object at this point that these needs are so minimal as to fail to distinguish *human* life from animal life in general. It will be argued, and correctly, that human life is defined by the symbolic wealth of conscious and self-conscious social being. The life-grounded perspective completely agrees. However, it insists not on a gulf between the symbolic and the material, the organic and the social, but rather on their integral unity. Human consciousness is an emergent property of the evolved structure of our brains in historically developed and symbolically mediated social relations. Hence a second set of minima follows from our conscious, social nature. In order to develop our imaginative, cognitive, communicative, and materially creative capabilities we require, in addition to the material inputs required by healthy organic existence, institutional and symbolic inputs that depend more directly on social organization. The most obvious life-requirement of *human,* as opposed to mere, life, is education. In the absence of any education whatsoever we would not even develop the most basic social capability of language use. In addition, we require, especially while young, love and care from adult guardians, so that we develop the capabilities to trust, cooperate, and interact lovingly and in non-instrumental ways with others. We also require institutions that enable us to play, that expose us to artistic creations of all sorts, so that our capabilities to move creatively and to imagine develop. In addition, humans require institutions that allow us to find individually meaningful and socially valuable work, so that our practically creative capabilities may be realized. Finally, since human nature is *social*-organic, we require political institutions that enable all citizens of different societies to participate in the formulation of the public policies that determine their lives (and these institutions include economic institutions, as I will explain in Part Three below).

There is a final dimension of human life-requirements whose fundamental connection to full human development is too rarely noted. This final dimension is free time. By free time I do not refer in the first instance to the simple quantity of time outside of labour at the disposal of individual subjects. Having a quantity of time at one's free disposal is the material condition of free time, but free time itself, in the life-grounded sense, refers to an experience of time itself as free, as an open matrix of possibilities for life-activity. This meaning contrasts with the "modularized" experience of time in advanced consumer capitalist societies today. (Van der Poel, 1997, pp. 171-94). Here, although there is a greater quantity of empty time at the disposal of people as compared to earlier periods of industrial society, this empty time is not experienced as an open matrix of possibilities, but as a series of 'modules' to be filled largely through the consumption of pre-structured forms of entertainment and leisure. Leisure time is simply the mirror-image of work time– both are essentially structured by external market forces and in neither is imagination, creativity, individuality, or valuable contributions to others developed as the steering value of the practices. Yet it is imagination, creativity, individuality, and valuable contributions to others that really mark out human life as distinctive, and distinctively valuable, for only in the human being is the capacity to positively delight in the value that one's creations and work have for others fully realized. Yet, if life is by and large a pre-determined sequence of activities determined by external forces, none of these capabilities can be *freely developed* (which is not to say that they cannot be developed at all). Hence, the final minimum life-requirement to be prioritised by a life-grounded economy is free time. The qualitative, experiential essence of free time depends, as I said, on having available a quantity of non-work time.

Could it not be objected, however, that these minima are purely arbitrary, relative to a set of philosophical premises about human nature which have no sure claim to veracity. The best way to respond to this important objection is to subject it to an empirical test. The empirical test in this case involves the objector asking him or herself if there is a rationally defensible sense to any conception of human life as *gaining* in value by *reducing* any of these minima to the point where the capability in question cannot be realized. To put the point bluntly: is it rationally defensible to maintain that life *improves* if people have to drink polluted rather than clean water, have less rather than sufficient nutrients in their food, or no access rather than access to health care? If anyone argues 'yes' and means it then they should lead by example and disconnect their water system from the local water treatment plant and not replace its life-protective function with an alternative, starve themselves, and get rid of their health insurance. At this point it is a virtual certainty that the well-educated sceptic will give up their objection or maintain it in a purely verbal form without a verifying change of practice. The same argument holds for the second and third classes of life-requirement. Can a life improve if one's abilities to think, imagine, create, and contribute positively to the lives of others is reduced rather than expanded? On what defensible conception of human life can it be better to have less education than is required for full self-development? Or to be imprisoned in the narrow mindedness that comes from having no access to the artistic and cultural creations of others of one's own or different cultures? Or to have been brutalised while young rather than loved? Or to be forced by circumstances to repeat the same mindless task rather than to develop meaningful capabilities that make a positive difference to others' lives through one's work? Or to be forced at gunpoint to execute the decisions of an authoritarian government rather than freely determine through peaceful debate with one's fellow citizens the laws and policies all will obey? The same again holds for free time. What understanding of human being would permit the objector to infer that the experience of life as the mechanical repetition of routine is better than experiencing the future as an open matrix of possibility? Once again, since the argument concerns real life-activity and its social and natural conditions, the usual empty thought experiments of philosophy which do nothing but obfuscate real material life will not satisfy the challenge. The challenge can only be answered by citing a real example. The real example, furthermore, cannot simply refer to different contents, or ways of eating, acting, educating and so forth. Differences of content, cultural or individual, are differences of what Doyal and Gough call 'need-satisfiers.' (Doyal and Gough, 1991, pp. 155-9) What is required is an example of a human life that is better for being deprived of one of the minima examined above, not one particular way of satisfying them. I am confident that such an example cannot be produced on the terms stipulated by the test.

Let me now sum this section up. In all three cases it is clear that the degree to which we can satisfy these minimum life-requirements depends largely upon the structure of economic institutions. What is available to eat and drink, the extent of people's educational and work opportunities, the diversity and accessibility of cultural institutions, and the quantity of time people must devote to work are all determined in general by the principles that determine how a society allocates its resources, what it produces, how it distributes and uses what is produced. Moreover, while not mechanically determined by economic institutions, the psychological dispositions according to which personal motivations are formed is essentially bound up with the reward structure of a given society. Since rewards are also resources, these structures of motivation also cannot be understood outside of the regulating value-system of the economy in any given society. As we will now see in the next section, the regulating principles of the GCMS are at odds with these life-grounded economic principles.

PART 2: THE LIFE-BLIND GLOBAL CAPITALIST MARKET SYSTEM

In the previous section I argued that economic institutions and practices form a life-grounded mediation between the natural field of life-support and socio-cultural, symbolic and temporal fields of higher human capability development, expression, and enjoyment. Economic goods in this life-grounded conception are objects and services that satisfy life-requirements in the three domains specified. This understanding of an economy is, however, completely foreign to the ruling value-system of the global market economy as well as the still dominant neo-classical theory that explains its dynamics and justifies its outcome and reward structure. To begin this part it is first essential to understand the neo-classical conception of an economy, the meaning of economic 'good,' and the underlying value system that justifies both as well as the motivating reward structure whose internalization helps to reproduce the system. Once this understanding of economic institutions and justifying value-system has been made clear, the precise reasons why the GCMS is life-blind will be apparent. This part will conclude with a clear recapitulation of these reasons supported by the example of the opposition between market rationality and life-requirements in the current debate over the 'economic costs' of global warming.

To get a clear grasp of what neo-classical economics understands economies, economic goods, and optimal economic dynamics to be, let us turn again to the work of von Hayek, who explicates the normative presuppositions that remain submerged in neo-classical economics proper. For von Hayek an economy is "in the strict sense of the term ... a complex of activities by which a given set of means is allocated in accordance with a unitary plan among the competing ends according to their relative importance." (von Hayek, 1973, p. 107). For von Hayek then an economy is a process through which means are allocated between competing ends. As I noted in the first section von Hayek simply presupposes the existence of the people whose activity creates these productive units, i.e., they are simply assumed to be there with competing ends. By assuming what must be explained– how there are people with competing ends– von Hayek simply makes the life-ground disappear. That is, since his theory just ignores the fact that (at the very least) the natural life-requirements of people must be satisfied by their productive activity before there can be any competing ends, he frees his formalistic definition of the economy from having to take into account the *necessary* ends or purposes any economy must satisfy.

The importance of this freedom his abstraction allows him only becomes clear when we shift focus from the basic idea of an economy to his conception of a generalized economic system. In any free generalized economic system, von Hayek makes clear, "there can exist ... no single ordering of needs."(von Hayek, 1973, p.113). As with his understanding of economies, so too his understanding of needs is purely formalistic, in that it refers simply to whatever means anyone requires to pursue any project whatsoever. It thus fails to distinguish between needs as life-requirements, instrumental system needs, and mere consumer demand. Given his claim that there can be no single ranking of needs, it is immediately apparent that these differences simply do not exist for von Hayek. In fact, he believes that a free, or market-based, economic network can only exist if the crucial distinction between needs as life-requirements, instrumental system needs, and mere consumer demand is absent:

> A policy making use of the spontaneously ordering forces therefore cannot aim at a known maximum of particular results, but must aim at increasing, for any person picked out at random, the prospects that the overall effect of all changes required by that order will be to increase his chances of attaining his ends ... the common good in this sense is not a particular state of things but consists in an abstract order which in a free society must leave undetermined the degree to which the several particular needs will be met. (Von Hayek, 1973, p.114)

In other words, a society that relies on the market to allocate resources *must not* distinguish between the different types of need discussed above, as well as the difference between needs and consumer desires. What this means in the concrete is that a wealthy market society cannot decide to reallocate resources from luxury consumption to even basic need satisfaction, if that decision requires arguing in advance that, say, the need for inner city housing for the homeless is objectively prior, in the normative sense, than the luxury demand of the rich to build ever bigger estates.

I will return to the important issue of what von Hayek means by 'spontaneous forces' below. For the moment the problems with this formalistic and abstract account of economies and needs must be spelled out more clearly. First of all, if we examine von Hayek's position from the life-grounded perspective, its *material irrationality* is clear. For any system of *human* thought that fails to distinguish between the conditions of existence of human beings and the contingent ends that they may form assuming they are alive and able to think contradicts its own conditions of possibility. Von Hayek could have written the work that he wrote, or he could have written another. In order to do either a or b, he had to satisfy his basic natural and social life-requirements. The choice between book a and book b is contingent, and any society that forced him to write one rather than the other is, anyone would agree, unfree in that dimension of freedom. However, a society that prioritises the satisfaction of those general life-requirements is not only not unfree, it has in fact prioritised the material conditions of anyone's being free to do anything at all. Assuming the availability of resources sufficient to satisfy the social minima of life-requirements for all, the society that mandates as a foundational economic principle that those minima will be satisfied does not determine particular individual ends in an authoritarian way, but rather ensures the material conditions for the free development, realization, and enjoyment of individual capabilities. Any theory which cannot distinguish between the necessary conditions of possibility of choice and the objects of choice that are available if and only if those conditions of possibility (what Keith Graham aptly calls 'constraints of precondition– Graham, 2002, pp. 152-158) is materially irrational.

This material irrationality is not simply the result of a category mistake between conditions of possibility of choice and the objects of choice. It is the result, rather, of the very abstraction from life-requirements as the necessary condition of their being any economy at all, in any sense of the term. If it is not possible to rank needs, then it is not possible to argue that it is more important to produce nutritious food, say, than luxury automobiles. If there is no way of ranking needs then there is no way of ranking needs, and one group's demand for luxury automobiles is as necessary as *everyone's* nutritional life-requirements. But if there is no way to distinguish between life-requirements and mere consumer demands, it follows that it would not be irrational to prioritise the production of one to the detriment of the production of the other, from within the framework that von Hayek constructs. If the spontaneous order of the market system selects for increased investment in luxuries for the rich, to the detriment of the poor, there is no objective basis to argue against that decision, provided only that no central governmental authority has interfered with the spontaneous order. Nor can we look to the self-correcting mechanism of the market to ensure the life-requirements of the poor are met. So long as there are enough people left to work and a minimum of unemployed to prevent wage inflation, nothing in the market mechanism of self-correction will channel investment back into basic food production to prevent starvation of the surplus poor. Indeed, economic science in one of its founding texts affirmed periodic famine as a necessary corrective to the numbers of poor. (Malthus, 1998, pp. 72-100)

The problem here, as should be evident, is that the understanding of economic 'good' at work here is detached completely from the life-ground of value. An economic "good" in neo-classical theory is any commodity for which there is demand (or for which demand can be created, through advertising, etc). As DeMartino explains the basic neo-classical assumptions in this regard, "The market brings together ... consumers and firms. Consumers come to the market with ... money, in pursuit of maximum satisfaction given the constraint imposed by their income ... firms ... come ready to supply the goods and services that [consumers] desire. When firms supply these goods, they are not fulfilling some moral obligation to meet social needs ... [but rather] seek maximum return on their investment, maximum profit.(DeMartino, 2000, p.56) Note that good is anything that satisfies a demand, and that demands, as we saw in von Hayek, cannot be prioritised according to any objective ranking of importance. That does not mean, however, that there is *no* ranking of values in the GCMS. Since the goal of firms is not to fulfill needs, but to maximise profits, it follows that the priority ranking of 'goods' in the GCMS is according to return on investment, or, in terms of the money-value that returns to firms upon sale of their product, regardless of what contribution the good makes to life-value.

It therefore follows as a general rule of value in the GCMS that money-value rules over life-value. In other words, the GCMS makes investment decisions according to a money, and not life-grounded value system. The substitution of the money for the life-ground of value is crucial to understanding its life-blind tendencies. It is a necessary consequence of the money-grounded value system according to which investment priorities are determined that market agents and the governments that facilitate market transactions (by establishing the legal framework that is necessary for the spontaneous market order to develop) cannot detect problems that *successful* investments cause for life-value. Since 'good' in this system is detached from the life-ground, and 'success' means realizing a profit, harms to life, when these are profitable, register as the good aimed at by the investment. As McMurtry explains, "investment proceeds solely by the principle of netting maximum monetary gains for private market agents by production of commodities for individual consumers, or money sequencing with no consumable good. Investment outcome will, for the universal true faith, be optimal by a doctrinally postulated equilibrium of the deist mechanism that is assumed as the 'regulating hand.'(McMurtry, 2000, p.134). The problem of course, is that the 'regulating hand,' what von Hayek calls a 'catallaxy,'(spontaneous order) measures equilibrium only as an optimal state of supply and demand. It cannot, therefore, in principle, measure, by its economic metric, life-damage when it is a consequence not of intentional designs but the spontaneous process of market transactions themselves.

Let us take the example of the private automobile. Automobile markets are in equilibrium when as many people as possible can afford an automobile at prices that returns profits to the producers. Given ideal conditions of formal freedom to produce and consume, von Hayek's spontaneous forces will constantly adjust price until equilibrium is achieved. Let us assume that every adult in the society desires an automobile and equilibrium is attained when 80% of adults can afford a car. Equilibrium means, from the standpoint of distribution, Pareto-optimality (where no one's preferences can be further satisfied without someone else's being compromised). Once this equilibrium is attained a 'good' economic outcome, indeed, the best possible in the GCMS, has been achieved. This outcome can only be called 'good' however, if the real life costs– pollution, increased morbidity due to traffic accidents and smog, destruction of arable land by the construction of suburbs and freeways, etc) are factored out, as we have seen they necessarily are by neo-classical standards of economic evaluation. Thus what are costs in a life-grounded economy exist only as externalities, even though, if we extrapolate the logic at work here, these externalities could progress to the point where they threaten life as such.

This conclusion can be borne out by turning to the example of the 'economic costs' of global warming. My example here is a report recently prepared by the Ministry of the Environment of the current Canadian Government. My goal here is not to criticise the specific conclusions of the report but to uncover the essential life-blindness of its conception of the economy and 'economic rationality.' The Report, "The Cost of Bill C-288 to Canadian Families and Businesses" was an attempt to quantify the impact on the Canadian economy if the government were to meet its Kyoto Treaty Commitments (as demanded in Bill C-288). As should be clear, "costs" are defined in terms of money costs to business and family income. Life costs, as we will see, are not an independent variable in the report.

The introduction to the report, written by John Baird, the current Canadian Minister of the Environment, asserts that "Canadians want balanced solutions to environmental protection and economic growth. Balance means making sure that economic decisions are environmentally responsible. But balance also requires that environmental decisions be economically responsible." (Drummond et. al., 2007, p. 2). If balance must be established between two factors, then it follows that those two factors are independent of each other (otherwise there would be nothing to balance). Thus it follows that Baird, and the report that follows, assumes that the environment and the economy are independent systems external to one another whose interests can be opposed to one another.

The life-blind nature of this construction is immediately evident. Human life and life-activity, including, as I argued above, economic activity, is always activity that occurs within and depends upon the natural life-field. Since human life is compatible with many forms of economic activity, but is intolerant of natural conditions that fail to satisfy its organic conditions of existence, it is obvious, if one begins from the life-requirements of human beings, that the life-supporting capacity of the natural life-filed is of necessary prior importance to the economy. No economy that systematically undermines the life-supportive capacity of the natural world can persist past the point where that life-supportive capacity has been undermined. So it is again materially irrational to construct the economy as an independent system of value which has interests equal and opposed to the human life interest in a life-supportive environment. Yet, that is exactly what the report proceeds to do.

The Minister urges that environmental decisions be responsible to "economic growth." But what does "economic growth" mean in the context of the report. It means growth of Canadian GDP as measured by the money value of the goods and services produced in the country each year. Like the neo-classical understanding of economic goods examined above, however, the report conceives economic goods in a strictly life-blind way, as whatever can be sold, regardless of its positive or negative impact on life-value. As the report asserts, "Gross Domestic Product is the best available indicator of the overall health of the Canadian economy, as it measures the market value of the goods and services produced in the Canadian economy." (Drummond et. al., 2007, p. 18). Yet this assertion simply ignores a growing literature within the field of economics that argues that GDP is not only not the best, but not even a good, measure of economic health. As pioneered by Nobel Laureate Amartya Sen, this argument rejects the usefulness of GDP as a measure of economic health because it does not explain how money wealth is distributed, and therefore masks potentially serious inequalities of income, nor does it tell us what income is invested in, nor what people are able to 'do and be' with whatever share of the national income they control. (Sen, 1999, pp. 290-291). In the general terms developed here, GDP is a completely life-blind measure of economic health.

To explain this point through an example, consider the main driver of Canadian economic growth in the past 3 years, oil sands development in Northern Alberta. The high price of oil has made extraction of crude oil from the oil sands 'economically' viable. The massive investments being made around Fort McMurray has created a jobs boom throughout Alberta. On the one hand, paid employment is an instrumental system need in the GCMS, and so the growth in employment must be counted as a partial life-good. This partial life-good, however, is undermined by the long-term environmental, and therefore, by extension, long-term human life-costs. First, oil sands extraction is thermodynamically irrational, requiring more energy input to its extraction than it yields. Second, it requires massive amounts of water to produce the steam utilised to generate the chemical reaction that separates the oil from the sand. As a result the Athabasca River and its watershed is threatened (and therefore the whole project too, since it cannot continue without water). Finally, oil sands extraction is a massive producer of greenhouse gases (and thus the primary reason why successive Canadian governments have shied away from a serious effort to meet Kyoto targets).(Polaris Institute, 2007). In sum, when judged from a life-grounded perspective the oil sands industry is driven by short-term money-value thinking. Over the long term its environmental costs will far outweigh the short term gains in employment for those who work in the industry. However, judged from the perspective of GDP, oil sands development appears as a great contributor to the overall 'health' of the Canadian economy.

Now, since implementing measures to reduce overall greenhouse gas emissions will cost the Canadian economy money-value (i.e., reduce GDP) the report concludes that it is not feasible to meet those targets by the dates stipulated in the treaty. This conclusion is of course true so long as the understanding of 'economy' 'economic good' and 'economic health' is understood in a life-blind way. Once we re-ground our conceptions of those crucial terms in life-value, growth of life-value, and sustainability of the growth of life-value, the material irrationality of the GCMS, its value system, and supporting science (neo-classical economics) becomes apparent. The problem, however, is not in demonstrating this long-term material irrationality, but in discovering an alternative that both serves long-term life-interests better than the GCMS, can be realised without a massive increase in life-costs over the short to medium term of its introduction, and workable as a system of human interaction and coordination. I will now to turn the basic structure of such an alternative in the final part.

PART THREE: A LIFE-GROUNDED NEGOTIATED COORDINATION ECONOMY

The ultimate line of defence for proponents of the GCMS has two flanks. On the one hand it will be argued that to even contemplate fundamental changes to the ruling economic order is to attack the very foundations of human freedom itself. Indeed, von Hayek's conception of the market system as a spontaneous order is essentially a defence of market freedom as the very essence of human freedom. According to von Hayek, the superiority of the market system to known alternatives is that rests on each agent's ability to respond to local circumstances without having to try to anticipate or understand global conditions. Each motivated by their own interests take care as best they can of the conditions immediately affecting them, and in this way– provided a sound enabling framework of law is in place– the system itself spontaneously adjusts to changing conditions in such a way that much higher degrees of complexity and productivity are possible. As he writes, "What the general argument against interference thus amounts to is that, although we can endeavour to improve a spontaneous order by revising the general rules on which it rests, and can supplement its results by the efforts of various organizations, we cannot improve the results by specific commands that deprive its members of the possibility of using their knowledge for their purposes." (Von Hayek, 1973, p. 51). There is an important conflation of distinct issues at work here which must be teased out if the argument regarding alternatives that follows is to be properly understood.

The essential conflation upon which the plausibility of von Hayek's argument rests is a conflation between governance of an economic system for definite ends and "commands." The use of the term 'command' is tendentious, designed to lead the reader to associate any attempt to frame and govern economic activity according to shared ends, and authoritarian command economies that explicitly rule out individual freedom at all levels. This conflation is of the most serious magnitude, for if it goes unnoticed, the social forces generated by the catallaxy– market forces under the control of no one– end up the ruling power of society. Hayek asserts that the catallaxy operates by each person "using their own knowledge for their purposes," and this is true to some extent. What is left unsaid here is how those purposes are formed, and what general conditions must be obeyed by persons if they are to have any hope of successful functioning within the spontaneous order. As soon as we look carefully at what actually occurs in the GCMS it becomes clear, however, that the system does not reproduce itself via free individuals freely using their knowledge to satisfy their purposes, but is in fact a system of constraint on both the formation and pursuit of individual purposes. For as the money-grounded value system of the GCMS makes clear, only such purposes as are likely to make a profit for investors will find the means of pursuit, and whether they are successfully achieved or not depends on the overall state of market forces, not individual knowledge or initiative. It is only when society prioritises the satisfaction of the basic life-interests of people, as I argued in Part Two, that they are in a position to formulate and freely develop their capabilities. Since the satisfaction of these interests is at best accidental in the GCMS, it cannot plausibly be defended as a system that rests upon and maximises individual human freedom. Individuals are instruments of the economic system, and not the other way round, as would be required by a fully free democratic society.

One need not take my word for this. The most recent update on the Millennium Goals from the United Nations concludes that progress has been very uneven towards the poverty-reduction and social and human development targets, but where greatest success has been achieved it has not been through the neo-classical model of deregulated globalization, but rather through *consciously governed* economic development. It notes that "several developing countries are demonstrating that rapid and large-scale progress towards the MDGs (Millennium Development Goals) is possible when strong government leadership and policies and strategies that effectively target *the needs of the poor* are combined with adequate financial and technical support from the international community. ... In general, strategies should adopt a wide-ranging approach that seeks a pro-poor economic growth, including the creation of a large number of additional opportunities for decent work. This in turn will require comprehensive programs for human development, particularly in education and in health." [emphasis added] (United Nations, 2007, p.5). The point is clear– those countries have taken the clearest steps towards satisfying the MDG's that have consciously governed their economic development in an explicitly need– and therefore life– grounded way.

The unstated role of the life-ground of value is obvious here. However, simply governing economic activity according to the priorities of life-requirement satisfaction is a necessary but not sufficient condition of fully life-grounded economy. As I emphasised in Part One, human beings are social-organic beings, and their life-requirements include the ability to meaningfully participate in the institutions through which public policy– and crucially economic policy– is developed. Otherwise the full material (natural and social) conditions for the free development, realization, and enjoyment of life-capabilities in individually meaningful and socially valuable ways are not satisfied. Thus, a life-grounded economy must be a democratic economy and a democratic economy, contrary to Von Hayek, requires some form of planning beyond the general normative framework specified by the life-grounded minima defended in Part One. But that– planning– the neo-classical opponent will reply, has been historically proven to be impossible without massive life-costs, both in terms of the loss of individual civic freedom and overall economic efficiency and social complexity. Thus my argument seems to hit a dead end. Unless a defensible alternative to the failed command economies of the Stalinist world can be found, external governance of market forces seems to be the best alternative to the unregulated, money-steered, GCMS. There is, however, such an alternative and it is found in Pat Devine's model of a negotiated coordination economy.

I will spell out the basic structure of a negotiated coordination economy as a response to what could be called the 'objection from possibility.' This objection argues that socio-economic dynamics, on the national and international scale, have reached such a degree of complexity that they cannot be plausibly governed from within in a democratic way. The information burdens that would be imposed on democratic planning agencies would be impossible to bear. Any convincing answer to this objection must satisfy three criteria.

- First, it must explain how a model of democratic planning could cope with the information burdens that destroyed the one attempt known to humanity of a planned modern economy, the Stalinist model of centralized bureaucratic planning. That is, it must provide a credible explanation of what information would substitute for the price mechanism in signalling to planners and productive units what the most efficient allocation of resources would be. Second, it must prove that it would not invest preponderant political and social power in an authoritarian party or movement. That is, it must provide a credible model of social and political organization that would transform the separation of political from economic power typical of capitalism in such a way that society was democratized without damaging the equal life-interests of citizens. Third, it must prove that the process of transformation does not rely upon utopian theories of revolutionary reconstruction of society but is intrinsically linked to practices and processes that actually exist but are only partially realized today.

Devine interprets his model of negotiated coordination of economic life as a middle path between the extremes of laissez-faire 'freedom' from external regulation (von Hayek's catallaxy) and central bureaucratic control over the totality of social life. Both, Devine believes, have proven to be historic failures. The collapse of the centralized command economy has been interpreted, however, not only as a practical refutation of 'actually existing socialism' but further, as a practical refutation of the possibility of an efficient and innovative planned economy of any form. What Devine rejects is the inference from the failure of *centralized* planning to the impossibility of *de-centralized, democratic* planning.

The first point that must be understood about his model is the distinction between market forces and market exchange. Devine's model seeks to replace the rule of market forces over economic life without replacing market exchange between productive units. As I noted above, market forces are the unintended outcomes of individual productive units making decisions in their own self-interest in an economy typified by zero-sum competition (someone's gain is someone else's loss). These forces are the unmentioned real power exercised over people's life horizons– what will be available for consumption, how much it will cost, how much people will earn, what sort of work they will be able to find, how much time they will have to devote to paid labour- that, once understood, demonstrate that the GCMS is not a system of freedom but coercion. The problems generated by blind market forces are the necessary consequence of what is essential to the market system, namely, atomised decision making. However, these market forces are in principle separable from market exchanges. Market exchanges are simply interactions between economic agents in which mutual interests are coordinated and satisfied.(Devine, 1988, p. 23). There is no incompatibility, Devine argues, between market exchange and a democratically planned economy. The difference between a negotiated coordination economy and a capitalist market economy is that the decisions of individual productive units would be coordinated with other social interests within the framework of a democratically determined set of economic and social priorities. Within that framework, however, individual units of production would be free to make their own decisions about how to best produce their output. Overall economic activity would be coordinated within an agreed upon plan but most decision making power would be, as far as possible, decentralized. In short, by embedding market exchanges in a democratically determined set of economic priorities, the valuable complexity and responsiveness of a spontaneous order can be separated from the life-blind and coercive consequences of money-steered market forces.

Decentralized decision making power is the key to avoiding the information deficits that destroyed centrally administered systems. The model of organization that Devine envisages relies upon a feedback loop between local producers and higher level bodies of political authority. In simplified form the model would look like this. Society-wide deliberations would begin at the local level and generate a set of national socio-economic priorities. These deliberations would involve all parties with an interest in their outcome and the final choice would be the outcome of political negotiation. The final decision as to the national priorities would be made by the national assembly, which would then inform the national planning commission. Macroeconomic goals (the rate of savings, the distribution of income between wages, taxes, and revenue for individual production units, rent on use of natural resources, etc) would be determined centrally. The national planning commission would then produce a set of alternative plans that would be the focus of national deliberation. Responsibility for realizing the objectives of the chosen plan, however, would be decentralized. Individual production units would be free to govern themselves within the broad objectives established by the plan. Thus Devine's model combines quantitative and qualitative information that will be used by production units, planning authorities, political institutions, and social interests to determine the match (or lack thereof) between planned and actual economic performance. As he argues, "Claims on resources in the form of purchasing power and prices that reflect costs of production are indispensable quantitative indicators of what constitutes socially useful production. However, qualitative considerations are equally indispensable. The interaction of representative institutions, community interests and consumer/user interests would generate the qualitative knowledge that has to be taken into consideration ... when deciding on what constitutes the social interest in any given situation."(Devine, 1988, p.217). Devine does not propose that price signals be abolished in favour of pure technocratic planning of the economy. Rather, he seeks to embed price signals in a richer institutional environment in which interests that currently have to bang at the negotiation door to gain a hearing are formally incorporated from the beginning.

From the perspective of the life-grounded value system defended here, what must be added to this is that negotiated coordination, if it is to fully free the current economic system from its life-destructive tendencies, must win people to agree that the three social minima defended above form the essential normative frame of the democratic planning exercise. That is, unless people as active participants to the plan continue to be motivated by the same sorts of demand as typify current behaviour, there will be no necessary life-value savings or development. The ultimate justification of any economic outcome, no matter what the form of the interactions that generate that outcome, is that it demonstrably satisfies peoples fundamental life-interests. If those life-interests remain confused with unlimited consumer demand on energy, resources, and social wealth in the form of capability-disabling consumer products, then the negotiated coordination economy, although it would be more democratic than the market order catallaxy, would not solve the fundamental life-crises that humanity confronts. However, as the problem of winning people over to a life-grounded perspective involves specific political and philosophical problems that have there own complexity, I will have to set them aside here and focus only on answering the objection from possibility from an economic angle.

Thus, to resume the explanation, a negotiated coordination economy would consciously shift the governance of economic life from unintended market forces to decentralized planning bodies working with firms. Firms rely on price signals to make day to day adjustments to production, but these price signals are themselves embedded in a normative framework defined by the democratically agreed upon plan (which is in turn embedded in life-grounded objectives) The gradual effect of the spread of negotiated coordination would be to supplant private self-interest with solidaristic commitment to democratically determined economic goals. Individual units of production would still be expected strive to produce as efficiently as possible and to generate revenue sufficient to cover costs plus generate a surplus. Part of the surplus would be taxed (to fund investment in life-serving public goods and social infrastructure) while the rest would be used to cover investments in plant and equipment. In accordance with the life-grounded interpretation of the negotiated coordination economy, priority would have to be assigned to minimising instrumental system needs so that overall demand on energy and resources would be gradually reduced. Motivation would be supplied by the intrinsic value of work and political participation that was demonstrably valuable to oneself and one's fellow citizens. The economy would be dynamic, but dynamic in a planned, life-grounded way, oriented by a deliberatively achieved set of overall objectives within the framing objective of satisfying the fundamental life-interests of human beings.

The key institution required for the transformation of atomised decision-making on the basis of narrow self-interest into conscious democratic decision making in the interests of creating the socio-material conditions for free development of vital capabilities is what Devine calls the 'negotiated coordination body.' These bodies would mediate between individual production units and the central political and planning institutions in which overall priorities are democratically generated and decided upon. As he describes them, "the composition of the negotiated coordination bodies would be determined by applying the principle of self-government– representation of all affected interests. ... [they] would be responsible for deciding how changes in the capacity of their branch of production should be achieved and how differential performance between units within each branch should be dealt with." (Devine, 1988, p. 261). In an ideal unregulated capitalist system production units open and close according to profitability. In theory the decision to close is taken by management and simply imposed on the workers and the broader community. In reality, however, the decision to close a plant involves the owners in a complex set of negotiations with workers and different levels of government. The reality of negotiations in a complex modern economy lends plausibility to Devine's argument. What he is proposing is an extension of processes that already exist and are central to the functioning of actual national and local economies in the GCMS, not *ex nihilo creation* of a new social order.

The difference between the type of negotiation that goes on now and that which Devine proposes is thus a difference of degree, not kind. Negotiated coordination bodies would not only involve representatives of the different units of production but wider community interests and representatives of higher level planning and government bodies. Let us say, for example, that there are five steel mills in a country but that cheaper imports have created surplus domestic capacity such that there is need for only three plants. In a laissez-faire economy the two most unprofitable plants would be closed. In a command economy all might be kept going artificially in order to maintain full-employment. In an actual economy which plant would be closed would be the outcome of complex negotiations between management, workers, and governments, but the final decision would ultimately rest with management, which retains the right to cease to use its property. In Devine's model all affected interests would be represented, not just workers and management but the wider community interests as well. Arguments and proposals would be made in the negotiated coordination body and competing interests balanced and reconciled. Let us suppose that an unproductive factory is located in a region that was historically poorer than the national average and had fewer prospects for economic revitalization. By the logic of market forces that historical asymmetry would not factor into the decision. In a negotiated coordination economy, however, local interests could argue that the unproductive plant be allocated the resources to improve efficiency and thus become competitive. One of the more productive plants in a region where it would be easier to shift employees to other activities could be closed, solving the problem of domestic overcapacity while not unfairly burdening the interests in the wealthier region. In this way a hard decision can be made but, since all affected interests are equally represented, the costs could be actively consented to and social solidarity maintained.

The problem of imports touched upon here raises the important question of how Devine's model could accommodate problems generated by the internationalization of market forces in the actual GCMS. To be sure this problem adds another layer of complexity to his model but not an insuperable layer. As the actual functioning of the GCMS makes clear, the nation state remains an essential institution even in a world of highly mobile capital. Capital cannot simply set up shop wherever it pleases. As even von Hayek agrees, a market order cannot exist without law, and the creation of law remains the exclusive right of national governments. In order to internationalise a negotiated coordination economy it is therefore not necessary to create a world planning authority. Rather, the second-order coordination problems (i.e., coordination problems between national economies) can be solved through negotiations between states. The substitution of democratically determined plans for more market forces as the steering value of negotiated coordination economies would gradually overcome the power assymetries (between rich and poor nations, between multinational corporations and nations desperate for investment) that tend to favour richer countries in negotiations today. Although the complexities involved in coordinating economic activity across borders in an equitable and democratic way would be challenging, the reality of trade negotiations today proves that they would not be insurmountable. The difference, again, is a difference of the goals and justifying values of negotiation. Today, those goals are opening economies to international investment in the interests of multinational corporations profitability. In a negotiated coordination system the goal would be maximum efficient use of the worlds resources as measured by life-values (minimal energy use for maximal real life-requirement satisfaction, adjusted to the asymmetries in wealth that structure the world as we live, i.e, priority would be placed on reducing the energy consumption of the wealthiest areas and the savings used to develop, in a life-grounded way, those areas that have been subject to the worst forms of exploitation and human underdevelopment).

In liberal-capitalist democracy the principle of self-government– that all affected parties ought to be represented in decisions that affect them such that any costs imposed upon them can be freely accepted– is limited to the public sphere of politics and law. Self-government does not extend into the structure of forces that determine socio-economic life. People thus find that their life-horizons are determined by the outcomes of market forces over which they have no formal or substantive control. The alternative to such coercion is a democratic economic system governed through conscious negotiated coordination. Yet it seems doubtful whether the type of conscious commitment to social priorities Devine's model requires is a real possibility given the inevitability of differences of opinion and interest actually operative in society.

- The great strength of Devine's proposal, however, is precisely that he is not a utopian in the pejorative sense of the word, naively hoping that different interests can immediately transform themselves and concur around a binding set of goals and values. What he does commit himself to is the belief– evidenced by actual negotiations today– that people are capable of opening their consciousness to arguments made from opposed perspectives, listening and making reasonable counter-arguments, uncovering identities of interest that are initially hidden by one-sidedness or misunderstanding, and thus producing, over time, sets of social objectives that are, as far as possible, in everyone's real life-interest. There will be costs, but the costs, since they will be freely accepted and compensated, will be experienced as bearable and not coercive and unjust. As he argues, "the model of negotiated coordination is prefigurative, in that it anticipates a society in which people in principle wish to act in the social interest and the problem for them is to decide together what that means in practice. At the same time, the model is able to accommodate situations in which this principle is not fully operative. ... It cannot legislate self-interest away, but neither does it reward it. Instead it institutionalizes the requirement that specific interests be brought up against one another, confronted with representatives of more general interests, and encouraged to arrive at an integrated view through negotiation." (Devine, 1988, p. 249). Just as planning failures generate the information necessary to spur the creative intelligence necessary to move beyond the impasses, so too the experience of confronting one's interests with other interests is capable of producing the reflective understanding necessary to recognize partiality of perspective and broaden self-interest outward towards more comprehensive values.

In short, Devine relies upon experience to cultivate the skills and capabilities necessary for successful negotiated coordination and points to the feminist movement as an example of self-transformation. Take the example of the women's movement. Patriarchal philosophy long derided women as incapable of self-government. Successful in their struggles, however, women transformed themselves from being the objects of patriarchal power to the subjects of their own liberation and produced, through this self-transformation, social, political, and cultural changes that would have been dismissed as impossible two or three centuries previously.(Devine, 1988, pp. 144-145). It was not lack of capability for self-rule that held women back, but rather lack of opportunity to develop the capability. The same holds true in principle for workers and other groups now prevented from exercising any democratic control over the economy. It is not that the problems are too technical for non-experts to make any valuable contribution to their solution, but rather that current power relations impede the development of the talents necessary to actively participate in the governance of economic life.

Thus the spread of democratic institutions into the governance of economic life can be envisaged as possible and realistic if it is gradual and evolutionary. However, social democratization is not simply a matter of establishing 'workers control' over production. Devine counts the interests of workers as a centrally important interest, but not, as Marx did, representative of the universal interest of humanity. Production units would be self-governing as far as possible, but the interests of workers would have to be meshed with wider community interests in any fully democratic social organization, as well as with the wider and deeper life-interests, not only of members of the local community, but the nation and world of life as a whole. Let us return to the example of the unproductive steel mill. Facing closure, it is reasonable to assume that the workers at the plant would vote in favour of keeping it open. Let us suppose that as part of the package of reforms they submit to the negotiated coordination body is a plan to reduce costs by using fuel in the coke ovens that is less expensive because it has a higher sulphur content. This plan would have to be defended against broader community and world long-term interests in healthy environment. It is thus highly unlikely that such a proposal could generate the broad-based agreement necessary to have it passed by the legislative bodies that are ultimately responsible for deciding upon the allocation of funds. The workers would thus be obliged to submit a new proposal or face closure.

These processes of negotiation at local and national levels can thus in principle avoid the authoritarian coercion typical of Stalinist societies by involving representatives of concrete social interests at each stage of planning and decision making. Final decision making authority, as I noted above, lies in the national assembly, and the content of any agreement is subject to demonstrable coherence with life-grounded objectives. Unlike present federal systems, however, in which power at each level (national, provincial-state, municipal) is separated, Devine's model of negotiated coordination relies upon a re-organization of the flow of power from local to national, bottom to top. The basic level of political organization is local. Power and information is first generated at the local level and then articulated into more general interests by deliberations at a higher levels. These generalized interests then form the basis for the national plan. The objectives of the national plan are in turn disseminated down the pyramid to local political and negotiated coordination bodies for implementation. Those affected by decisions are involved at every step of the process such that the national objectives and the local modes of implementation are legitimated by the actual consent of all affected interests. Hence democratic legitimacy is in principle reconciled with planning. The concrete problems experienced in the course of the implementation of the plan once again serve as the occasion for processes of social learning.

The real question raised by Devine's model, however, is not whether people would participate in a society that was in fact democratic, but whether it is reasonable to argue with them that they need to take political steps now to initiate processes of life-grounded, democratic social change. What real grounds are there for accepting that Devine's argument is rigorously plausible? Answering that question brings me to the final step in the argument.

The best evidence for the plausibility of Devine's model is the reality of planning and negotiation in the actual economy. As I noted at the beginning of Part Three, those poor nations that have consciously invested in need-satisfaction have gone the furthest towards meeting the MDGs. The Chinese economy, although currently developing in an ecologically unsustainable way, and relying upon authoritarian labour-discipline to keep wages low and investment flowing, is, notwithsatnding these real problems, another example of how planned development can alleviate poverty. In every capitalist nation, in fact, and even in the standard-bearer of open markets, the United States, planning and negotiation is ubiquitous. Price-signals are not self-evident in terms of what they imply at the level of corporate strategy. Corporations thus do not make investment or divestment decisions over night, but meet to discuss and argue about how best to respond to changing economic circumstances. They generate long-term forecasts and determine future courses of action accordingly. Nor do nations simply leave the course of their economic futures up to market forces exclusively, no matter what their leaders might profess at the level of justifying rhetoric. Every nation retains some degree of control over macroeconomic factors and all publish national budgets. National budgets set out economic priorities and encourage or discourage different forms of economic activity through tax rates and other sorts of direct and indirect regulation. Political parties and social movements plan party and-movement activities in accordance with agreed upon objectives. Governments, unions, social movements and businesses are constantly negotiating and re-negotiating the terms of economic life, who will benefit and who will suffer increased costs, as well as over which values ought to govern society. As Devine concludes, "in the most successful capitalist countries, even those apparently most ... market-oriented, the long-run development of the economy is not left primarily to the determination of market forces. Some degree of *ex ante* coordination is attempted, both within and between industries and sectors."(Devine, 1988, p. 52) Devine's model for a self-governing society is thus rooted in real processes of planning and negotiation central to actual economic life. On analogy with the universalization of civil and political rights over the past 300 years, it argues that those currently shut out of negotiation and planning, or those who voice is effectively marginalised when decisions are made, are formally and substantively included.

It is the gradual and evolutionary means of transformation favoured by Devine that lends his proposal credibility. Time is the philosopher's stone that changes impossibility into possibility. Devine does not ignore complexity, but instead locates the actual practices of negotiation and planning that make complexity and spontaneity work for human beings (to the extent that it does) and theorizes the means of extending and internalizing them. The more those processes are extended and internalized, the more the form of separation of economic and political power typical of capitalism is overcome, the more democratic social relations are. Success depends not upon the discipline of a revolutionary cadre or a class of philosopher-kings, but on the spread of the life-grounded basis of social solidarity.

REFERENCES

DeMartino, George, 2000. *Global Economy, Global Justice*. New York: Routledge.

Devine, Pat, 1988. *Democracy and Economic Planning*. Boulder, CO: Westview Press.

Doyal, Len, and Gough, Ian. 1991. *A Theory of Human Needs*. New York: Guilford.

Drummond, Don, et.al. 2007. "The Cost of Bill C-288 to Canadian Families and Business." Ottawa: Ministry of the Enironment.

Economist. 2006. "The Rich, the Poor, and the Growing Gap Between Them." www.economist.com/world/displaystory.cfm?story_id=70559/ (Accessed June 12th, 2007)

Graham, Keith. 2002. *Practical Reasoning in a Social World*. Cambridge: Cambridge University Press.

Malthus, Thomas. 1998. *An Essay on the Principle of Population*. Amherst, NY: Prometheus Books.

Marx, Karl. 1975. *The German Ideology*. Moscow: Progress Publishers.

McMurtry, John. 1998. *Unequal Freedoms*. Toronto: Garamond.

McMurtry, John. 2000. *Value Wars*. London: Pluto Press.

Milanovich, Branko. (2006). "Global Inequality: What it is and Why it Matters." DESA Working Paper No.26. New York: United Nations. www.un.org/esa/desa/papers/2006/wp26_2006.pdf (Accessed July 12th, 2007)

Nussbaum, Martha. 2006. *Frontiers of Justice*. Cambridge MA: Harvard University Press.

Polaris Institute. 2007. "Controversial Oil Substitutes Increase Emissions, Devour Landscapes." www.polarisinstitute.org/controversial_oil_substitutes_sharply_increase_emissions_devour_landscapes. (Accessed July 25th, 2007)

Sen, Amartya. 1999. *Development as Freedom*. New York: Knopf.

Smith, Adam. 1986. *The Wealth of Nations*. Harmondsworth, UK: Penguin Books.

Spring, Silvia. 2006. "Blood and Money." *Newsweek*. www.msnbc.com (Accessed, July 12th, 2007.

Von Hayek, Friedrich. 1973. *Law, Legislation, and Liberty. Volume One: Rules and Order*. Chicago: University of Chicago Press.

United Nations. 2007. "The Millennium Development Goals Report. New York: United nations.

Von Hayek, Friedrich. 1976. *Law, Legislation, and Liberty. Volume Two: The Mirage of Social Justice*. Chicago: University of Chicago Press.

Wade, Robert Hunter. (2003). "The Disturbing Rise in Poverty and Inequality: Is it all a Big Lie? *Taming Globalization*. David held, ed. Cambridge: Polity.

In: Political Economy Research Focus
Editor: Walter R. Levin, pp. 69-92

ISBN: 978-1-60456-154-8
© 2008 Nova Science Publishers, Inc.

Chapter 3

RELIGION AS ADAPTATION:
THE ROLE OF TIME PREFERENCE

Robert F. Mulligan
Western Carolina University
North Carolina USA

ABSTRACT

This paper argues that religion confers survival benefits on societies and individuals because it allows a general lowering of time preference. Time preference is one of the most basic economic concepts and a fundamental category of human action. Theories of interest, term structure, and opportunity cost all depend on time preference, which is also the basis for capital budgeting in modern finance. This paper establishes how and why the emergence of religious belief supported a reduction of time preference, allowing for employment of capital in time-consuming roundabout means of production.

The economic concept of time preference explains why belief in God conferred survival value as we evolved, and why it no longer does so. Time preference is the desire to enjoy immediate gratification. Though considered a universal determinant of human action, it has been observed to vary greatly in intensity across individuals. For example, time preference is especially high in children who lack experience and maturity, and in individuals with low life expectancy. Time preference is also high for criminals, and the general lowering of time preference both facilitates and is facilitated by the development of civilization and the increase in complexity of social relationships. The essence of low time preference is planning for the future, a willingness to delay gratification, and patience to wait for future benefits.

Once religious belief emerged among our distant ancestors, to be transmitted as a successful adaptation, it must have contributed to the reproductive success of the believers. Primitive humans experienced an appalling life expectancy. Homo sapiens evolved in an environment where infant mortality approached 100% and life expectancy *for those surviving infancy* was certainly below 20 years. Our remote ancestors had little reason not to consume all their seed corn at once, and deistic belief mitigated their natural tendency to enjoy whatever gratification they could immediately control. Religious belief enhanced the survival prospects of both individuals and communities by conditioning them to engage in longer-range planning through such beliefs as life-after-death, spirit survival, and reincarnation.

The survival benefit of religious belief is mostly lost once life expectancy lengthens to the point where, in and of itself, it results in lowered time preference and more responsible, more forward-looking behavior from the majority of agents in the community.

1. INTRODUCTION

The Austrian school's subjectivity and methodological individualism provide a distinctive view of time preference. The seminal writings on time preference are cited by Hoppe (2001:1): Jevons (1965), Mises (1949: chs. 18 & 19), Böhm-Bawerk (1959), Strigl (2001), Fetter (1902, 1914a, 1914b, 1914c, 1977), and Rothbard (1963). "What restricts the amount of saving and investment is time preference" (Mises 1949:483, 491). Kirzner (1996:6) distinguishes interest from a productivity return, because interest depends on time preference rather than on productivity. The more impatient an individual is for want-satisfaction, the higher their time preference, and the more they consume out of current income, meaning they save less and have less available for investment. For each individual, the division of real income into consumption and saving is determined by their subjective time preference. People with high time preference consume more of the income or output immediately, while those with low time preference save more. The income saved by low-time-preference individuals raises the community's wealth, acts as a reserve against unforeseeable catastrophes such as famines, clearly offering obvious survival benefits, and can be used for investment which permanently increases the community's wealth and productivity.

If an individual's time preference were zero, all the individual's income would be saved and available for investment. If an individual's time preference were infinite, no income would be saved. Mises defines the rate of time preference, which he also calls originary interest, as the ratio between the present values of present and future goods:

> "Originary interest is the ratio of the value assigned to want-satisfaction in the immediate future and the value assigned to want-satisfaction in remote periods of the future. It manifests itself in the market economy in the discount of future goods as against present goods. It is a ratio of commodity prices, not a price in itself. There prevails a tendency toward the equalization of this ratio for all commodities. In the imaginary construction of the evenly rotating economy the rate of originary interest is the same for all commodities (1949:526)."

Time preference varies significantly across individuals. It is generally thought to be highest for the extremely young and the extremely old, but much lower for the middle-aged. Children have high time preference because of their limited experience and cognitive development (Mischel 1958, 1961a, 1961b, 1961c; Mischel, Shoda, and Rodriguez 1989; Hoppe 2001:4.) Time preference is also thought to be especially high for the poor (Banfield 1974, 1977), criminals (Wilson and Herrnstein 1985), and for borrowers.

A person just informed of a terminal illness, leaving them with a suddenly lowered life expectancy, would naturally experience an abrupt increase in time preference. This is the

Ikiru effect, from Akira Kurosawa's (1910-1998) 1952 film from an original script by Kurosawa, Shinobu Hashimoto, and Hideo Oguni. In Ikiru, ("to live,") Takashi Shimura (1905-1982) delivers his lifetime performance as municipal bureaucrat Kanji Watanabe. When he first learns he has terminal stomach cancer, he embarks on an extravagant but ultimately unsatisfying round of conspicuous consumption. Shimura's character finds personal redemption through seeing a stalled urban renewal project to fruition. For some, this increase in time preference accompanies an increase in interest in religion.

Increasing peoples' time preference leads to more impulsive and short-sighted decision-making and weakens community cohesion. This paper will examine the extent to which the emergence of religion among our distant ancestors contributed to enhancing their sociability and improved their reproductive and survival opportunities. The remainder of this paper is organized as follows: Section 2. "Religion as a Sociobiological Adaptation," introduces the debate among sociobiologists, theologians, and philosophers over whether religion confers evolutionary advantages; Section 3. "Benfits of Minimally Inconsistent Narratives," explores how religious belief may minimize information processing burdens and facilitate social consensus; Section 4. "Religious Practice versus Religious Belief," clarifies the difference between these two related concepts; Section 5. "Group Cohesion," discusses how communal rituals could enhance survivability of the social group; Section 6. "Subjectivity of Time Preference," introduces the economic concept of time preference; Section 7. "Monotheism as a Beneficial Adaptation," argues that belief in one god contributes to social coordination of preferences, including time preference; Section 8. "The General Rate of Time Preference," explains the arbitrage process which leads to one time preference rate which dominates a social group; Section 9. "High versus Low Time Preference," develops the implications high or low time preference has for individuals and groups; Section 10. "High Time Preference and Persistent Poverty," explores why high time preference is particularly damaging; Section 11. "Unresolved Problems," acknowledges some particularly vexing issues which remain and suggests some areas for future research; and finally, Section 12. "Conclusion," presents some concluding comments.

2. RELIGION AS A SOCIOBIOLOGICAL ADAPTATION

The anthropological study of religion searches for objective benefits which enhanced our ancestors' survival and reproductive opportunities (Atran 1990, 2002). The extreme contrasting view of Dawkins (2006) and others (Harris 2004; Dennett 2006) is that religion evolved only as a byproduct of other, actually desirable adaptations, and like the appendix serves no useful purpose. Byproduct theory (Boyer 1994, 2001; Barrett 2004; Bloom 2004) views religion as a nonfunctional "spandrel" (Gould and Lewontin 1979), something which evolved as a consequence of other features which provided adaptational advantages, but provides none itself.

Atran's argument for religion as an evolutionary adaptation which survived in society because it enhanced our ancestors' survival opportunities is two-pronged: first, religion shared by a community allows individuals to rapidly construct "minimally counterintuitive narratives" (Atran and Norenzayan 2004a, 2004b; Norenzayan and Atran 2004; Norenzayan et al 2006) to explain and respond to observed phenomenon; and second, communal religious observances increase the degree of group cohesion, which in turn promotes the development of society and social cooperation. This second hypothesis interfaces intimately with constitutional political economy. Inspired chiefly by Hayek (1952, 1960, 1973, 1976, 1979), this literature searches for evidence of spontaneously emergent institutions, behaviors, and cooperative arrangements (Atcheson 1988; Benson 1991, 1992, 1994, 1999; Ellickson 1991; Bailey 1992).

The economic study of spontaneous order is chiefly associated with Hayek, though the emergence of undesigned orders, institutions, and cooperative arrangements had been noted earlier by Hale (1713), Mandeville (1729), Hume (1739, 1777, 1779), Smith (1759, 1776), and Ferguson (1767) (Ratnapala 2001). Menger (1871, 1883:156-158; 1892) proposed the development of commodity money by participants in primitive barter economies as a spontaneous order and Mises (1912), with the regression theorem, explained how fiat money evolves from commodity money. Polanyi (1941, 1945, 1948, 1951) exerted strong influence on Hayek (Jacobs 1999).

It becomes inevitable to consider religious belief and other cultural manifestations as evolutionary adaptations as soon as we realize that not all religious beliefs are equally adaptive, that is, not all offer the same increased survival and reproductive opportunities. However, Altran's argument is largely independent of the specific content of religious belief, which varied across social groups in primitive times as it does today. In the absence of religious belief, our ancestors would have faced the far greater burden of constructing correct naturalistic explanations on very short notice. One requires a sophisticated knowledge of natural science before this naturalistic strategy could even begin to work, and in primitive times the risks in the short term were too great, of being devoured by predators, of being killed by other humans, or merely dying of exposure to the elements. Furthermore, in many cases community acceptance of a naturalistic hypothesis might be ultimately unavoidable, but could generally not be realized without fatal delay. Atran-Nourenzayan "minimally counterintuitive narratives" suggested by the community's religious tradition benefited individuals directly in guiding immediate responses to an extremely harsh environment, and served to coordinate the community's reaction as well, in an efficient manner which conserved energy, time, and resources, allowed the social group to respond quickly when called for, and facilitated group acceptance of psychologically satisfying explanations stemming from the group's cultural tradition. Furthermore, the cognitive burden imposed by simultaneously constructing naturalistic and supernaturalistic narratives better enabled us to survive in the long run by supporting evolution of a more sophisticated and powerful brain.

Supernatural belief seems to be evoked naturally as a response to the inevitability and ubiquity of death in primitive times (Norenzayan and Hansen 2006) which is perhaps too painful and final to be dealt with otherwise. Darwin (1871) noted the nearly universal belief in supernatural agents and de Unamuno (1921) suggested belief in consciousness after death was an essential feature of consciousness itself, which is inherently unable to conceive of its own absence. Boyer (2001) argues to the contrary, that such unconfirmable beliefs as in God or an afterlife cannot contribute to an organism's survival ability.

Some early brain adaptations which clearly had survival value were a *belief in agency, causal reasoning,* and *theory of mind. Belief in agency* enables us to detect and avoid predators, but we habitually overinvoke our awareness of agents both animate and inanimate. When someone is startled by leaves rustled by the wind, they may waste some energy, which is costly to the organism, but the same timely reaction to leaves rustled by a crouching predator can save the organism's life and allow for transmission of the adaptation through the species' genes. Heider and Simmel (1944; Heider 1958) established that humans instinctively impute agency even to inanimate objects, to the point where it appears to be a fundamental aspect of human behavior, explanation, and language. Religion imputes agency to supernatural entities, which may or may not exist. Many are invisible and imperceptible, though primitive humans often worshiped inanimate natural or artificial objects, such as idols.

Causal reasoning results in our constructing narratives, sometimes subconsciously, to explain and make sense out of our experience. More importantly, narratives serve to integrate our experience. Religion partially automates this process, and shared beliefs would seem to naturally minimize competition among potential alternative narratives within a social group, conserving energy in social intercourse and allowing communities to reach consensus more rapidly and efficiently. Constructing narratives involving long-lived or immortal supernatural entities automatically influences individuals with high time preference to at least conceive of the possibility of extending their own time horizon and lowering their time preferences to better accord with those of the deities they worship and propitiate. *Theory of mind* allows us to understand the actions and intentions of others, to predict how others will act in response to a given situation, and to influence and respond to the behavior of others. Very young children have not yet formed a theory of mind, and cannot understand how others can possess false beliefs. Theory of mind enables us to form expectations of how deities and spirits in which we believe will act in response to external events and our own contemplated actions, including sacrifice and transgression, and enables us to have insight into what may propitiate these entities, whether they actually exist or not. Our ability to get in the mind of possibly non-existent long-lived supernatural agents shows us the way to transition from the high time preference of primitive barbarism, to the lower time preference of primitive agriculture and beyond.

James (1902) saw religion as fostering stronger emotional ties among individuals and strengthening the bonds of community. In his view, religion greatly increases individual loyalty to the group of fellow believers, who confirmed their bonds of community in communal rituals. If this is the case, then the survivability of the strengthened community and the enhanced survivability of the individuals in it would both be enhanced by religious belief. Iannaccone and Makowsky (2007) conducted a series of simulations which demonstrated beneficial clustering of religious groups allows for faster growth because it makes it easier, in terms of lowered transaction cost, for individuals with similar religious beliefs to engage in exchange, intercourse, or other social interaction. Interaction with people of different religions imposes higher transaction costs because both parties do not share a common belief, and may have drastically different ethical standards and behavioral patterns. The information burden which must be overcome before social interaction can proceed prevents some interaction, and makes other interaction more costly. One faces less uncertainty about social partners' past experience and future behavior because one shares the ritualistic practices of the religion with them. Less predictability makes exchange outside one's religious group more costly.

For a species with low life expectancy, which ours certainly was in primitive times, deistic belief imposes lowered time preference, that is, more patience and willingness to save and invest. Even worship of the local deities of the early bronze age improved temporal continuity and focused social energy. More sophisticated religious practices probably accompanied the transition to agriculture between the middle and late stone ages. Barbaric hunter-gatherers of the middle stone age would likely pray for good weather and bountiful hunting, focusing their energies in the immediate future. There was no reason for primitive hunters not to consume their prey in its entirety, because there was no means of preserving any surplus. Once a people engages in agriculture, as started to happen during the late stone age, their attention starts to lengthen to extend from one harvest cycle to the next. An agricultural society might benefit by reserving more of their product as seed corn, and religious practice might implement this time preference by reserving part of the harvest for sacrifice to the community's local deity or as religious alms. The priestly class would store the surplus grain for their own use, for use as seed corn in the future, or against the possibility of famine. The more foresightful the behavior of individuals in a community, and the longer their time-horizon, the more resources are saved instead of being immediately consumed. Saving output allows for time-consuming, capital-using, roundabout means-of-production, which are more productive and lift a community above subsistence. Once a community saves some of its output or income, its wealth is virtually guaranteed to grow more rapidly than groups which save less. Religious belief spread because social groups which engaged in it also engaged in lower-time-preference behavior, outcompeting groups without the religious beliefs necessary to coordinate a general lowering of time preference.

This explains how religious belief removes the incentive to consume the community's seed corn immediately. The survival benefit of religious belief is mostly lost once life expectancy lengthens to the point where, as in modern society, it results in lowered time preference even in the absence of religious belief. Agriculture necessitated the development of astronomy under priestly sponsorship among the Babylonians, Assyrians, and Chaldeans. Any flaws in calendar astronomy are cumulative, and after a mere century under a flawed calendar, a farmer looking up at the sky at noon on the longest day of the year, will be struck by the fact that not only will it be nighttime, it will be snowing (Beckmann 1971). Religious beliefs in such a society would be difficult to maintain in the light of conflicting natural evidence. By the end of the copper stone age, the priestly class was entrusted with the calendar, astrological divination, and the scheduling of ritual feasts they presided over, all compelling them to develop the science of astronomy.

Since religion contributes to lowering time preference, and lowered time preference necessarily improves the social group's survival opportunities, it should be clear that religion is a highly successful evolutionary adaptation. It is possible that some religions developed which promoted high time preference, but if so, these would have been selected out.

3. EVOLUTIONARY BENEFITS
OF MINIMALLY INCONSISTENT NARRATIVES

Religion suggests minimally inconsistent narratives for the social group to utilize as explanations, and which guide the cultural inheritance over time. In order for the narrative-generating capacity of religious belief to contribute to group survival, it must improve survivability better than alternatives. Wilson (2002) argues that religious practice imposes costs on participating individuals, including alms, energy, sacrifice, and acceptance of false or unverifiable beliefs. However, for successful religious groups, the benefit to individuals need only outweigh the cost. Some religions do not pass this test, or in a changing environment do not continue to pass this test, and are abandoned, or the group which follows the religion becomes extinct, outcompeted by a group with a religion more successfully adaptive to prevailing conditions. One plausible reason why religion evolved, especially in light of the extraordinary time and energy devoted to elaborate and sophisticated rituals, architecture, hierarchical institutions, cultural artifacts, etc., is that in primitive social groups, the time and energy devoted to elaborate rituals and sacrifices were more than outweighed by the incessant savings of time and energy offered by recurrent group adoption of simple, consistent, "minimally counterintuitive narratives" dictated by the community's religious tradition.

Even when these explanatory narratives diverged from factual reality, they always had the immediate advantage that they were nearly certain to be accepted without question throughout the social group and that they were likely to meet individuals' most urgent psychological needs. Thus, the community's energy will not be wasted debating the meaning of events it experiences, and the whole society can agree rapidly and almost costlessly on the appropriate response to a given event. Sosis (2004) emphasizes the cultural content of religious practice and argues that specific elements of belief have to have a certain internal consistency to work together for the individual. One's religious faith acts as a kind of aesthetic cultural framework against which additional beliefs must be evaluated. Aesthetically dissonant or culturally incompatible hypotheses are likely to be rejected, even if factually true. The adaptational benefit here would be to shield the individual from the agnostic's staggering burden of having to justify all beliefs about the external environment as they arise. The content of primitive religious beliefs evolves spontaneously like property rights (Bailey 1992) and other cooperative arrangements (Benson 1991, 1999). These spontaneously evolved institutions are thought to survive only if they enhance the survival opportunities of the societies in which they emerge, and if they confer competitive advantage over other institutional arrangements. A social group with less competitive institutions and religious beliefs may adopt those of its faster-growing neighbors, may merge with them, or may be outcompeted to extinction. In each case, the less adaptive institutions are always evolutionary dead ends.

In the absence of a spontaneously emergent cultural tradition, such as a social group's religious belief, which allows for the generation of minimally inconsistent narratives, members of the social group would have had to devote far more time and energy to constructing these narratives, and because narrative construction occurs cooperatively in a social context, further time and energy would then need to be devoted to discussion and persuasion aimed at attaining the assent of others in the social group. Religious belief seemingly automates this extraordinarily cumbersome and expensive process. Agents thus freed from the burden of constructing their own narratives and achieving consensus, would necessarily have more time and energy to devote to long-range planning and speculative foresight, and ceteris paribus, would necessarily have lower time preference.

4. RELIGIOUS PRACTICE VERSUS RELIGIOUS BELIEF

The investigator has to distinguish religious belief from religious practice and ritual. Belief may not actually be coerced and can only flourish in a liberal society recognizing the sovereignty of the individual conscience (Mises 1957:337-340). Belief cannot be observed directly, but only inferred from literary sources, including scriptural texts, theological texts such as commentaries, and secular literature, or from architectural relics, and other archeological remains. Religious practice is revealed much more directly from the same evidence than actual belief. Except for rare first-hand accounts of beliefs of specific authors, evidence of belief generally has to be evaluated as prescriptive rather than descriptive, while the same artifacts provide descriptive evidence of religious practice.

The evolution of ritual practice is imposed from above as an adjunct to governmental authority. Often the ruler is himself a deity like Pharaoh or the Roman emperor, or is high priest of the state religion, or is closely associated with, though separate from, the priestly class.

Human sacrifice is a particularly problematic practice. The story of Abraham and Isaac becomes understandable as a narrative of the transition beyond human sacrifice. Human sacrifice is described in the bible as a practice of pagan cults and neighboring peoples (Deuteronomy 12:31, 18:10–13; 2 Kings 21:6; Ezekiel 20:26-31; 23:37). Judaism evolved from primitive fertility cults, some of which practiced human sacrifice (Davies 1956). Judith 5:7 relates that Abraham abandoned the numerous gods of his fathers to worship the universal God Jehovah. Apart from the moral indignation it evokes, human sacrifice is a particularly expensive religious practice, and it is not surprising that religions prohibiting it would have an evolutionary advantage. Once it was abandoned, it becomes understandable for an oral tradition to develop in which Jehovah commands human sacrifice as a demonstration of unconditional obedience, but rejects the human sacrifice once it is offered. Faced with a history of making human sacrifice, but having abandoned the practice in the relatively recent past as too expensive and morally repugnant, the priestly class would likely construct a narrative in which the deity rejected that kind of sacrifice. Given this hypothesized origin, the fact that Jehovah misleads Abraham with regard to his intentions, becomes understandable and acceptable in light of the moral instruction He provided the patriarch.

5. GROUP COHESION

Once primates began to live in social groups, natural selection began to balance the benefits of cooperative defense, hunting, and child-rearing behaviors against the cost of intragroup competition. Brain size and social group size tend to have evolved together (Dunbar 1996). The larger brain confers evolutionary advantages on the species, and is necessary to handle the volume, complexity, and sophistication of social interactions which increase geometrically with the size of the social group. The larger the social group, the greater the percentage of brain weight devoted to the neocortex or neomammalian brain. Macaque monkeys, who interact in social groups of approximately twenty, have neocortexes which account for 50% of their brain weight. More advanced, intelligent, and social than macaques, chimpanzees live in groups of approximately fifty, and have neocortexes which account for approximately 65% of the brain. In humans the neocortex accounts for 80% of brain weight and includes the language centers.

Hauser (2006) concludes that primates are evolutionarily hard-wired to adopt and practice rules of morality. Although the content of these rules can vary across human societies, survival and reproductive benefits of primate's receptiveness of morality point to an evolutionary cause. De Waal (2006) observes a number of moralizing behaviors in primates: *empathy, reciprocity, social hierarchy,* and *peacemaking. Empathy* is displayed by the comforting of the psychologically distressed or physically injured. It is so commonly observed among primates as to constitute the norm. Occasionally empathy has been observed in other species, but normally does not extend outside the social group except in primates. It has been observed in other mammals, but seems fairly exceptional except for primates. *Reciprocity,* exhibited by non-human primates most strikingly in mutual grooming, suggests observance of the Golden Rule. *Social hierarchy* is observed most strongly in primate societies where the dominant breeding males and females are related to most other members of the social group. Primates' observance of social hierarchy contributes predictability of behavior within the group, and its violation is typically punished, in extreme cases by banishment. *Peacemaking* has been observed through reconciliation among males who have fought each other, and through females distracting, discouraging, and disarming males to prevent them from inflicting more serious injury when they fight. These social behaviors comprise a "stylized morality" which forms a foundation for human morality and religion (de Waal 1982, 1996, 1997, 2005). These are cooperative behaviors which serve group interests by minimizing harm to individuals in the group.

In addition to making cooperative behavior easier to facilitate, social interaction allows for development of other evolutionary adaptations like language and abstract reasoning abilities.

An emerging school of literary criticism, *literary Darwinism* (Carroll 2004; Gottschall and Carroll 2005) posits first that language skills and narrative conceptualizations are evolutionary adaptations which provided survival and reproductive advantages, and second that literature appeals to readers by offering them survival and reproductive advantages, either through enhanced information-processing ability or by providing examples of successful reproductive strategies. This would explain why most adult literature has always dealt with romantic relationships. Literary Darwinism is chiefly inspired by biologists such as J.B.S. Haldane (1932), Desmond Morris (1967), and especially Edward O. Wilson (1975, 1978, 1998).

Apparently religious belief helps maximize the benefits of social cohesion while minimizing the destructive aspects of group life. Individuals living in groups are observed to engage in deception, politicking, coalition formation, and various other activities which are generally discouraged by religion. Although the argument is made that primates' needs to engage in and overcome these negative behaviors forced us to develop larger brains, religion seems to act as a brake against unbridled wantonness. Sosis and Ruffle (2003) found that religious kibbutzim in Israel were more cohesive and survived external stresses better than their secular counterparts. If the degree of social cohesion confers a survival benefit on groups, the puzzle is why these groups have not continued to completely dominate human society (Sosis 2004). It may be that the solution to this puzzle is the observation that religious groups have in fact dominated human history, and that the secular character of modern society is merely a short-term aberration.

6. SUBJECTIVITY OF TIME PREFERENCE

The time preference of one individual can influence the time preference of others (Rothbard 1963: 147-159, 1977; Hoppe 1989, 1993, 2001:6-7). As low time preference individuals save and effect capital accumulation, making the structure of production more productive and roundabout, the marginal utility of present goods tends to fall relative to future goods. This tends to lower everyone's time preference ceteris paribus, though there will always be a range of high and low time preferences within the social group. In addition, as capital accumulates through the saving of low-time-preference individuals, the relative scarcity of labor increases, and ceteris paribus, wage rates rise. The higher wage rate tends to raise the supply of present goods and lower the time preference of previous nonsavers. As wealth and income increase, life expectancy rises, increasing the marginal utility of future goods over present goods, further lowering individual time preference, ceteris paribus.

Individual time preference can exhibit magnitude inconsistency, much like risk preference. Risk preference is magnitude-inconsistent if an individual is more or less risk-averse for small values or larger ones (Arrow and Fisher 1974), and time preference can be inconsistent over different magnitudes, and also over the dimension of different time periods. After arbitrage, however, a social group will have a general rate of time preference, and any inconsistency at the individual level will be minimized, if not eliminated completely.

Religion can also influence time preference rates in a society. Religious practices such as veneration of the dead and ancestor worship, apart from serving individuals' psychological needs, generally lower believers' time preferences by directing their actions toward gratification outside the immediate present, and even outside their current temporal life. If religious belief includes afterlife rewards for particular modes of behavior during life, it provides a powerful mechanism not only for extending the individual's time horizon, lowering their time preference, but also for coordinating the subjective preferences of otherwise disparate individuals. Among several competing societies with religious beliefs, the one imposing the most socially beneficial and cohesive behavioral rules on the individual would have an adaptational advantage over the others. Normally the most adaptive behavioral rules would be those minimizing harm to others in the society, often through formal prohibition in the form of a divinely-ordained moral code.

For the priestly class which administers a religion, as for the temporal ruler, the time horizon will be longer, that is they will have lower time preference themselves and impose a lower time preference on the community, the more secure against competitive threats, is their monopoly on wealth extraction from the productive members of the community. The priestly class could both enhance the wealth-creating potential of the community, and maximize their security against internal and external threats, such as from new religions, by suppressing social innovation, which introduced uncertainty, and by extracting a relatively low portion of the community's wealth. In contrast, an insecure ruler with a short time horizon will try to transfer wealth rapidly from subjects. The archetypal contrast is between the secure English King Henry II and his far less secure son John (Mulligan 2004:49-57). A priestly hierarchy anticipating possible overthrow would behave similarly. Rulers, like priestly classes, face strong incentives to protect their own income, and their citizens' persons, productive activity, and property (Holcombe 1994:8-9).

If the ruler's time preference impacts the governed (Hoppe 2001:15-39; see also Rothbard 1977:172-184 and Hoppe 1989:ch. 9), this must also be true for the religious practices of primitive societies. Religious beliefs in immortal, or at least long-lived, gods would focus the community away from immediate self-gratification toward longer time horizons. Belief in spirit survival, life-after-death, reincarnation, and ancestor worship would justify decisions based on a time horizon longer than adult life expectancy, which in primitive times was pathetically brief. It is interesting to speculate that the antediluvian macrobian lifespan of Adam (Genesis 5:5) and Methuselah (Genesis 5:27) may have originated as an artifact of the initiation of lower time preference beliefs among a people with relatively low life expectancy and high time preference.

7. MONOTHEISM AS A BENEFICIAL ADAPTATION

Though not clearly related to time preference per se, monotheism seems to have been a highly effective evolutionary adaptation which emerged much later. Monotheism seems to offer the advantage of a single explanation for many phenomena. In addition, although there were places where Jehovah was not worshiped, to the ancient Hebrews there was no place He was not absolutely sovereign. This feature, which characterizes many of the world's great religions, has tremendous benefits for traders who travel far and wide. Many primitive deities seem to have been associated with particular places, times, and specific objects. They may have been thought to possess superhuman and supernatural powers, but they could be escaped by distance. Even gods associated with the heavens were only found in particular planets, constellations, winds, or other meteorological phenomena. Apollo could be counted on to return with the dawn, but he did not govern the night sky, and his sister Artemis only hunted when the moon was visible. The Philistine deity Baal, worshiped by Queen Jezebel (2 Kings 10:21), died at the end of every spring, to be born again following the harvest. One of the earliest monotheistic religions was the Pharaoh Akhenaten's worship of the Aton, which Freud (1939) suggested as the origin of Judaism. Abraham's spontaneous discovery of monotheism (Genesis 15:17) seems to have occurred during the middle bronze age, predating Akhenaten by several centuries.

The advanced ancient civilizations each had a sophisticated and intricate pantheon of gods which presumably evolved over millennia from time immemorial. These pantheons are no longer worshipped, but continue to be celebrated as a profoundly valuable cultural inheritance. Each god of these pantheons had its own specific attributes and preferences, and some would contribute more to lowering time preference among believers than others. A certain amount of unproductive arbitrage among followers of different cults would still be present among followers of pantheistic religion. Monotheism automatically offers a higher level of coordination among individuals' time-preference.

As an example for the relative lack of coordination of preferences implicit in a pantheistic religion, it is only necessary to consider the Greeks. The Olympian gods gave mixed signals at best. This may have expressed the bewildering variety of natural phenomena facing the Greeks in ancient times. In the *Iliad*, Apollo smites the Greeks with a plague in book 1, taking the side of the Trojans in retribution for the abduction by the Greeks of one of his priestesses. In book 3, Aphrodite also assists the Trojans by rescuing Paris after he is defeated in combat by Menelaus. Later, in book 5, Aphrodite and Ares are wounded by the Greek warrior Diomedes, counseled in battle by Athena and Hera. A nephew of Hercules and grand-nephew of Zeus, Diomedes is deified when finally killed in battle. Hercules and Diomedes are the only mortals ever to wound any of the gods. In book 8, the gods abandon both sides, disgusted by the violence the mortals inflict on one another, suggesting, not surprisingly, that the immortals enjoy lower time preference than mortals. Poseidon encourages the Greeks in book 13, and Aphrodite switches sides when she helps beautify Hera in preparation for Hera's seduction of Zeus in book 14, known as the deception of Zeus. Hera distracts Zeus through this seduction to provide the Greeks an opportunity to attack Troy. Since the gods war among themselves in the *Iliad*, attempting to propitiate them would be a tricky task for any mortal, something even Odysseus never attempted.

Apollo, profoundly virtuous and Christ-like in the *Alcestis* of Euripides, assumes human form and gains greater empathy for mortals through his experience. It is striking that in the *Alcestis*, he becomes the only immortal in the Olympic pantheon who grows in moral stature. He directed the establishment of colonies in Asia Minor, including Troy, which explains why he protects the Trojans in the *Iliad*, and also in Magna Graecia, consisting of Sicily and southern Italy. Apollo is the god of the sun, of wisdom, music, literature, and healing. As king of the muses he grants inspiration and he gives prophecy through the Delphic oracle. But he is also the bringer of plagues, which makes him somewhat similar to Jehovah. Unlike Jehovah, the Olympian gods possess human weaknesses and appetites. They are simultaneously easier for us to identify with and rather appalling role-models, often exhibiting irresponsibility, moral incontinence, and other high-time preference behaviors, which seems puzzling in light of their immortality. Apollo seemed to have inherited a constitutional weakness for romantic infidelity from his father Zeus, in marked contrast to his exceptionally chaste twin sister Artemis. Apollo was not particularly attracted to other immortals, but he had a marked carnal weakness for beautiful young mortals of both genders. Occasionally deceptive with his lovers, he was often highly vindictive in response to rejection, such as with Daphne, Castalia, Cassandra, and Coronis. Even when he meant no harm, mortals he loved often suffered hideously and fatally as a result. The Greek myths often present moral instruction in the form of cautionary narratives, but in them, the gods are as morally flawed as any mortal. And Apollo is one of the least objectionable among the Olympians. Asclepius, son of Apollo and ancient god of medicine, was the most-worshiped deity in the ancient Greek world. His character was unimpeachable. Zeus slew him for resurrecting the dead with his healing arts, but revived him as a constellation in response to human intercession. It was in retaliation for the death of Asclepius that Apollo slew the Cyclopes who fashioned thunderbolts for Zeus. Zeus punished Apollo by making him serve Admetus in the guise of a mortal shepherd, setting the stage for the *Alcestis*. Interestingly, the desire for healing addresses particularly immediate needs, and is consistent with very high time preference, as described by the Ikiru effect. Panacea, daughter of Asclepius and goddess of the cure, would normally only be propitiated in thanksgiving for a successful cure. Her cult was subsidiary to those of Asclepius and Apollo.

8. THE GENERAL RATE OF TIME PREFERENCE

The time preference rate predominating in any community is reached through arbitrage among many individuals, high-time-preference borrowers and low-time-preference lenders. Lenders compete to offer borrowers lower interest rates while borrowers compete to offer lenders higher interest rates, resulting in the substitution of an objective, observable, exchange-value-determined, market interest rate, for the subjective, unobservable, individual, rate of time preference. The prevalence of a market rate of interest must be counted among the other spontaneously-evolved institutions Menger (1883:155-159) cites.

Clark (2007) argues that saving and investment exceeded a critical threshold only about 1800 in England, and in his view, the reason this happened was that the English population, after centuries of natural selection, finally became sufficiently dominated by the numerous offspring of the wealthy. This population segment inherited less wealth because of population growth, but inherited their ancestors' low time preference. This enabled them to save rather than consume the social surplus immediately, and their willingness to invest in capital-intensive production technologies enabled the explosion of wealth which was the Industrial Revolution. Prior to this time, poverty was endemic everywhere because as Malthus (1798) observed, any growth in wealth was rapidly outpaced by growth in population. Clark's hypothesis requires time preference to be heritable, and it remains unclear whether it can be. Many preferences can be taught, but that is diametrically opposite to genetic transmission.

Differences in general time preference across countries or societies can be partially attributed to demographic differences. American time preference is generally higher than in Japan. To a large extent this difference can be explained by the older median population in Japan. Exceptionally poor countries which have realized high savings rates have experienced phenomenal economic growth, particularly Korea and postwar Japan. Poor countries which have not protected private property have low savings rates and stagnant or even retrogressive economies. If savings are invariably confiscated, there can be no benefit from delaying gratification. In effect, the economic growth rates of modern national economies can be considered analogous to proxies for evolutionary adaptiveness of social groups in primitive times, including religious belief and general time preference.

Although time preference appears to originate within the organism, external factors can change or influence time preference. Hoppe (2001:3-5) notes time preference is determined by "external, biological, personal, and social or institutional" factors. Such external factors as property-right security, physical security generally, and observed behavior of others in the community, affect individuals' time preference. Lower time preference, a willingness to delay gratification, is generally associated with greater predictability in the external environment, which can come either from objective changes in the external environment, or from the individual gaining knowledge and experience – that is, time preference can be influenced by both internal and external factors. This observation argues for the superiority of common law and other spontaneously evolved institutions, which change slowly and incrementally, over positive legislation, which can change abruptly (Rizzo 1985; Mulligan 2004, 2005). The continuity of customary law and institutions, including religion, is preferable from this perspective to the flexibility of positive law and revolutionary change. This explains why religious believers normally resist innovation.

Production requires time (Menger 1871:68), and only lower time-preference individuals with a willingness to invest the time required can improve technological productivity and increase a society's wealth. Cash flow and subsistence considerations ensure that a person with zero income and savings would display higher time preference, that is, a greater desire or impatience for immediate gratification, than the same person with above-subsistence resources, and that the person's time preference would fall as resources rise farther above subsistence. Thus, time preference was higher in primitive societies, and fell as civilization progresses. Only as individuals came to value and recognize property rights, could they exercise entrepreneurial awareness for and implement more productive, roundabout, capital-using production methods. Owning property and lowering time preference interact in a virtuous circle. Those with lower time preference are likely to acquire property through saving and investment, and those with property experience more intensively the potential benefits of saving and deferring gratification, thus being influenced to lower their time preference still further.

9. High versus Low Time Preference

Böhm-Bawerk suggested the cultural level of a nation is mirrored by its overall time preference, which he saw as inversely proportional to a people's intelligence and moral strength (Schumpeter 1951:182). Banfield (1974:61-62) considers time preference the principal underlying distinction between upper and lower classes. The upper class possesses property and low time preference, which results in higher economic productivity, educational attainment, and the amassing of greater wealth. The lower class has little or no property and high time preference, resulting in lower economic productivity, educational attainment, and wealth accumulation. Differences in time preference also account for a higher incidence of criminality among the lower class. Criminals have high time preference and prefer the immediate reward of a crime even at the risk of a delayed and uncertain punishment.

Time preference also illuminates class mobility. High time preference upper-class individuals are likely to squander their wealth on immediate gratification and thereby descend into the lower class, whereas low time preference lower-class individuals are likely, through thrift and industry, to delay gratification, accumulate wealth, and rise to the upper class. Social mobility can impact a social group systematically if its general rate of time preference changes, and religious belief would have generally lowered time preferences for the groups which adopted it.

Though crime is only one of many high time preference behaviors, others including risk-taking, incivility, insensitivity, unreliability, untrustworthyness, rebellious behavior, self-destructive behavior, sexual libertinism, certain eating disorders, and extreme sports, (quite a mixed bag, many of which include some kinds of criminalized behavior as extremes), the systematic relationship between criminality per se and high time preference is well documented (Banfield 1974:140-141, 1977; Wilson and Herrnstein 1985:49-56; Hoppe 2001:31, note 31). Most, if not all, of these high-time-preference behaviors, are generally discouraged by most major religions.

The progress of civilization is a process of capital accumulation and the substitution of voluntary exchange for coercion and violence (Elias 1968; Hoppe 2001:6). Hoppe (2001:7) likens the lowering of social time preference which accompanies the transition from barbarism to civilization to the lowering of individual time preference which accompanies the transition from childhood to adulthood. Actual or supposed social degeneration can lead to individuals raising their time preference, a phenomenon which can be compared to the transition from adulthood to old age, the Ikiru effect. A perception of social degeneration can become a self-fulfilling prophecy, if individuals adopt an attitude of "après nous le déluge," attempting to consume all resources immediately. Festinger, Reicken, and Schachter (1956) studied millenarian and messianic cults which predicted the imminent end of the world. Cult members exhibited typical high-time-preference behaviors as long as they could maintain belief in the cults' central prophecies in the face of repeated disconfirmation. This demonstrates that religion can impose high time preference on believers as well as low time preference. Unfortunately for these groups, since high time preference impairs a group's survival opportunities, such religions fail to spread widely.

A religion preaching a moral code of living in the moment would tend to increase time preference among its followers. Thus reputation and repeated-deal arrangements would be less valuable, social sanctions such as ostracism less effective, and acceptance and implementation of moral norms less pervasive, lowering social cohesion. In this insecure environment, "crimes" such as vigilantism, unlicensed gun possession, and construction of unlicensed castles, would often be "undertaken to exercise social control (Ellickson 1991:213; Acheson 1988; de Soto 1989)." When the community fails to provide acceptable levels of security, individuals will take matters into their own hands.

10. HIGH TIME PREFERENCE AND PERSISTENT POVERTY

The liberal order generally lowers individual time preferences by providing individuals the opportunity to discover and exploit roundabout means of production, which cannot be relied on in the absence of secure rights to own, use, dispose of, and transfer, land, capital, and one's own labor services, including embodied entrepreneurial talent and human capital. Lack of secure and transferable property rights prevents third-world nations from accumulating wealth and productive capital (de Soto 1989). This incidentally compels them to persist in the high-time-preference state which predated civilization, even though these societies are often deeply religious. The cause of this may be laid at the feet of the developed world, whose development lending activities are hostile toward private property, entrepreneurial innovation, and low time preference: "expropriation is the right of any country (World Bank 1976:13)." This forces third-world entrepreneurs to exhibit high-time-preference behavior and extract whatever wealth they can immediately, because otherwise they may lose everything.

This attitude toward individual rights, that they are privileges granted by, and only exercised at the sufferance of the government, is highly suggestive of the *droit administratif*. A.V. Dicey (1885:213-267) suggests the tradition of French and continental administrative law or *droit administratif* is fundamentally opposed to the Anglo-American concept of the rule of law. Government does not enjoy a privileged position under the rule of law, but does under *droit administratif*. An extreme view would be that under *droit administratif*, the government is above the law. Dicey notes *droit administratif* possesses many advantages, especially from the point of view of administrative efficiency. These advantages accrue, however, to the governing classes rather than to the governed. Though not necessarily an atavistic survival, the principle of the government being above the law points back to an origin in theocratic government where religious freedom was not tolerated. This now secular legal philosophy is especially compatible with that of development planning, which assumes that the international development lenders' staffs of technocrats are better able to direct the third world's economic progress than the uncoordinated activity of those nations' citizens. The possibility is not conceived of, that the international technocrats and the developing nations' citizens might have different preferences, including different time preferences. Because Anglo-American common law is not a planned order, it is fundamentally at a variance, not only with the philosophy of legal positivism (Rizzo 1985), but also with the imperatives of development planning or central economic planning. Positive legislation may change overnight, and necessarily imposes high-time preference. In contrast, customary law, because it can only evolve slowly and incrementally, imposes low time preference along with greater predictability of behavior. This advantage is invariant to any shortcomings in the content of customary law, and is merely a property of the fact that the mode of changing the law limits the speed and degree of change.

The well-known problem of the commons can be described as a failure of institutional structure which imposes higher time preference on individuals. The free or below-cost provision of a public good, in this case grazing land, results in individual users making more intensive use of the low-cost public good. The fact that such highly intensive use causes perceptible degradation and shortening of the expected useful life of the public good, leads users to try and extract as much value added as possible, resulting in even more rapid and complete destruction of the public resource. Artificially imposing higher time preferences creates incentives for collectively undesirable behavior (Smith 1988:86-87). The free rider problem results when provision of public goods is substituted for established customary security of property rights (Hardin and Baden 1977; Olsen 1993; Hoppe 2001:17).

Similarly, in the transition economies of the former Soviet Union, where state-owned property has been privatized but the government has imposed a moratorium on the transfer of ownership, owners attempt to extract value by using the resource so intensively they degrade its value. Since they cannot sell the property anyway, there is no incentive to preserve the resource for possible future sale, and the only incentive is to maximize the immediate yield. This tendency is aggravated by the significant possibility of future nationalization. In the Ukraine, agricultural land is being abandoned as the crop yield falls and owners are unable and unwilling to invest in improvements and complementary capital equipment (Krasnozhon 2005). Overwork of agricultural land in the short run results in soil exhaustion, abandonment to nature, and in extreme cases, total loss of topsoil.

Religious beliefs and rituals would influence individuals to make better, lower-time-preference use of common property and any resources for which rights of disposal and transfer were not well-defined. In primitive times, this would have included a far greater sphere than after the emergence of law and property rights. In effect, religious ostracism would dissuade individuals from overgrazing a common pasture or degrading other common resources. Such societies would have possessed a clear adaptational advantage over those who had not implemented any mechanism for limiting the overuse and degradation of common resources. The need for, and advantage from, such institutions, increased exponentially during the transition from the hunter-gatherer cultures of the middle stone age to the agricultural societies of the new stone age, starting approximately 11,000-8,500 B.C.

11. Unresolved Problems

The literature on religion as an evolutionary adaptation has two contradictory explanations. One strand argues that religion provides an adaptive benefit because it minimizes the information processing burden on the individual and leaves us free to utilize our brain capacity for other, more beneficial uses. This strand of research emphasizes the benefits of religion in offering an expectation of uniform behavior in the community group through "minimally inconsistent narratives." Such uniformity of behavior should have improved group cohesion. Weber (1905) and Tawney (1926) believed that particular religious beliefs, through validating and encouraging economically beneficial behavior at the individual level, contributed to the success of the social group. These desirable behaviors improved group cohesion and the predictability of individual behavior, making it easier for individuals to coordinate their plans.

A contrasting research stream argues that religion enables us to form larger social groups, which imposes a greater information processing burden on the individual, and promotes development of a larger neocortex. One argument is that the cognitive burden imposed by requiring the simultaneous construction of naturalistic and supernaturalistic narratives better enabled us to survive in the long run by supporting evolution of a more sophisticated and powerful brain. It should be clear that both accounts cannot be simultaneously true, unless additional explanations can be marshaled, and this unresolved conflict in the evolution of religion literature is both a major difficulty and a fruitful area for further research.

A possible resolution is to distinguish short-run from long-run costs and benefits. It seems arguable that religious belief saves energy, time, and uncertainty in the short run, facilitating immediate responses and rapidly-formed social consensus. Here the benefit is chiefly in the short run. Any conflict between religious belief and empirical evidence can often be overlooked until it becomes critical and generates sufficient cognitive dissonance. When conflicts between religion and reality had to be resolved in the longer run, the information processing burden imposed by particularly abstract theological reasoning, and perhaps more importantly by discussion, argument, and debate within the social group, may well have contributed to enlargement of the neocortex, as well as improving the efficiency of its utilization. Clearly, more evidence needs to be found which can be applied to either confirming or disconfirming this hypothesis.

It appears especially unlikely that this longer-term reasoning could have been engaged in by people with notably high time preference. High-time-preference individuals live in the moment and do not characteristically deliberate or philosophize. In contrast, low-time-preference individuals can still be alert to immediate threats like predators. Religious belief, and fundamental cognitive categorizations like belief in agency for inanimate objects, would enable low-time-preference individuals to respond immediately. It may well have been that religion allowed the low-time-preference individuals to survive, flourish, and reproduce. They are the group which engaged in theological deliberation and debate, but this could have been possible only after immediate threats had been addressed. The low-time-preference savers are the group which makes the more intensive use of the available neocortex, and in whom it likely evolved. They are the ones with the comparative advantage in entrepreneurial planning.

12. CONCLUSION

Though time preference is necessarily subjective, it should be influenced by objective external factors such as a culture's religious ritual and social interaction. Societies varied in their general attitudes to saving, investment, and consumption, and in primitive times, the major impetus coordinating individual time preference was religious practice.

Religious belief confers survival benefits on societies and individuals which adopt it to the extent it allows a general lowering of time preference. Although religious belief can be arbitrary in the sense that it is not subject to naturalistic justification, religious practice enhances the survival and reproductive opportunities of the societies that it serves to shepherd through adverse selection. Only the most adaptive religious practices survive and contribute to the ongoing evolution of a cultural tradition. The emergence of religion and morality supported a reduction of time preference, allowing for employment of capital in time-consuming roundabout means of production.

Although belief in God conferred survival value as we evolved, it no longer does so. Human longevity has expanded to the point where our time horizon is relatively long and our time preference is relatively low by historical standards. The general lowering of time preference both facilitates and is facilitated by the development of civilization and an increasing complexity of social relationships. The essence of low time preference is planning for the future, a willingness to delay gratification, and patience to wait for future benefits.

Once religious belief emerged among our distant ancestors, to be transmitted as a successful adaptation, it must have contributed to the reproductive success of the believers. Primitive humans experienced an appallingly low life expectancy, and many early religions were fertility cults. The more primitive fertility cults focused on human reproduction, but as agriculture developed at the start of the new stone age, fertility cults emerged which focused on agricultural activities such as the timing of planting and harvesting. Our remote ancestors had little reason to conserve resources for the future because their future was much more uncertain and dangerous than ours. Religion successfully mitigated their natural tendency to enjoy whatever gratification they could immediately control. Successfully adaptive religious beliefs enhanced the survival and reproductive prospects of both individuals and communities by conditioning them to engage in longer-range planning through such beliefs as life-after-death, spirit survival, and reincarnation.

Religious practices which did not confer survival benefits, if adopted, clearly would have disadvantaged communities which may have died out as a result. The tremendous and costly application of resources to non-productive activities such as human sacrifice or pyramid building likely contributed either to the abandonment of those practices or extinction of the culture. The Egyptian pyramids were built during the third, fourth, and fifth dynasties, conventionally dated from approximately 2700-2400 B.C., and Egyptian culture and religion continued to flourish without building more pyramids for nearly three thousand years before pantheistic religion was supplanted in Egypt by forcible conversion to Christianity, and nearly four thousand years before forcible conversion to Islam.

Sociobiologists studying the problem of religion as an evolutionary adaptation are hard-pressed to point to survival benefits it necessarily offers today, and many question whether it ever necessarily provided any evolutionary benefit. Researchers arguing for the adaptive benefits of religious belief cite such characteristics as group cohesion, the facilitation of ready explanations, and impacts on cognitive burden. Some feel religion benefits a species by lowering the cognitive burden through simple, intuitive, though usually objectively false or unverifiable, explanations. Others feel religion imposes a dual burden of simultaneous acceptance of two explanations, a naturalistic one and a religious one, for every event, but this added burden is beneficial because it contributes to the evolution of a more powerful brain.

It is clear that the examination of time preference helps sort out the issues of whether religion offers adaptive benefits, why it does so, and whether the benefits continue. Religious beliefs need not lower time preference and therefore confer adaptive benefits, though those beliefs most familiar to us, such as after-death-survival, spirit-survival, immortality of the gods, and reincarnation, obviously act to lower time preference. We have little cultural memory of religious practices which may have increased time preference, if any ever existed anywhere, perhaps because societies with such practices were adaptationally disadvantaged. Natural selection was hard on beliefs which encouraged high time preference. The survival benefit of religious belief is mostly lost once life expectancy lengthens to the point where, in and of itself, it results in lowered time preference and more responsible, more forward-looking behavior from the majority of agents in the community.

REFERENCES

Acheson, J.M. 1988. *The Lobster Gangs of Maine.* Hanover, New Hampshire: University Press of New England.

Arrow, Kenneth J.; Fisher, Anthony C. 1974. "Environmental Preservation, Uncertainty, and Irreversibility." *Quarterly Journal of Economics* 88(1): 312-319.

Atran, Scott. 1990. *Cognitive Foundations of Natural History: Towards an Anthropology of Science.* Cambridge and New York: Cambridge University Press; Paris: Editions de la Maison des sciences de l'homme.

Atran, Scott. 2002. *In Gods We Trust : the Evolutionary Landscape of Religion.* Oxford and New York: Oxford University Press.

Atran, Scott; Norenzayan, Ara. 2004a. "Religion's Evolutionary Landscape: Counterintuition, Commitment, Compassion, Communion." *Behavioral and Brain Sciences* 27: 713-770.

Atran, Scott; Norenzayan, Ara. 2004b. "Why Minds Create Gods: Devotion, Deception, Death, and Arational Decision Making." *Behavioral and Brain Sciences* 27: 713-770.

Bailey, M.J. 1992. "Approximate Optimality of Aboriginal Property Rights." *Journal of Law and Economics* 35: 183-198.

Banfield, Eric. 1974. *The Unheavenly City Revisited.* Boston: Little, Brown, and Company.

Banfield, Eric. 1977. "Present-orientedness and Crime." In Barnett, Randy E.; Hagel, John (eds.) *Assessing the Criminal: Restitution, Retribution, and the Legal Process.* Cambridge MA: Ballinger.

Barrett, Justin. 2004. *Why would Anyone Believe in God?* Lanham, Maryland: AltaMira.

Beckmann, Petr. 1971. *A History of Pi.* Colorado Springs: Golem Press.

Benson, Bruce L. 1991. "An Evolutionary Contractarian View of Primitive Law: the Institutions and Incentives Arising Under Customary American Indian Law." *Review of Austrian Economics* 5: 65-89.

Benson, Bruce L. 1992. "The Development of Criminal Law and Its Enforcement: Public Interest or Political Transfers." *Journal des Economistes et des Etudes Humaines* 3: 79-108.

Benson, Bruce L. 1994. "Are Public Goods Really Common Pools: Considerations of the Evolution of Policing and Highways in England." *Economic Inquiry* 32: 249-271.

Benson, Bruce L. 1999. "An Economic Theory of the Evolution of Government and the Emergence of the State." *Review of Austrian Economics* 12(2): 131-160.

Bloom, Paul. 2004. *Descartes' Baby: How the Science of Child Development Explains What Makes Us Human*. New York: Basic Books.

Böhm-Bawerk, Eugen von. [1884-1921] 1959. *Capital and Interest, Kapital und Kapitalzins*. South Holland, Illinois: Libertarian Press.

Boyer, Pascal. 1994. *The Naturalness of Religious Ideas: a Cognitive Theory of Religion*. Berkeley: University of California Press.

Boyer, Pascal. 2001. *Religion Explained: the Evolutionary Origins of Religious Thought*. New York: Basic Books.

Carroll, Joseph. 2004. *A Literary Darwinism: Evolution, Human Nature, and Literature*. New York: Routledge.

Clark, Gregory. 2007. *A Farewell to Alms: a Brief Economic History of the World*. Princeton: Princeton University Press.

Darwin, Charles. 1871. *The Descent of Man, and Selection in Relation to Sex*. London: John Murray.

Davies, (Rev.) A. Powell. 1956. *The Ten Commandments*. New York: New American Library.

de Soto, Hernando. 1989. *The Other Path: the Invisible Revolution in the Third World*. New York: Perennial Library.

Dawkins, Richard. 2006. *The God Delusion*. Boston: Houghton Mifflin.

Dennett, Daniel C. 2006. *Breaking the Spell: Religion as a Natural Phenomenon*. New York: Viking.

de Waal, Frans B.M. 1982. *Chimpanzee Politics : Power and Sex among Apes*. Baltimore: Johns Hopkins University Press.

de Waal, Frans B.M. 1996. *Good Natured: the Origins of Right and Wrong in Humans and Other Animals*. Cambridge: Harvard University Press.

de Waal, Frans B.M. 1997. *Bonobo: the Forgotten Ape*. Berkeley: University of California Press.

de Waal, Frans B.M. 2005. *Our Inner Ape*. New York: Riverhead Books.

de Waal, Frans B.M. 2006. *Primates and Philosophers: How Morality Evolved*. Princeton: Princeton University Press.

de Unamuno, Miguel. [1921] 1972. *The Tragic Sense of Life in Men and Nations* (trans. Kerrigan, Anthony.) Princeton: Princeton University Press.

Dicey, Albert Venn. [1885] 1915. *An Introduction to the Study of the Law of the Constitution* (new 8th ed.) Indianapolis: Liberty Classics.

Dunbar, Robin Ian MacDonald. 1996. *Grooming, Gossip, and the Evolution of Language*. Cambridge: Harvard University Press.

Elias, Norbert. [1968] 1978. *The Civilizing Process: a History of Manners, Über den Prozess der Zivilisation*. New York: Urizen Books.

Ellickson, R.C. 1991. *Order Without Law: How Neighbors Settle Disputes*. Cambridge: Harvard University Press.

Ferguson, Adam. [1767] 1966. *An Essay on the History of Civil Society*. New ed. Edinburgh: Edinburgh University Press.

Festinger, Leon; Riecken, Henry W.; Schachter, Stanley. 1956. *When Prophecy Fails: a Social and Psychological Study of a Modern Group that Predicted the Destruction of the World*. New York: Harper and Row.

Fetter, Frank A. 1902. "The Roundabout Process of the Interest Theory." *Quarterly Journal of Economics* 17(1): 163-180.

Fetter, Frank A. 1914a. "Interest Theories Old and New." *American Economic Review* 4(1): 68-92.

Fetter, Frank A. 1914b. "Capitalization versus Productivity, Rejoinder." *American Economic Review* 4(4): 856-859.

Fetter, Frank A. 1914c. "Davenport's Competitive Economics." *Journal of Political Economy* 33: 555-562.

Fetter, Frank A. 1977. *Capital, Interest, and Rent: Essays in the Theory of Distribution*. Kansas City: Sheed, Andrews and McMeel.

Fisher, Irving. 1896. "Appreciation and Interest." *Publications of the American Economic Association* (New York: Macmillan) 11: 23-29, 92-92.

Freud, Sigmund. 1939. *Moses and Monotheism, Der Mann Moses und die monotheistische Religion*. New York: Institute of Psycho-analysis.

Gottschall, Jonathan; Carroll, Joseph (eds.) 2005. *The Literary Animal: Evolution and the Nature of Narrative*. Evanston: Northwestern University Press.

Gould, Stephen Jay; Lewontin, Richard. 1979. "The Spandrels of San Marco and the Panglossion Paradigm: a Critique of the Adaptationist Programme." *Proceedings of the Royal Society of London Series B* 205: 581-598.

Hale, Matthew. [1713] 1971. *History of the Common Law of England*. New ed., Chicago: University of Chicago Press.

Hardin, Garett; Baden, John (eds.) 1977. *Managing the Commons*. San Francisco: William H. Freeman.

Harris, Sam. 2004. *The End of Faith: Religion, Terror, and the Future of Reason*. New York: W.W. Norton.

Hauser, Marc D. 2006. *Moral Minds: How Nature Designed Our Universal Sense of Right and Wrong*. New York: Ecco Press.

Hayek, Friedrich A. 1952. *The Sensory Order: an Inquiry into the Foundations of Theoretical Psychology*. Chicago: University of Chicago Press.

Hayek, Friedrich A. 1960. *The Constitution of Liberty*. Chicago: University of Chicago Press.

Hayek, Friedrich A. 1973. *Law, Legislation and Liberty*, vol. 1, *Rules and Order*. Chicago: University of Chicago Press.

Hayek, Friedrich A. 1976. *Law, Legislation and Liberty*, vol. 2, *The Mirage of Social Justice*. Chicago: University of Chicago Press.

Hayek, Friedrich A. 1979. *Law, Legislation and Liberty*, vol. 3, *The Political Order of a Free People*. Chicago: University of Chicago Press.

Heider, Fritz. 1958. *The Psychology of Interpersonal Relations*. New York: John Wiley & Sons.

Heider, Fritz; Simmel, Marianne. 1944. "An Experimental Study of Apparent Behaviour." *American Journal of Psychology* 57(2): 243-59.

Holcombe, Randall G. 1994. *The Economic Foundations of Government*. New York: New York University Press.

Hoppe, Hans-Hermann. 1989. *A Theory of Socialism and Capitalism*. Boston: Kluwer.

Hoppe, Hans-Hermann. 1993. *The Economics and Ethics of Private Property*. Boston: Kluwer.

Hoppe, Hans-Hermann. 2001. *Democracy-the God that Failed*. New Brunswick, New Jersey and London: Transaction Publishers.

Hume, David. [1739] 1979. *A Treatise of Human Nature*. New ed., Oxford: Clarendon Press.

Hume, David. [1777] 1975. *Enquiries Concerning Human Understanding and Concerning the Principles of Morals* (2nd ed.) New ed., Oxford: Clarendon Press.

Hume, David. [1779] 1947. *Dialogues Concerning Natural Religion*. New ed. Indianapolis: Bobbs-Merrill.

Iannaccone, Laurence R.; Makowsky, Michael. 2007. "Accidental Atheists? Agent-based Explanations for the Persistence of Religious Regionalism." *Journal for the Scientific Study of Religion* 46(1): 1-16.

Jacobs, Struan. 1999. "Michael Polanyi's Theory of Spontaneous Orders." *Review of Austrian Economics* 11(2): 111-127.

James, William. 1902. *The Varieties of Religious Experience: a Study in Human Nature*. Cambridge: Harvard University Press.

Jevons, William Stanley. 1965. *Theory of Political Economy*. New York: Augustus M. Kelley.

Kirzner, Israel M. 1996. *Essays on Capital and Interest: an Austrian Perspective*. Cheltenham, United Kingdom: Edward Elgar.

Krasnozhon, Leonid. 2005. "Lessons of Privatization: Property Rights in Agricultural Land in Ukraine." In *Property Rights: the Essential Ingredient for Liberty and Progress*. Great Barrington, Massachusetts: American Institute for Economic Research. *Economic Education Bulletin* 45(5): 123-136.

Malthus, (Rev.) Thomas Robert. [1798] 1826. *An Essay on the Principle of Population* (sixth ed.) London: John Murray.

Mandeville, Bertrand. [1729] 1988. *The Fable of the Bees or, Private Vices, Publick Benefits*. New ed. Indianapolis: Liberty Classics.

Menger, Carl Friedrich. [1871] 1976. *Principles of Economics, Grundsätze der Volkswirtschaftslehre*. New York: New York University Press.

Menger, Carl Friedrich. [1883] 1985. *Investigations into the Method of the Social Sciences with Special Reference to Economics, Untersuchungen über die Methode der Socialwissenschaften und der Politischen Oekonomie insbesondere*. New York: New York University Press.

Menger, Carl Friedrich. 1892. "On the Origins of Money." Foley, C.A. (trans.) *Economic Journal* 2: 239-55.

Mischel, Walter. 1958. "Preference for Delayed Reinforcement: an Experimental Study of a Cultural Observation." *Journal of Abnormal and Social Psychology* 56: 57-61.

Mischel, Walter. 1961a. "Preference for Delayed Reinforcement and Social Responsibility." *Journal of Abnormal and Social Psychology* 62: 1-15.

Mischel, Walter. 1961b. "Delay of Gratification, Need for Achievement, and Acquiescience in Another Culture." *Journal of Abnormal and Social Psychology* 62: 543-552.

Mischel, Walter. 1961c. "Father-absence and Delay of Gratification: Cross-cultural Comparisons." *Journal of Abnormal and Social Psychology* 63: 116-124.

Mischel, Walter; Metzner, R. 1962. "Preference for Delayed Reward as a Function of Age, Intelligence, and Length of Delay Interval." *Journal of Abnormal and Social Psychology* 64: 425-431.

Mischel, Walter; Shoda, Y.; Rodriguez, M. L. 1989. "Delay of Gratification in Children." *Science* 244: 933-938.

Mises, Ludwig von. [1949] 1998. *Human Action: a Treatise on Economics* (5th ed.) Auburn: Ludwig von Mises Institute.

Mises, Ludwig von. [1957] 1969. *Theory and History: an Interpretation of Social and Economic Evolution.* New Haven: Yale University Press. Reprint, New Rochelle, New York: Arlington House.

Morris, Desmond. 1967. *The Naked Ape.* London: Jonathan Cape.

Mulligan, Robert F. 2004. "Spontaneously Evolved Social Order versus Positive Legislation in English Constitutional History." *Review of Austrian Economics* 17(1): 41-65.

Mulligan, Robert F. 2005. "The Common Law Character of English Charters: Spontaneous Order in the Constitutions of Clarendon (1164)." *Constitutional Political Economy* 16(3): 285-311.

Norenzayan, Ara; Atran, Scott. 2004. "Cognitive and Emotional Processes in the Cultural Transmission of Natural and Nonnatural Beliefs. In Schaller, M.; Crandall, C. (eds.) *The Psychological Foundations of Culture* (pp 149-169). Hillsdale, New Jersey: Lawrence Erlbaum Associates.

Norenzayan, Ara; Hansen, I. G. 2006. "Belief in Supernatural Agents in the Face of Death." *Personality and Social Psychology Bulletin* 32: 174-187.

Norenzayan, Ara; Atran, Scott; Faulkner, J.; Schaller, M. 2006. "Memory and mystery: The cultural selection of minimally counterintuitive narratives." *Cognitive Science* 30: 531-553.

Olson, Mancur. 1993. "Dictatorship, Democracy, and Development." *American Political Science Review* 87(3): 567-576.

Pipes, Richard. 1999. *Property and Freedom.* New York: Alfred A. Knopf.

Polanyi, Michael. 1941. "The Growth of Thought in Society." *Economica* 8(33): 428-456.

Polanyi, Michael. 1945. "The Planning of Science." *Political Quarterly* 16(4): 316-28.

Polanyi, Michael. 1948. "Planning and Spontaneous Order." *Manchester School of Economic and Social Studies* 16: 237-268.

Polanyi, Michael. 1951. *The Logic of Liberty: Reflections and Rejoinders.* Chicago: University of Chicago Press.

Ratnapala, Suri. 2001. "Eighteenth-century Evolutionary Thought and its Relevance in the Age of Legislation." *Constitutional Political Economy* 12: 51-75.

Rizzo, Mario J. 1985. "Rules versus Cost-benefit Analysis in the Common Law." *Cato Journal* 4: 865-884.

Rothbard, Murray N. [2004] 1963. *Man, Economy, and State* (2d ed.) Auburn: Ludwig von Mises Institute.

Rothbard, Murray N. 1977. *Power and Market*. Kansas City: Sheed Andrews McMeel.

Schumpeter, Joseph Alois. 1951. *Ten Great Economists*. New York: Oxford University Press.

Smith, Adam. [1759] 1981. *The Theory of Moral Sentiments*. New ed. Indianapolis: Liberty Classics.

Smith, Adam. [1776] 1981. *An Inquiry into the Nature and Causes of the Wealth of Nations*. New ed. Indianapolis: Liberty Classics.

Smith, T. Alexander. 1988. *Time and Public Policy*. Knoxville: University of Tennessee Press.

Sosis, Richard. 2003. "Why aren't We all Hutterites? Costly Signaling Theory and Religious Behavior." *Human Nature* 14: 91-127.

Sosis, Richard. 2004. "The Adaptive Value of Religious Ritual." *American Scientist* 92:166-172.

Sosis, Richard; Ruffle, Bradley. 2003. "Religious Ritual and Cooperation: Testing for a Relationship on Israeli Religious and Secular Kibbutzim." *Current Anthropology* 44: 713-722.

Strigl, Richard von. 2001. *Capital and Production*. Auburn: Ludwig von Mises Institute.

Tawney, Richard Henry. [1926] 1962. *Religion and the Rise of Capitalism; a Historical Study*. Gloucester, Massachusetts: P. Smith.

Weber, Max. [1905] 1930. *The Protestant Ethic and the Spirit of Capitalism, Protestantische Ethik und der Geist des Kapitalismus* (trans. Parsons, Talcott). New York: Scribners.

Wilson, David Sloan. 2002. *Darwin's Cathedral: Evolution, Religion, and the Nature of Society*. Chicago: University of Chicago Press.

Wilson, Edward O. [1975] 2000. *Sociobiology: the New Synthesis*. Cambridge: Harvard University Press.

Wilson, Edward O. 1978. *On Human Nature*. Cambridge: Harvard University Press.

Wilson, Edward O. 1998. *Consilience: the Unity of Knowledge*. New York: Alfred A. Knopf.

Wilson, James Q.; Herrnstein, Richard J. 1985. *Crime and Human Nature*. New York: Simon and Schuster.

The World Bank. 1976. *Questions and Answers / The World Bank*. Washington: The World Bank.

In: Political Economy Research Focus
Editor: Walter R. Levin, pp. 93-108

ISBN: 978-1-60456-154-8
© 2008 Nova Science Publishers, Inc.

Chapter 4

THE ECB'S MONETARY POLICY. DOES IT FIT TO ALL EMU MEMBERS?

Adolfo Maza[*], Blanca Sánchez-Robles[†] and José Villaverde[‡]
Department of Economics, University of Cantabria, Avda. de los Castros,
s/n 39005-Santander, Spain

ABSTRACT

This paper analyses some issues related to the design and potential asymmetric effects of the monetary policy in the Eurozone. Our analysis of monthly data from January 1999 to November 2005 by cointegration techniques suggests that the design of the monetary policy by the European Central Bank (ECB) can be characterized by a model that comprises a Taylor rule, in which a higher weight is given to the goal of price stability than to the expansion of output. Next, we try to assess whether the single monetary policy has similarly suited all the members of the European Monetary Union (EMU) to the same extent. We conclude that the costs associated to the single monetary policy are not the same for all of them. In particular, the higher the inflation rate in a particular country, the larger the costs entailed by the loss of monetary independence.

Keywords: Monetary policy, Taylor rule, European Central Bank, European Monetary Union
JEL Classification: E43, E52, F33, F36

---

[*] E-mail: adolfo.maza@unican.es
[†] blanca.sanchezrobles@gmail.com
[‡] villavej@unican.es

INTRODUCTION

The final phase of the European Monetary Union (EMU), together with the physical launching of the Euro in 1999, has led to a dramatic change in the economic scenario for the members of the Eurozone. As the theory of the Optimal Currency Areas (OCA) argues, the single currency entails both advantages (benefits) and disadvantages (costs) for the EMU members. Among the benefits it is worth mentioning the reduction of transaction costs, the suppression of the uncertainty associated with exchange rate fluctuations, and the higher efficiency brought about by a more dynamic trade between the countries belonging to the area. One of the main drawbacks of EMU, on the other hand, is the loss of monetary policy at the national level as a potential tool to expand or contract the aggregate demand (Emerson, 1992); in effect, since January 1999 the monetary policy has been established globally, for the whole Eurozone, by the European Central Bank (ECB).

The costs associated with the loss of monetary independence might not be the same for all the countries in the Eurozone. The extent of these costs is related to the transmission mechanism[1]: asymmetries in this mechanism (see, for example, Clausen and Hayo, 2006) across the members of the monetary union might be critical in determining the effects of a common monetary policy. Generally speaking, the larger the economic differences –in size, openness, the credit channel, the response of bank lending, the phase of the business cycle, the industry mix and so on- between a member country and the rest of the Eurozone, the higher the potential costs for that member, both in terms of output and inflation. If these countries are precisely the less advanced countries of the EMU, this fact could delay the process of national convergence within the area. In more technical terms, if the probability of a country facing an asymmetric shock rises, the cost of the lack of monetary autonomy will increase (for a discussion on the issue of asymmetric shocks see, for example, Sánchez-Robles and Cuñado, 1999; Maza and Villaverde, 2006).

The purpose of this study is twofold. On the one hand, we intend to obtain some insights into the way in which the monetary policy of the ECB is designed. On the other, we try to get a feeling of some of the costs associated with the loss of monetary autonomy for particular EMU countries.

The structure of the paper is as follows. Section I provides a brief survey of the literature. Section II estimates a model of the determination of the interest rate by the ECB from January 1999 to November 2005. This section also computes the interest rates that, according to the model, would be optimal for each of the 12 countries that made up the EMU, and measures the differences between these interest rates and those determined by the ECB. Finally, Section III presents our conclusions.

---

[1] The transmission mechanism (see, for example, Favero *et al.*, 1999) refers to the way changes in monetary policy affect aggregate demand and, thus, output and inflation. This mechanism, which works through the way changes in the official interest rate affect market rates, asset prices, expectations and the exchange rate, is characterised, as a general rule, by long, variable and uncertain time lags, thus making it difficult to foretell the effects of monetary policy on the levels of economic activity and prices.

I. A Brief Survey of the Literature

There are many papers, both at the theoretical and the empirical level, that have analysed the way in which central banks design their monetary policy. An approach that has been widely used in the last few years characterizes the implementation of monetary measures through the use of rather simple rules of monetary policy. An important paper in this regard is Taylor (1993). This author establishes a rule in order to capture the behaviour of the interest rate of reference for the case of the USA Federal Reserve System (FED) over the years 1987-1992. This rule can be expressed formally by the following equation:

$$r_t = (R_t + i_t) + \beta (i_t - i^*) + \delta (y_t - y^*) \tag{1}$$

in which r_t is the nominal interest rate at time t, R_t is the real interest rate in equilibrium, i_t is the effective rate of inflation, y_t is the actual rate of growth of output, i^* is the targeted inflation rate, y^* is the potential rate of output growth and β and δ are unknown parameters. Taylor did not estimate these parameters. Instead, he assumed a pre-established weight of $\beta - 1 = \delta = 0.5$. He also presupposed a figure of 2% for both the targeted inflation rate and the real interest rate in equilibrium.

Subsequent papers have used this approach in trying to assess to what extent the monetary policies implemented by different central banks follow equation (1) –known as Taylor's rule- or some alternative of it. For example, Persson and Tabellini (1997) include the credibility of monetary institutions in the equation. Clarida *et al.* (1997a) introduce expectations of the variables considered.

Other studies have entered variables that capture the tendency of central banks to adjust their interest rates gradually, avoiding sharp fluctuations. These papers (for instance Clarida *et al.*, 1999) presume some sort of inertia between the interest rate in time t and the lagged interest rate.

Orphanides (2002) estimates another version of the baseline equation, using lead values of the variables. He also replaces the growth rate of the Gross Domestic Product (GDP) by the deviation of the unemployment rate from its target in the long run, arguing that the correlation between these indicators is high. Clarida *et al.* (1997b) have used the rate of growth of the Index of Industrial Production as a substitute for the rate of growth of GDP.

Most of the results obtained in these pieces of research show that, in general, monetary policy in the last few decades may indeed be characterized as following the Taylor rule, with values of the coefficients that are quite similar to those suggested by Taylor.

Many of these papers focus on the monetary policy implemented by the FED. More recently, though, other papers (see, among others, De Grauwe *et al.*, 1999, De Grauwe, 2000, De Grauwe and Piskorski, 2001 and De Grauwe and Senegas, 2004) have turned their attention to the countries belonging to the EMU, especially Germany. One example of these papers is Faust *et al.* (2001), which compares the monetary policy of the Bundesbank with that implemented by the ECB in its two first years of operation. According to this research, interest rates in the Eurozone are comparatively lower than those that would hypothetically be determined by the Bundesbank; this result is due to the higher weight that the ECB gives to economic growth compared to that of the Bundesbank.

Galí (1998) analyses the potential impact of the monetary policy of the ECB on the Spanish economy. The instrument employed is an index of monetary tension that reflects the discrepancies between the interest rate that would be obtained from a Taylor rule in two different scenarios: the EMU and Spain. His results suggest that the costs associated to the loss of monetary policy are small if the ECB follows the Taylor rule, and if the degree of synchronization of the business cycle and the inflation rate between Spain and the rest of the Eurozone is large.

Finally, we can add that there are recent papers that handle the issue from the point of view of game theory (Debrun, 2001; Aksoy *et al.*, 2002; Angelini *et al.*, 2002; Fatum, 2003).

Debrun (2001), for example, confirms the idea popularized by different authors about the similarity in the lines of performance between the ECB and the Bundesbank ("Twin Sister Hypothesis"). This paper proposes a model of relative weights attached to individual preferences in the joint objective function of the bank, where countries bargain over the reference interest rate.

Aksoy *et al.* (2002) analyse the impact of the asymmetries (and the tensions these asymmetries cause) between the member countries of the Eurozone within the framework of the design of the monetary policy by the ECB. This work asserts that, on average, the preferences of larger countries appear to be more weighted than the preferences of smaller countries in the design of the ECB's monetary policy.

Angelini *et al.* (2002) employ a simple econometric model applied to Germany, France and Italy. The model is composed by an aggregate demand function, an aggregate supply function and a loss function with the parameters of each country. This paper shows that "the performance of a central bank that chooses the nominal interest rate to minimize a standard quadratic loss function of area-wide inflation and output gap improves significantly if the reaction function includes national variables - as opposed to the case in which the interest rate reacts to area-wide variables only" (p. 3). In this framework the Italian case is especially significant, because it is the country presenting greater deviations with respect to the European average.

Finally, Fatum (2003) presents an examination of the monetary policy in the Eurozone from the perspective of a game of strategic delegation. Under the assumption that the median voter theorem is too restrictive to capture some important aspects of monetary policy, mainly the preferences, this article demonstrates that strategic delegation within the Eurozone leads to a solution of the game in agreement with the preferences of the countries that present a greater degree of aversion to inflation.

II. THE MODEL

As is well known, from 1 January 1999 the monetary policy in the Eurozone has been designed and implemented by the ECB. As for the preferred framework for conducting monetary policy[2], the Board of the ECB established in 1998 an inflation target of less than 2%. In addition, it sketched some guidelines for the monetary policy, establishing as the main

---

[2] Other common alternatives are to target monetary aggregates or even the exchange rate.

control variables the quantity of money M3[3] and a wide set of indicators -the evolution of production, the exchange rate, the aggregate demand, the situation in the labour market and the fiscal policy stance- that are crucial to ascertain the nature of the economic shocks impinging on the countries of the Eurozone.

These guidelines were revised in May 2003. The reform, however, did not alter the spirit underlying the concept and goals of the monetary policy of the ECB. One of the main changes is that the ECB will try to ensure an inflation rate near to (instead of less than) 2% in the medium run. This modification is tantamount to an implicit recognition of the asymmetries existing between the members of the Eurozone.

If we look briefly at the monetary policy implemented by the ECB from January 1999 to November 2005 we can distinguish two periods (Figure 1). In the first one we observe an upward trend of the interest rates, due in turn to inflationary pressures. In the second period, starting at the beginning of 2001, monetary policy becomes more expansionary -in order to foster the Eurozone economy of the members of the EMU- and the interest rate decreases progressively.

A. The Monetary Policy of the ECB

We have designed several models to characterize the monetary policy of the ECB. Since an important pre-requisite in the construction of the model is the homogeneity in the data, we have taken these data from the same source as the ECB does, i.e. the Statistical Office of the European Union, EUROSTAT.

In order to determine the equation to be estimated we have followed a procedure that goes from the general to the specific: from a very general specification that comprised a large number of regressors, and a reasonable number of lags, we have discarded those variables that were not statistically significant. Finally, we have arrived at a more parsimonious representation of the data generating process[4].

In the end, we have used as regressors in the final estimation the following: the growth rate of the Harmonized Consumption Price Index (to capture inflation), and the growth rate of the Index of Industrial Production (as a proxy of output). This last variable has turned out to be more adequate than GDP in the estimations. We have worked with the differential of both variables with respect to an annual growth rate of 2%. In the case of inflation this figure stems directly from the guidelines of monetary policy established by the ECB. With regard to industrial production, we have tried out alternative growth scenarios, concluding that the outcomes were quite similar.

---

[3] M3 includes currency in circulation, overnight deposits, deposits with agreed maturity up to 2 years, deposits redeemable at notice up to 3 months, repurchase agreements, money market fund (MMF) shares/units and money market paper and, finally, debt securities up to 2 years.

[4] In order to choose the best specification we have employed different criteria, as, for example, the Akaike Information indicator.

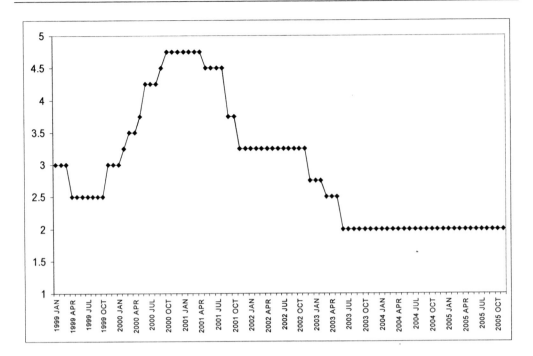

Figure 1. The interest rate in the Eurozone. (Jan 99 – Nov 05)

In addition, we have worked with lagged values of the variables, in order to capture the delay associated with the process of decision making and implementation of the different measures by the ECB. The number of lags that performed best in the estimation was four[5].

The final equation estimated to characterize the monetary policy of the ECB is as follows:

$$IR_t = C + \beta_1 DPI_{t-4} + \beta_2 DIPI_{t-4} + \beta_3 DU + \beta_4 DV + z_t \qquad (2)$$

where IR_t is the interest rate at time t, C stands for the intercept, DPI is the differential of the Harmonized Consumption Price Index growth rate with respect to the reference value of 2%, $DIPI$ is the differential of the Industrial Production Index growth rate with respect to a hypothetical scenario of 2% and DU is a dummy variable intended to capture the change in the trend of the monetary policy alluded to above. In addition, and as can be seen in equation (2), we have included another dummy variable (denoted as DV) with the aim of controlling the change in the pattern of the ECB monetary policy occurring in 2003[6]. Finally, z is the error term and β_1, β_2, β_3, β_4 are parameters to be estimated.

From the econometric point of view, the main problem underlying the estimation of equation (2) is the possibility of the data being non stationary. To deal with this we have performed a set of tests in order to search for the existence of unit roots in the variables we are working with. Although the standard test for unit roots is the augmented Dickey-Fuller

---

[5] The results are not very sensitive to changes in the lags.
[6] The poor situation of the German economy could be behind the change in the pattern of the ECB's monetary policy. An alternative explanation for this change could be that the dollar/euro exchange rate was increasing, which might have led the ECB to establish a lower interest rate in order to avoid the inflows of capitals.

(ADF), for the sake of robustness we have also used the Kwiatkowski-Phillips-Schmidt-Shin (KPSS) test. The results obtained by applying these two tests are reported in Table 1. According to the ADF test all variables are integrated of first order, I(1). In addition, the non stationarity of the interest rate and Harmonized Consumption Price Index growth rate variables are confirmed when the KPSS test is computed; however, in this case the Industrial Production Index growth rate variable seems to be I(0).

The next step has been to determine whether the series are cointegrated. Since the residuals obtained from equation (2) are stationary (see the last column of Table 1), we can conclude that this seems to be the case. Accordingly, we have estimated an Error Correction Model (ECM)[7] following the Three Steps procedure devised by Engle and Yoo (1991)[8].

First, we estimate equation (2), which represents the underlying long run relationship in the series. Second, we have estimated the following ECM model which captures the short run dynamics and the adjustment towards the equilibrium:

$$\Delta IR_t = \phi_1 + \phi_2 \Delta DPI_{t-4} + \phi_3 \Delta DIPI_{t-4} + \phi_4 DU + \phi_5 DV + \gamma \hat{z}_{t-1} + w_t \tag{3}$$

Finally, we have corrected the parameters obtained in equation (2) in order to obtain an asymptotically efficient estimation of β. The correction procedure has been to estimate the following equation:

$$\hat{w}_t = \delta_1 \left(\hat{\gamma} DPI_{t-5} \right) + \delta_2 \left(\hat{\gamma} DIPI_{t-5} \right) + \delta_3 \left(DU \right) + \delta_4 \left(DV \right) + u_t \tag{4}$$

where $\hat{w}$ are the residuals from equation (3). The point estimates of δ allows us to correct the values of β by means of the equation:

$$\hat{\beta}^* = \hat{\beta} + \hat{\delta} \tag{5}$$

Table 1. Unit root tests

	Interest rate (IR_t)	DPI_{t-4}	$DIPI_{t-4}$	Residuals of equation (1)
ADF	-1.71	-2.46	-1.83	-5.00*
KPSS	0.60*	0.57*	0.23	0.12

ADF test under H0: variable is nonstationary.
KPSS test under H0: variable is stationary.
* = significant (rejection of the unit root hypothesis) at 5% level.
Sources: EUROSTAT, ECB and own elaboration.

---

[7] An alternative would be to estimate a VAR model. The results are very similar in both cases.
[8] The Two Steps procedure of Engle and Granger (1987) is not appropriate for this case since the t statistics it provides are biased and inconsistent when the series have unit roots. The Three Steps procedure allows us to circumvent this problem. In addition, we have also analysed the data with the technique of Johansen and Juselius (1990). Results are similar to those yielded by the Three Steps analysis.

Table 2. Long Run dynamics of the interest rate

Dependent variable: interest rate (IR_t)		
	Coefficient	t Statistic
Intercept	3.59	36.10***
DPI_{t-4}	0.86	2.34**
$DIPI_{t-4}$	0.13	1.98**
DU	0.15	3.71***
DV	-1.48	-51.92***
Adjusted R^2	0.88	

*** = Significant at 99%; ** = Significant at 95%;
Sources: EUROSTAT, ECB and own elaboration.

Table 3. Short run dynamics of the interest rate

Dependent variable: interest rate growth (ΔIR_t)		
	Coefficient	t Statistic
Intercept	-0.09	-2.36**
ΔDPI_{t-4}	0.06	0.62
$\Delta DIPI_{t-4}$	0.03	1.99**
DU	0.15	2.97***
DV	0.06	1.36
ECT	-0.11	-1.83*
Adjusted R^2	0.30	

*** = Significant at 99%; ** = Significant at 95%; * = Significant at 90%.
Sources: EUROSTAT, ECB and own elaboration.

Now we can compute the true t statistic and apply traditional inference procedures, taking into account that the standard errors of the parameters are those obtained in the computation of (4).

The results obtained from the equations (2) and (3), which show the long run and short run dynamics, respectively, are displayed in Tables 2 and 3.

As Table 2 suggests, a rise in the inflation rate is correlated with increases in the reference interest rate of the Eurozone. The same happens with the differential of industrial production. The point estimates of both variables are positive and significant at 5%. According to our results, a 1% change in the inflation differential entails an increase of the interest rate of 0.86%, whereas a 1% change in the growth differential pushes the interest rate upwards by around 0.13%. These results seem to be in accord with the very definition of the ECB monetary policy, which posits price stability as its main goal.

As regards the short run dynamics (Table 3) the point estimate associated with the error correction term (ECT) suggests that about 11% of the discrepancy between the actual value of the interest rate and its long run equilibrium value is corrected in each period.

B. Individual Country Differences

Regarding the second question formulated at the beginning of the paper, the discrepancies in the results of the monetary policy when individual countries of EMU are considered[9], we have replaced in equation (2) the aggregate data for the Eurozone with the figures corresponding to each of its members. Thus, we can compute the optimal interest rate that would result for each country if it could handle its own autonomous monetary policy. Of course, we are assuming that this hypothetical central bank of the individual member state follows the same Taylor rule as the one obtained for the ECB. This is, perhaps, a strong assumption, but is useful in order to assess the implications of the ECB monetary policy on each of the members. In addition, when a country expresses its desire to join the EMU, it is implicitly accepting the way in which the ECB conducts its monetary policy. Hence it does not seem unreasonable to argue that the individual country would follow a monetary rule similar to that used by the ECB[10].

Table 4 reports the optimal interest rates for each of the members of EMU in the last month considered in this study, November 2005, and, even more significant, the average for the period between January 1999 and November 2005; in the same way, this table shows the differentials between the optimal interest rate of each EMU member and the one established by the ECB. The Appendix displays the monthly results for the whole period under study.

Table 4. Optimal interest rates by countries

	Average January 1999-November 2005		November 2005	
	Optimal interest rate	Differential to ECB interest rate	Optimal interest rate	Differential to ECB interest rate
Germany	2.98	0.84	3.66	1.66
France	3.25	0.94	2.93	0.93
Italy	3.60	0.86	3.32	1.32
Netherlands	4.02	1.22	2.78	0.78
Belgium	3.43	0.79	3.76	1.76
Luxembourg	4.17	1.50	5.88	3.88
Ireland	5.83	2.89	2.65	0.65
Spain	4.37	1.49	4.38	2.38
Greece	4.62	1.72	4.30	2.30
Portugal	4.20	1.48	3.11	1.11
Austria	3.62	0.87	3.97	1.97
Finland	3.54	0.72	2.86	0.86

Sources: EUROSTAT, ECB and own elaboration.

---

[9] This issue is also analysed, although from a different point of view, in, for example, Ramaswamy and Slok (1998).
[10] Taylor rules for the individual countries for a period of time before the EMU could be estimated and, then, used to compute "optimal" interest rates for the period after the EMU. However, the main problem in this case is the change in the economic scenario that the EMU implies for its member states.

Taking into account that the interest rate of reference of the ECB was 2.00% in November 2005, it can be seen that the smallest differentials between the hypothetical optimal interest rate and the official interest rate correspond to Ireland, Netherlands, Finland and France. If we consider the whole period January 1999 – November 2005, the countries presenting the smallest differences are Finland, Belgium, Germany, Italy, Austria and France.

However, the opposite can be said, considering again the whole period under analysis, of the Southern European countries together with Luxembourg and The Netherlands. These were, generally speaking, the countries exhibiting the highest inflation rates around that time. The case of Ireland is remarkable: the differential is almost three percentage points. In turn, this can be attributed to the high rates of inflation prevailing in Ireland in the first years of our sample; in the last months of our sample period, however, the inflation rate was much lower and, as we mentioned in the previous paragraph, the optimal interest rate for Ireland is much closer to the interest rate determined by the ECB. Other countries in which the deviations are also noticeable are Greece (1.72), Luxembourg (1.50), Spain (1.49), Portugal (1.48) and The Netherlands (1.22); in the last case, however, the situation is very similar to that of Ireland, the ECB's interest rate being quite akin to the optimal for The Netherlands in the last months. In other words, the loss of the monetary autonomy seems to have been especially onerous for those countries that have suffered higher rates of inflation (as, for example, Ireland, Greece, Spain and Portugal); if these countries were able to control inflation (as Ireland did in the last months of our sample period), the cost of losing monetary policy independence would not be very important.

Moreover, we can observe the similitude between the monetary policy implemented by the ECB and the one that would have been put into practice by France and Germany (see Appendix for a more detailed comparison). In this regard, the hypothesis of the *twin sister* seems to gain support with our analysis, although it should be not restricted to the Bundesbank but to a combination of the French and German Central Banks. However, the similarity between the optimal interest rate for these countries and the one determined by the ECB has gradually diminished, especially in the last months of our sample period. To be precise, the differences between the optimal interest rate for Germany and France and the reference interest rate of the ECB increases notably from mid 2004. Three tentative explanations can be found to this change of approach, at least as regards to the German case: 1. The appointment of Mr. Jean-Claude Trichet as president of the ECB; 2. The improvement in the situation of the German economy; 3. The belief that changes in the interest rate do not seem to affect the German economy to any great extent; instead, it is gradually being accepted that this country has to undertake structural reforms in order to improve its economic situation.

Finally, the analysis of the optimal interest rates by countries suggests that all of them call for increases in the interest rate at the end of 2005. Although it exceeds the time horizon considered in this paper, it is well known that these increases in the ECB interest rate have indeed taken place during 2006.

III. CONCLUSIONS

We can summarize the main findings of this paper as follows:

1. Our analysis of the monetary policy implemented by the ECB since January 1999 suggests that this institution follows a Taylor rule, in which the weight that corresponds to the inflation rate is higher than that pertaining to economic growth.

2. The euro area-wide monetary policy does not have the same impact on all member countries; this means that the costs associated with the loss of monetary autonomy (in terms of the timing and magnitude of the responses of real output and inflation) vary between different Eurozone countries. In order to obtain a crude indicator of them we have computed optimal interest rates for each of the members of EMU, assuming independence in their own design of the monetary policy and a Taylor rule similar to the one we found for the ECB. By and large, costs seem to be larger for countries that exhibit higher inflation rates, especially Ireland, but also Greece, Spain, Portugal, Luxembourg and Netherlands. In contrast, costs seem to be moderate for core EU countries such as France and Germany.

Although these results are still tentative, they already provide some interesting insights. In particular, the costs associated to the single monetary policy are not the same for all members of EMU. Generally speaking, it seems that these costs might be higher for less developed countries, thus hindering the national convergence process in Europe.

APPENDIX: DETAILED RESULTS BY COUNTRIES

Table A.I. Optimal interest rates for particular countries

	Germany	France	Italy	Netherl.	Belgium	Luxemb.	Ireland	Spain	Greece	Portugal	Austria	Finland
1999 JAN	2.51	2.46	3.50	2.90	2.60	3.13	6.62	3.45	6.86	4.12	3.50	4.20
1999 FEB	2.18	2.03	3.05	3.15	2.37	3.52	6.70	3.36	6.48	3.58	3.31	3.95
1999 MAR	1.98	2.37	3.05	3.09	2.42	2.82	5.38	3.36	6.20	4.33	3.06	3.22
1999 APR	1.81	1.99	2.31	2.97	1.65	1.89	5.89	3.46	5.97	4.25	2.28	2.67
1999 MAY	1.84	1.94	2.69	3.33	2.41	-0.01	6.35	3.37	5.14	3.89	2.15	2.85
1999 JUN	1.61	1.93	2.42	3.54	2.01	1.33	5.14	3.13	4.65	3.80	2.22	3.00
1999 JUL	1.96	2.19	2.66	3.56	2.49	2.04	4.49	3.59	3.49	4.09	2.23	2.95
1999 AUG	2.27	2.10	2.41	3.16	2.50	3.01	4.69	3.70	3.52	3.86	2.30	3.65
1999 SEP	1.86	2.06	2.44	3.13	2.08	3.08	5.15	3.56	3.79	3.57	2.63	3.12

Table A.I. Continued

	Germany	France	Italy	Netherl.	Belgium	Luxemb.	Ireland	Spain	Greece	Portugal	Austria	Finland
1999 OCT	2.05	2.16	2.74	3.83	2.21	2.34	5.33	3.67	3.35	3.64	2.54	3.46
1999 NOV	2.02	2.11	3.07	3.34	2.05	1.14	5.32	3.89	3.39	3.04	2.28	3.43
1999 DEC	2.47	2.34	3.59	4.03	2.79	4.77	4.82	4.15	3.03	3.44	2.97	3.01
2000 JAN	2.62	2.52	3.28	3.43	2.96	3.71	6.16	4.23	3.21	2.97	2.63	3.64
2000 FEB	2.77	2.79	3.43	3.20	3.48	3.26	6.44	3.89	3.46	2.84	3.22	3.35
2000 MAR	2.97	2.94	3.72	3.47	3.66	3.31	6.42	4.51	3.43	3.38	4.34	3.84
2000 APR	3.25	3.31	4.11·	4.10	4.42	4.96	7.37	4.62	4.22	3.56	4.43	5.59
2000 MAY	3.37	3.80	3.63	3.37	2.12	6.60	5.09	4.47	4.26	3.60	3.61	4.46
2000 JUN	3.73	3.66	4.14	3.44	4.81	4.91	6.38	5.21	4.89	3.44	4.59	5.23
2000 JUL	3.50	3.85	4.41	3.43	4.61	5.49	7.46	5.15	5.67	1.91	4.86	5.53
2000 AUG	3.24	3.32	4.20	3.72	4.49	4.96	8.97	4.86	5.12	2.09	4.41	4.68
2000 SEP	3.33	3.77	4.72	4.24	4.75	4.82	8.59	5.35	5.05	3.54	3.88	5.87
2000 OCT	3.35	3.64	4.54	4.03	4.72	5.66	8.65	5.23	4.55	3.93	4.61	5.73
2000 NOV	3.64	3.85	4.27	4.54	3.82	6.82	8.55	5.14	4.54	3.97	5.46	5.62
2000 DEC	3.29	4.10	5.00	4.27	4.96	4.46	8.86	5.58	4.98	5.23	4.80	6.16
2001 JAN	3.77	3.91	4.27	4.50	5.31	4.41	7.83	5.16	4.66	5.21	4.98	6.45
2001 FEB	3.51	3.90	4.25	4.79	5.06	5.53	8.67	5.16	5.48	5.29	4.63	6.92
2001 MAR	3.52	4.05	4.42	4.31	5.17	6.10	9.69	5.64	5.92	4.94	4.13	6.90
2001 APR	4.16	3.53	4.98	4.14	5.45	6.54	8.53	5.30	5.36	4.97	3.66	5.25
2001 MAY	3.61	3.31	4.13	5.75	4.98	4.96	8.34	4.17	4.70	5.62	4.94	5.28
2001 JUN	3.86	3.26	3.26	6.12	4.11	4.91	9.90	3.75	4.90	5.97	4.17	4.64
2001 JUL	3.57	3.25	3.70	6.21	3.79	5.61	8.56	4.02	3.82	7.39	4.20	4.89
2001 AUG	3.66	3.67	3.89	6.79	3.82	4.37	7.43	4.43	4.12	6.51	4.43	3.87
2001 SEP	4.03	3.87	3.98	6.51	3.96	5.03	5.64	4.76	4.81	6.30	4.33	4.38
2001 OCT	4.08	3.80	4.07	6.15	4.41	4.38	7.09	4.72	5.20	6.12	4.18	4.08

Table A.I. Continued

	Germany	France	Italy	Netherl.	Belgium	Luxemb.	Ireland	Spain	Greece	Portugal	Austria	Finland
2001 NOV	3.25	3.69	3.65	6.15	4.09	4.06	4.95	3.32	5.19	5.61	4.40	3.59
2001 DEC	3.58	3.85	2.66	5.99	3.80	3.56	6.32	3.84	4.79	4.97	4.00	4.05
2002 JAN	2.93	3.10	3.09	6.23	3.21	3.82	5.69	3.46	5.15	5.17	3.83	3.55
2002 FEB	2.55	3.07	3.39	5.30	2.75	3.50	4.22	3.87	4.26	5.50	3.97	3.18
2002 MAR	2.13	2.36	2.72	5.58	2.85	3.15	3.79	3.14	3.91	5.46	2.83	2.97
2002 APR	2.17	2.39	2.63	6.29	2.30	2.08	5.90	2.94	3.38	5.13	2.90	2.35
2002 MAY	3.02	3.49	2.98	5.90	3.32	3.39	6.85	4.08	5.27	4.91	3.30	3.08
2002 JUN	2.55	3.29	3.55	5.34	3.28	3.26	4.97	4.24	4.84	4.27	2.89	2.99
2002 JUL	2.86	3.21	3.25	5.20	3.64	2.26	7.62	4.25	5.74	4.12	2.77	3.59
2002 AUG	2.82	3.62	3.47	5.16	3.29	3.73	5.92	4.99	5.82	5.46	3.42	4.74
2002 SEP	2.18	2.68	3.57	4.81	3.26	2.82	8.77	4.55	4.71	4.43	3.36	3.36
2002 OCT	2.16	2.70	3.18	5.24	2.40	3.64	7.19	4.19	4.84	4.58	3.39	3.69
2002 NOV	2.57	2.77	3.72	5.09	3.05	3.18	6.70	4.86	4.80	5.07	3.12	4.48
2002 DEC	2.52	2.94	3.63	4.97	3.02	3.80	6.43	4.61	4.69	4.80	3.17	3.25
2003 JAN	2.53	3.11	4.17	5.02	3.30	4.17	6.84	4.67	4.73	4.66	3.18	2.96
2003 FEB	2.92	3.12	3.97	5.45	3.38	5.00	6.87	5.42	4.94	5.12	3.05	3.65
2003 MAR	3.06	3.41	4.38	4.51	2.74	4.59	6.96	5.28	5.12	4.54	3.41	3.80
2003 APR	2.75	3.36	4.13	4.11	2.88	4.62	4.57	5.30	5.53	4.73	3.11	4.08
2003 MAY	2.56	3.26	4.27	3.93	3.14	5.17	5.58	5.04	4.67	5.05	3.71	3.44
2003 JUN	2.89	3.84	3.69	4.83	3.26	5.24	7.01	5.19	4.75	5.73	3.53	4.34
2003 JUL	2.90	3.85	4.04	3.87	2.93	5.77	4.99	4.99	4.69	4.53	3.84	2.97
2003 AUG	2.47	3.11	4.42	3.10	2.95	4.63	6.47	4.68	4.21	4.30	2.88	3.09
2003 SEP	2.31	2.63	3.50	3.11	2.14	4.09	4.78	3.98	5.09	4.65	2.19	2.56
2003 OCT	2.02	2.94	3.84	2.71	2.95	2.95	4.46	4.31	4.84	4.17	2.41	2.38
2003 NOV	2.50	3.23	4.14	2.80	3.24	3.62	5.41	4.34	4.86	3.98	2.65	2.87

Table A.I. Continued

	Germany	France	Italy	Netherl.	Belgium	Luxemb.	Ireland	Spain	Greece	Portugal	Austria	Finland
2003 DEC	2.31	3.05	4.11	3.30	3.02	4.60	6.58	4.37	4.13	4.39	3.13	2.81
2004 JAN	2.19	3.59	3.82	3.02	2.92	4.54	4.40	4.23	5.10	4.70	2.92	2.83
2004 FEB	2.65	3.77	4.04	3.21	2.80	3.50	6.32	4.09	4.44	3.95	2.82	2.35
2004 MAR	2.94	3.76	3.93	3.42	3.19	3.64	5.99	4.28	4.03	4.06	3.00	2.58
2004 APR	2.80	3.94	3.80	2.83	3.58	3.59	6.44	4.10	4.61	3.84	3.12	2.83
2004 MAY	2.84	3.39	3.30	2.99	2.73	3.98	4.18	3.50	4.02	3.14	2.77	2.39
2004 JUN	2.49	3.39	3.86	2.44	2.99	3.97	3.76	3.71	4.24	2.76	3.29	2.22
2004 JUL	2.71	3.47	3.57	3.00	2.91	4.34	3.99	3.94	4.78	3.97	3.38	1.70
2004 AUG	3.45	3.77	3.62	3.13	3.30	4.15	3.88	4.04	4.77	3.33	3.45	1.37
2004 SEP	4.02	4.64	3.95	3.49	3.93	4.70	3.54	4.91	4.62	3.54	4.43	2.19
2004 OCT	3.92	4.57	3.82	3.68	3.65	6.80	4.05	5.09	4.28	4.96	4.49	2.65
2004 NOV	3.88	4.12	3.49	3.20	3.98	5.39	5.22	4.66	4.59	3.65	4.36	2.73
2004 DEC	4.08	3.69	3.19	3.08	4.07	5.51	1.99	4.65	4.08	3.22	4.53	2.73
2005 JAN	4.02	3.93	3.63	3.13	3.96	4.54	4.19	4.78	4.08	3.04	4.28	2.56
2005 FEB	4.06	3.71	3.39	3.00	4.57	5.16	2.80	4.51	3.96	2.66	4.81	2.89
2005 MAR	3.45	3.78	3.16	3.20	4.13	5.22	2.74	4.90	4.64	3.36	4.80	2.23
2005 APR	3.78	3.96	3.25	3.25	3.49	5.19	3.62	4.55	4.21	3.45	4.51	3.01
2005 MAY	3.38	3.43	3.04	2.45	3.66	4.34	4.05	4.38	5.27	3.49	4.22	1.94
2005 JUN	3.49	3.31	3.00	3.04	3.30	4.31	3.65	4.35	4.52	3.38	4.12	1.78
2005 JUL	3.35	3.25	3.07	2.62	3.57	3.66	2.94	4.64	3.39	2.90	4.37	2.64
2005 AUG	3.16	3.46	3.54	2.88	3.49	4.62	3.23	4.66	4.04	3.58	4.21	3.03
2005 SEP	3.13	3.10	3.35	2.35	3.60	5.30	4.04	4.20	4.09	2.65	4.06	1.39
2005 OCT	3.57	3.15	3.11	2.84	4.27	3.48	3.69	4.34	4.04	2.41	4.00	1.47
2005 NOV	3.66	2.93	3.32	2.78	3.76	5.88	2.65	4.38	4.30	3.11	3.97	2.86

Sources: EUROSTAT, ECB and own elaboration.

REFERENCES

Aksoy, Y., De Grauwe, P., & Dewachter H. (2002). Do Asymmetries Matter for European Monetary Policy? *European Economic Review, 46* (3), 443-469.

Angelini, P., Giovane, P., Silviero, S., & Terlizzese, D. (2002). Monetary Policy Rules for the Euro Area: What role for national information? *European Central Bank,* February 2002.

Clarida, R., Galí, J., & Gertler, M. (1997a). Monetary Policy Rules and Macroeconomic Stability: Evidence and Some Theory. *Quarterly Journal of Economics, 115,* 147-180.

Clarida, R., Galí, J., & Gertler, M. (1997b). Monetary Policy Rules in Practice: Some International Evidence. *European Economic Review, 42,* 1033-1068.

Clarida, R., Galí, J., & Gertler, M. (1999). The Science of Monetary Policy: a new Keynesian perspective. *Journal of Economic Literature, 37,* 1661-1707.

Clarida, R., Galí, J., & Gertler, M. (2002). A Simple Framework for International Monetary Policy Analysis. *Journal of Monetary Economics, 49,* 879-904.

Clausen, V., & Hayo, B. (2006). Asymmetric monetary policy effects in EMU. *Applied Economics, 38* (10), 1123-1134.

De Grauwe, P. (2000). Monetary Policy in the Presence of Asymmetries. *Journal of Common Market Studies, 38* (4), 593-612.

De Grauwe, P., & Senegas, A. (2004). Asymmetries in Monetary Policy Transmission: Some Implications for EMU and its Enlargement. *Journal of Common Market Studies, 42* (4), 757-773.

De Grauwe, P., Dewachter H., & Aksoy, Y. (1999). The European Central Bank: Decision rules and macroeconomic performance. *CEPR Discussion Paper*, n° 2067.

De Grauwe, P., & Piskorski, T. (2001). Union Wide Aggregates Versus National Data Based Monetary Policies: Does it Matter for the Eurosystem. *CEPR Discussion Paper*, n° 3036.

Debrun, X. (2001). Bargaining over EMU vs. EMS: Why Might the ECB be the Twin Sister of the Bundesbank? *Economic Journal, 473,* 566-590.

Emerson, M., Gros, D., Italianer, A., Pisani-Ferry, J., & Reichenbach, H. (1992). *One Market, one money.* Oxford: Oxford University Press.

Engle, R., & Granger, C. W. (1987). Cointegration and error correction: Representation, estimation and testing. *Econometrica, 55,* 251-276.

Engle, R., & Yoo, B. S. (1991). Cointegrating time series: A survey with new results. In R. Engle, & C. W. J. Granger, (Eds.), *Long run economic relationships: Reading in cointegration.* Oxford: Oxford University Press.

Fatum, R. (2003). One Monetary Policy and Eighteen Central Bankers: The European monetary Policy as a game of Strategic Delegation. *EPRU working paper series*, 2003-19.

Faust, J., Rogers, J., & Wright, J. (2001). An Empirical Comparison of Bundesbank and ECB Monetary Policy Rules. *International Finance Discussion Papers*, n° 705.

Favero, C. A., Giavazzi, F., & Flabbi, L. (1999). The transmission mechanism of monetary policy in Europe: Evidence from banks' balance sheets. *NBER Working Paper*, July 1999.

Galí, J. (1998). La política monetaria Europea y sus posibles repercusiones sobre la economía Española. *Universitat Pompeu FAPRa Working Paper*, December 1998.

Johansen, S., & Juselius, K. (1990). Maximum likelihood estimation and inference on cointegration with applications to the demand for money. *Oxford Bulletin of Economics and Statistics, 52,* 169-210.

Maza, A., & Villaverde, J. (2006). A State Space approach to the analysis of economic shocks in Spain. *Journal of Policy Modeling, 29* (1), 55-63.

Orphanides, A. (2002). Monetary Policy Rules and the Great Inflation. *American Economic Review, 92,* 115-120.

Persson, T., & Tabellini, G. (1997). Monetary Cohabitation in Europe. *American Economic Review, 86,* 111-116.

Ramaswamy, R, & Slok, T. (1998). The real effects of monetary policy in the European Union: What are the differences? *IMF Staff Papers, 45* (2), 374-396.

Sánchez-Robles, B., & Cuñado, J. (1999). Perturbaciones asimétricas y Unión Monetaria Europea: Las regiones españolas. *Papeles de Economía Española, 80,* 152-170.

Taylor, J. (1993). Discrètion versus Policy Rules in Practice. *Carnegie-Rochester Series on Public Policy, 39,* 195-214.

In: Political Economy Research Focus
Editor: Walter R. Levin, pp. 109-119

ISBN: 978-1-60456-154-8
© 2008 Nova Science Publishers, Inc.

Chapter 5

THE AUTOMATIC NATURE OF DISMISSALS IN SPAIN: DISMISSAL-AT-WILL UNDER CIVIL LAW

Miguel Á. Malo[*]
Universidad de Salamanca, Spain
Luis Toharia
Universidad de Alcalá, Spain

ABSTRACT

In this research, we explain that, in Spain, a relatively minor reform in unemployment benefits regulation has introduced a system to dismiss at will. Therefore, the fairness of the dismissal is not important in practice, although the whole legal system requiring a fair cause for dismissals remains. We present different empirical evidence supporting such statement.

Keywords: Dismissal, Labour Law, severance pay
JEL Classification: K310, J530, J320

1. INTRODUCTION

The main objective of this paper consists of analyzing the recent legal changes affecting dismissals passed in 2002 in Spain. The interest of this national case rests on how a 'minor' legal change can affect to incentives of workers and firms creating an automatic mechanism for firms to dismiss workers without fair cause.

This result is highly interesting because such automatic nature for dismissals explicitly exists only under the North-American employment-at-will doctrine. But how a Civil Law

[*] Author for correspondence: Miguel A. Malo, Universidad de Salamanca, Edificio FES – Campus 'Miguel de Unamuno', 37007 Salamanca, Spain. Tel.: +34 923 29 45 00 (ext. 3512); E-mail: malo@usal.es

system could include such automatic procedure? At first sight, it is difficult because of the traditional distinction in Continental Labour Law about fair and unfair causes for dismissals. The first type consists of two groups: fair reasons related to economic activity (economic dismissals) and fair reasons related to misconduct of the worker (disciplinary dismissals). In countries with a Labour Law developed under a system of Civil Law the catalogue of fair causes is complete and closed, and, therefore, any cause not included in the list of fair causes is considered as unfair. In the same way, a misuse of a fair cause (for example, alleging disciplinary reasons when there are economic reasons behind the dismissal) will be considered as unfair too.

Therefore, under a Civil Law system dismissals only can become 'automatic' developing a dismissal-at-will practice but not an employment-at-will doctrine. In other words, the legal framework will provide incentives to firms to use some legal mechanism where the fair or unfair cause for the dismissal is not relevant and to workers to accept the dismissal under these circumstances as a lesser evil. We will show that the Spanish case, in special, through a 'minor' legal reform implemented in 2002 is an example of this situation, explaining what are the incentives of firms and workers and the costs of this system for both.

The remainder of this chapter is as follows. In the next section, we describe the Spanish legal framework on dismissals, focusing on the 2002 legal reform, and the main prediction related to our interpretation of the effects of this legal reform. In the third section, we present some data discussing whether the empirical evidence supports the predictions of our interpretation. Finally, a conclusions section closes the article.

2. THE SPANISH LEGAL FRAMEWORK ON DISMISSALS

2.1. Background

The current legal rules on dismissals are compiled in the Workers' Charter, enacted at the end of 1980. The objective of this Charter was to develop a labour relations system adapted to the recently recovered democratic system (the current democratic Constitution is dated at the end of 1978). There have been different important reforms of the Workers' Charter. In 1984, the rules governing temporary contracts were changed, in order to foster employment (then, the Spanish unemployment rate was above 20 percent). In 1994, a new reform created a new type of dismissal and introduced limits to the use of temporary contracts (because they had reached around 30 percent of the stock of wage and salary workers). In 1997, a new open-ended contract was introduced with a lower severance pay in some cases and financial subsidies for the firms. And the last reform affecting the Workers' Charter has been agreed between employers and unions in 2006, in order to promote even more the new open-ended contract with a lower severance pay. However, a legal change related to dismissal (mainly to dismissal costs) was introduced in 2002, but not through a modification of the Workers' Charter, but the 45/2002 Act on unemployment benefits.

After this brief summary of the recent changes of the basic norms of the Spanish Labour Law we proceed to describe the legal framework related to dismissals.

The procedure to dismiss permanent workers in Spain is very different as between individual and collective dismissals.

First of all, we should remark that until 1994 collective dismissal was in practice the only way to dismiss workers on economic grounds. In Spain, a collective dismissal is called ERE (*Expediente de Regulación de Empleo*). The most distinctive feature of collective dismissals in Spain is the requirement of administrative approval, introducing important bureaucratic costs for this type of dismissal. If it has been agreed with workers' representatives the collective dismissal is always approved. If there is no agreement, the Public Administration decides. The most important issue of this bargaining is the severance pay, which has a minimum of 20 wage days per seniority year. There are no accurate data on this question, but many authors consider that the agreed severance pay are much higher than for individual dismissals, and that collective dismissal is the most expensive form of employment adjustment per dismissed worker (Toharia and Ojeda, 1999). The amount of individual dismissals is much higher than the amount of dismissed workers in collective dismissals (see, for example, Malo, 2005), which can be considered as an indirect proof of the disincentives related to the use of collective dismissals.

Before the 1994 legal reform of the Spanish Labour Law, there was only permitted one individual dismissal on economic grounds in firms with less than 50 workers, although it was very difficult to use this legal provision because the interpretation of the legal term 'economic grounds' was very restrictive (Toharia and Ojeda, 1999). Therefore, the only real way to dismiss one worker on economic grounds before 1994 was a 'collective' dismissal for only one person. Because of the relevant fixed costs of a collective dismissal (administrative authorization, negotiations with workers' representatives, ete.), it is obvious that there were strong incentives to use multiple individual dismissals instead of a collective dismissal in many cases. However, as disciplinary grounds were the only legal fair causes available for firms before 1994, firms 'disguised' economic dismissals as disciplinary ones. See Malo (2000) for a detailed explanation of the incentives to use disciplinary reasons instead of economic reasons for individual dismissals.

In 1994, the legislation on dismissals was changed[1] to allow 'small' collective dismissals to be legally considered as individual dismissals, but explicitly on economic grounds and not 'disguised' as disciplinary ones. The adjustment should be below the 10 per cent of the workforce. However, even after reform, it is controversial whether firms have enough incentives to allege economic grounds in these individual dismissals. The dismissal on disciplinary grounds has fewer requirements. No advance notice is required and no initial severance pay has to be deposited, and the rest of costs and requirements are equivalent for both types of dismissals. Even the interpretation by judges of the economic grounds is controversial, because judges have to evaluate whether there are enough economic reasons to dismiss a worker, and this is not a judiciary issue but a management one (Malo, 2000). Therefore, the application of the economic dismissal is subject to a higher legal uncertainty, and the probability of a sentence declaring the dismissal as unfair (even existing real economic grounds) increases. As there are incentives for an improper use of disciplinary reasons, the main part of dismissals are solved by agreement (on average, for the time period of our data base only around 20 percent of all individual dismissals reached the judicial stage). Presumably, even the declaration of non existent disciplinary reasons is agreed with the worker to receive unemployment benefits and the agreement eliminates any stigma for the worker related to the dismissals and the disciplinary reasons alleged. Even when a disciplinary dismissal is declared as fair, the worker can receive unemployment benefits and subsidies, but with a delay of three months.

---

[1] See Toharia and Malo (2000) to have a comprehensive description of the 1994 Spanish Labour Law reform.

In 1997, another legal reform affecting firing costs was passed in Spain. A new open-ended contract was introduced including a lower severance pay for individual dismissals on economic grounds declared as unfair by tribunals. We would like to stress that this decrease in firing costs is only relevant for these new contracts and not for the rest of workers with open-ended contracts. In addition, the legal definition of economic grounds in individual dismissals was clarified in order to facilitate their use by tribunals.

2.2. Legal Changes Introduced in 2002

As we explained above, in 2002 a new legal change was introduced in firing costs[2]. Now, the government tried to decrease the bureaucratic costs of individual dismissals. When a dismissal is considered as unfair (directly by the courts or indirectly by firms in pre-trial agreements), the firm had to pay the 'intervening wages' (in Spanish 'salarios de tramitación'), which consist of all wages from the date of dismissal to the judicial decision. When the legal procedure lasted for more than two months, the firm applied to the Public Administration for the reimbursement of all intervening wages in excess of this period. However, in 2002 the regulation of intervening wages was changed, introducing at the same time a new way to transfer the severance pay from the firm to the worker. When firms give the severance pay corresponding to unfair dismissal (45 salary days per seniority year or 33 days for new contracts introduced in 1997) until two days after the dismissal letter, then the firm will not have to pay intervening wages to the worker, even when the worker would file a suit against the firm for unfair dismissal.

Note that in this situation, firms recognise *de facto* that the dismissal is unfair (they are giving to the worker the severance pay for unfair dismissals), but they can save the cost of the intervening wages if the worker wants to go to the labour courts. As the worker has obtained the highest severance pay, why to go to the courts? Therefore, the new regulation introduces strong incentives to solve dismissals before to go to the labour courts and even before to go to the bargaining institutions.

It is important to note that whether the cause of dismissal is fair or unfair is not important any more, with the exception of those cases arriving to labour courts. But theses cases will be rather different and they, probably, will be related to other aspects of the dismissal beyond the monetary compensation for the worker, because he/she can not obtain more money going to the tribunals. As the cause is not more important, this system could be called as a dismissal-at-will system, but with a cost for the firm. The cost is paying the highest severance pay, 45 salary days (or 33 salary days for the new open-ended contracts introduced in Spain in 1997). Now, dismissals are 'automatic' for the firm but paying the severance pay for unfair dismissals. However, as we have explained before (Malo, 2000), in the most part of dismissals the agreed severance pay was 45. Therefore, with the 2002 legal reforms firms have obtained the automatism of dismissals without changing the above limit for severance pay, and even obtaining a decrease in bureaucratic costs related to dismissals, because they have not to pay the intervening wages and the dismissal process is usually solved in only two days. On the other hand, workers obtain in a very short time period the severance pay and they obtain rapidly the

---

[2] See García-Perrote (2003) for the legal details of this reform.

highest one[3]. For them, the cost is the lost of importance of the true cause of the dismissal, opening the door to a lack of legal protection.

2.3. The Effects on Dismissals and Severance Payments: Three Predictions

The above reasoning allows us to state three predictions which can be tested with suitable data.

First, if the 45/2002 Act has introduced the described incentives for firms and workers, we will see that the majority of dismissals in Spain follows this legal mechanism.

Second, if the 45/2002 Act has decreased firing costs (mainly the bureaucratic part of these costs) we will see more dismissals after the legal reform.

Third, those dismissals solved at bargaining institutions should be rather different and relatively more expensive affecting workers with a high bargaining power (otherwise, why would the worker persist in the case going to bargaining institutions?).

In the next section, we present an empirical analysis trying to check these predictions.

3. EMPIRICAL ANALYSIS

First of all, we must stress that the 2002 legal reform has dramatically modified the statistical data on dismissals in Spain. Before this reform, almost all dismissals arrived to the bargaining institutions and, therefore, their figures on dismissal cases were a very accurately information about the total amount of dismissals[4]. However, after the passage of the 2002 reform there are few incentives to go the bargaining institutions (because firms try to elude the payment of the bureaucratic costs offering to the workers the corresponding unfair severance pay) and their figures on dismissals are never more a proxy for the total amount of individual dismissals. However, we can circumvent this lack of data about the number of dismissals for 2002 using the administrative data on new beneficiaries of unemployment benefits by entry reason (the different types of dismissal are reasons included in these administrative data).

As the published information using this administrative data source, we will use micro-data from the Historical Register of Unemployment Benefits of the Public Employment Service in order to check the main predictions of our interpretation of the 2002 legal reform. Our empirical analysis is based on micro-data of entries in this Register between May 4th of 2002 and December 31st of 2004.

The entries in the unemployment benefits register can be considered a good approach to the amount of dismissals because practically all dismissed workers can apply for these benefits.

The first prediction can be checked with Table 1. This table shows in the first column the number of dismissals considering the entry in the Register during the whole period described

---

[3] Even they can immediately apply for the corresponding unemployment subsidies or benefits, and any importance is given to the cause of dismissal, either economic or disciplinary, because the firm, implicitly, has accepted that the cause was unfair.

[4] Only a very small fraction was solved before to go to bargaining institutions, and therefore administrative data from these institutions before 2002 provided an accurate estimation of the number of dismissals in Spain.

above, the distribution in the second column and the distribution without considering collective dismissals in the third column.

Table 1. Number of dismissal and characteristics of dismissed workers, by dismissal type. May 2002-June 2007

Type of dismissal	Number	%	% (w/o ERE)	% women	% above 45 years old	% below 30 years	Av. Age	Median Age
45/2002 Act	1396248	66.05	71.2	46.1	28.1	19.6	39.3	37.0
Objective*	229441	10.85	11.7	48.5	34.4	15.2	41.2	39.0
Bargaining institutions (SMAC)	150339	7.11	7.7	40.7	44.9	9.0	44.9	42.0
Labour courts	41369	1.96	2.1	43.7	42.7	10.8	43.1	42.0
Collective dismissals (ERE)	153767	7.27	-	30.3	68.3	4.0	49.7	52.0
Other	142838	6.76	7.3	48.7	23.6	24.0	37.5	35.0

Source: Micro-data of the Register of Unemployment Benefits of the Public Employment Service.
* Objective economic dismissals introduced in 1994 (art. 52 of the Workers' Charter).

Dismissals using the 45/2002 Act is the most important category: 59.4 per cent of all dismissals of the period and 65 per cent of all individual dismissals (i.e. excluding collective dismissals). Therefore, the first prediction is confirmed by the simplest examination of the data related to dismissals, showing that the majority of dismissals are automatic in Spain. In addition, if we consider that the second row includes objective economic dismissals accepted directly by workers, we will have that more than 80 per cent of all individual dismissals are accepted by workers without questioning the choice of the firm.

The second prediction is related to the number of dismissals, increasing after the passage of the 45/2002 Act. Figure 1 shows the evolution of the number of dismissals as a ratio respect to the total of workers with open-ended contract in the private sector. The blue line represents the ratio of dismissals respect to the total of workers using the administrative data from bargaining institutions to estimate the number of dismissals. The number of workers with open-ended contract in the private sector has been calculated with the Labour Force Survey. The blue line shows a clear decreasing trend from 2002 onwards. However, as we have seen before, after the passage of the 45/2002 Act almost 80 per cent of all individual dismissals never arrive to bargaining institutions. Therefore, these figures do not provide an accurate estimation of the evolution of this ratio. Using data from HSIPRE (as in Table 1) we have estimated the same ratio from 1998 onwards (see the pink line). Before the legislation reform both data sources provide a very similar estimation, but after the reform, the data from the Register of Entries in the Unemployment Benefits System show a clear increase in the dismissals ratio. This increase is not related to any economic downturn of the Spanish economy during these years (the unemployment rate has been around 12 per cent and even slightly decreasing from 2002). Although this is a simple 'before-after' comparison is not against the second prediction of our reasoning.

The third prediction was related to those dismissals going beyond the automatic procedure of the 45/2002 Act and arriving to bargaining institutions. Our prediction was that these cases are characterized by a stronger bargaining power of workers. We have considered that an effect of a larger bargaining power would be an increase in average severance payments. Figure 2 shows the average of severance payments for those dismissals solved by agreement in bargaining institutions and by agreement or sentence in labour courts. We see that after the passage of the 2002 legal reform there is not any change in the series related to labour courts, while the average severance payment in bargaining institutions increases in a very spectacular way, even doubling in the last years the average severance payment obtained in 2001. Therefore, after 45/2002 Act cases arriving to bargaining institutions are rather different than before. As the other cases are solved before to go to these institutions, we should observe relevant differences in workers characteristics. Coming back to Table 1, we can see that the average (and the median) age of workers with dismissals finished in bargaining institutions is above the age of workers dismissed using the 45/2002 Act (and above also those who accepted an economic objective dismissal). The severance payment is calculated as salary days per seniority year, and assuming a positive association between age and seniority we have that the average severance pay should increase. However, maybe it is not enough for the huge increase observed in Figure 2. Table 2 shows the entitlement period for unemployment benefits (strictly related to seniority) and the salary day used to estimate the unemployment benefits. We can see that both variables are clearly higher for those workers whose dismissals were finished in bargaining institutions. Again, data are not against the predictions of our interpretation of the effects of the 2002 legal reform.

Finally, with the micro-data from the Register of Entries in the Unemployment Benefit System we have estimated some logistic regressions in order to check whether the effects of the commented variables remain in a multivariate analysis. Table 3 shows two logistic regressions on the probability of an entry into the unemployment benefit system because of a dismissal according to the 45/2002 Act versus any other type of entry and the probability of an entry according to the 45/2002 Act versus any other type of individual dismissal (in other words, excluding the possibility of being dismissed through a collective dismissal).

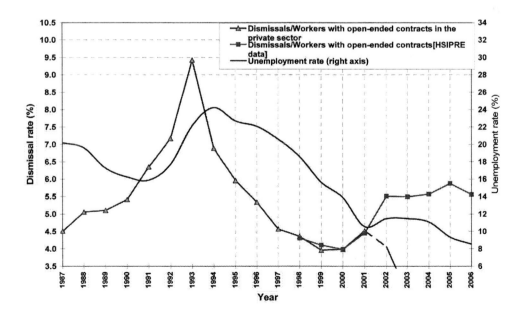

Figure 1.

**Table 2. Characteristics of dismissed workers by entitlement period and dismissal type.
May 2002-June 2007**

Type of dismissal	Number	% "short" entitl.	% "medium" entitl.	% "long" entitl.	Median entitl. period	Salary per day	
						Average (pta.)	Median (pta.)
45/2002 Act	1396248	26.5	44.1	29.4	16	4044	3571
Objective*	229441	21.6	44.0	34.4	18	3800	3477
Bargaining institutions (SMAC)	150339	15.1	35.2	49.8	22	4937	4243
Labour courts	41369	20.2	39.5	40.3	20	4241	3707
Collective dismissals (ERE)	153767	3.8	19.3	76.9	24	6365	6490
Other ·	142838	49.0	35.0	16.0	10	4023	3611

Source: Micro-data of the Register of Unemployment Benefits of the Public Employment Service.
* Objective economic dismissals introduced in 1994 (art. 52 of the Workers' Charter).

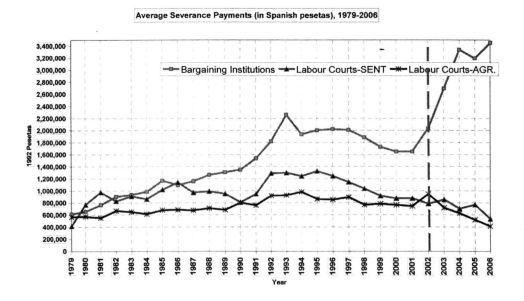

Figure 2.

The results (in terms of odds ratios) are rather similar in both estimations. Women have a lower probability of being dismissed through the 45/2002 Act, but the difference respect to male is rather small (around 1.1 lower). Age provides the same results as in the descriptive analysis of Table 1. Younger workers have a higher probability of being dismissed with the legal procedure introduced in 2002, while for older workers we have the opposite result. According to these results, the salary per day in the last job has an inverse relationship with the probability of being dismissed using the 45/2002 Act. This effect has a relevant size for the first logistic regression (i.e. considering all types of entries in the unemployment benefits

Table 3. Logistic regressions on the probability of an entry in the unemployment benefits system because of a dismissal according to the 45/2002 Act

Variables	Versus any other type of dismissal				Versus any other type of individual dismissal			
	Coeff.	Odds Ratio	1/O.R.		Coeff.	Odds ratio	1/O.R.	
Gender								
Male (&)								
Female	-0.1492	0.8614	1.1609	**	-0.0851	0.9184	1.0889	**
Age								
Less than 24	0.0676	1.0700		**	0.0786	1.0818		**
25-29(&)								
30-34	-0.0287	0.9717	1.0291	**	-0.0475	0.9536	1.0487	**
35-39	-0.0483	0.9528	1.0495	**	-0.0958	0.9086	1.1005	**
40-44	-0.1224	0.8848	1.1302	**	-0.1540	0.8573	1.1665	**
45-49	-0.2934	0.7458	1.3409	**	-0.2616	0.7698	1.2991	**
50-54	-0.5026	0.6050	1.6529	**	-0.3446	0.7085	1.4114	**
55+	-0.6349	0.5300	1.8868	**	-0.5106	0.6001	1.6663	**
Salary per day[†]								
Up to 2000(&)								
2001 to 3000	-0.0400	0.9608	1.0408	**	0.0043	1.0043		
3001 to 4000	-0.0542	0.9473	1.0557	**	0.0422	1.0431		**
4001 to 5000	-0.1877	0.8288	1.2065	**	0.0295	1.0300		**
5001 to 6000	-0.3294	0.7194	1.3901	**	0.0119	1.0120		
6001 to 7000	-0.5022	0.6052	1.6524	**	-0.0364	0.9643	1.0370	**
7001 to 8000	-0.6465	0.5239	1.9088	**	-0.0278	0.9726	1.0282	*
8001 to 9000	-0.8228	0.4392	2.2769	**	-0.0347	0.9659	1.0353	**
More than 9000	-0.9818	0.3746	2.6693	**	-0.1015	0.9035	1.1068	**
Entitlement period								
4 months(&)								
6 months	-0.0745	0.9283	1.0773	**	-0.0691	0.9333	1.0715	**
8 months	-0.1566	0.8550	1.1695	**	-0.1447	0.8653	1.1557	**
10 months	-0.2188	0.8035	1.2446	**	-0.1922	0.8252	1.2119	**
12 months	-0.2386	0.7877	1.2695	**	-0.2112	0.8096	1.2351	**
14 months	-0.2971	0.7430	1.3459	**	-0.2486	0.7799	1.2823	**
16 months	-0.3372	0.7138	1.4010	**	-0.2654	0.7669	1.3039	**
18 months	-0.3696	0.6910	1.4471	**	-0.2837	0.7530	1.3280	**
20 months	-0.3800	0.6839	1.4623	**	-0.2944	0.7450	1.3423	**
22 months	-0.3877	0.6786	1.4736	**	-0.3067	0.7359	1.3589	**
24 months	-0.7885	0.4545	2.2000	**	-0.5635	0.5692	1.7568	**
Year								
2002(&)								
2003	0.5991	1.8206		**	0.6809	1.9757		**
2004	0.9892	2.6892		**	1.0088	2.7422		**
2005	1.1571	3.1808		**	1.1867	3.2763		**
2006	1.4840	4.4103		**	1.5285	4.6115		**
2007	1.6485	5.1991		**	1.7750	5.9001		**
Constant	1.3020	3.6766		**	1.0960	2.9922		**
N	1966018				1812472			

Estimations include 11 occupational dummies and 17 regional dummies.

[†] *Salary per day* corresponds to the last job (in Spanish pesetas).

* The coefficient is statistically significant at 95 %

** The coefficient is statistically significant at 99 %

&: Reference.

Source: Micro-data of the Register of Unemployment Benefits of the Public Employment Service (may 2002-june 2007).

system) but it is much lower for the second logistic regression (which excludes collective dismissals, where workers usually have higher seniority and higher wages[5]). The results for the entitlement are in the same line. The same probability decreases for longer entitlement periods, but this decrease is much lower when excluding collective dismissals. The entry year (i.e. the date of the dismissal) has a positive effect, showing a sort of learning effect: in 2007 the probability of being dismissed using the 45/2002 Act is until 5 times higher than in 2002.

To sum up, the multivariate analysis confirms the results obtained with the descriptive analysis and it is according to the three predictions stated above.

4. CONCLUSIONS

In 2002, a 'minor' legal change concerning dismissals was introduced in Spain. So minor, that this change was not a modification of the Workers' Charter but a new Unemployment Benefits Act. However, the impact has been dramatic creating *de facto* a sort of dismissal at will mechanism under a Civil Law system, where, *de iure*, there is a clear distinction of fair and unfair reasons for dismissals.

Nevertheless, the irrelevance of the fairness of the dismissal causes is obtained supporting some costs: for firms, the costs is paying the highest legal severance pay (the corresponding unfair severance pay), and, for workers, the cost is a decrease of the legal protection against an unfair break of the labour contract. On the other hand, this 'dismissal-at-will2 system gives to workers a relatively easy access to the highest severance pay and a very rapid mechanism to claim unemployment benefits without going to bargaining institutions.

Any further legal change should consider this combination of pros and cons for workers and employers. In this vein, any proposal for decreasing firing costs should consider that workers will claim any sort of compensation for such decrease (as an increase in legal protection in terms of using *de facto* distinction of fair and unfair reasons for dismissals). In a similar way, any workers' claim about restoring *de facto* the distinction of fair and unfair reasons for dismissals should consider that employers will ask for a real decrease in severance payments.

ACKNOWLEDGEMENTS

The authors gratefully acknowledge the comments received participants of the workshop on 'The Economic of Dismissal Law and Employment Protection', held at the Utrecht School of Economics (22-23 June 2006). They are also grateful to the Spanish Public Employment Service for providing the data used. Miguel A. Malo acknowledges the financial support received from the 'Junta de Castilla y León' (research project SA020A05).

---

[5] See, for example, Malo and Toharia (1999) and Malo (2001).

5. REFERENCES

García-Perrote, I. (2003): *La Ley 45/2002 de Reforma de la Protección por Desempleo. La reforma de la reforma del despido, de los salarios de tramitación y del desempleo*, Valladolid: Editorial Lex Nova.

Malo, M.A. (2000): 'A Simple Model of Severance Pay Determination: The Case of Individual Dismissals in Spain', *Labour*, 14(2), 269-290.

Malo, M.A. (2001): "European Labour Law and Severance Pay Determination in Collective Redundancies", *European Journal of Law and Economics*, 12(1), 73-90.

Malo, M.A. (2005): "La evolución institucional del despido: una interpretación en términos de un accidente histórico", *Revista de Historia Económica*, vol. XXIII, n° 1, 83-115.

Malo, M.A. and Toharia, L. (1999): *Costes de despido y creación de empleo*, Spanish Ministry of Employment and Social Affairs, Madrid.

Toharia, L. and Ojeda, A. (1999) "The management of redundancies in Europe: the case of Spain", *Labour*, 13 (1), 1-31.

Toharia, Luis and Malo, Miguel A. (2000). "The Spanish Experiment: Pros and Cons of the Flexibility at the Margin", in G. Esping-Andersen and M. Regini (eds.), *Why Deregulate Labour Markets*, Oxford: Oxford University Press, pp. 307-335.

In: Political Economy Research Focus
Editor: Walter R. Levin, pp. 121-134

ISBN: 978-1-60456-154-8
© 2008 Nova Science Publishers, Inc.

Chapter 6

THE POLITICAL ECONOMY OF HUMAN AND PHYSICAL CAPITAL ACCUMULATION IN ECONOMIC GROWTH

*Alberto Bucci**

University of Milan, Italy

ABSTRACT

Using a balanced-growth model with physical and human capital accumulation where the equilibrium allocation of skills between alternative uses (production of goods and education) is endogenously determined, this article analyzes quantitatively the long run effects of changes in the saving rate and in income distribution (i.e., in the shares of physical and human capital in income) on investment in human capital, growth of income, and the ratio of human to physical capital (all these variables being measured in efficiency units). It is assumed that in the long run the ratio of physical to human capital is constant, so that these two production factors can grow at the same rate. This rate is a function of the economy's exogenous technological and preference parameters and depends positively on the share of skills invested in human capital formation. In equilibrium, we also find that population growth is neither necessary nor conducive to economic growth and that the level of real income in efficiency units depends linearly on the level of human capital in efficiency units and is independent of population size.

Keywords: Economic Growth; Human and Physical Capital Investment; Political Economy; Scale Effects

JEL Classification: I20; J22; J24; O41

---

* Author's Address: University of Milan, Department of Economics, via Conservatorio 7, I-20122 Milan, Italy. Tel.: ++39/ (0)2/50321.463; Fax: ++39/ (0)2/50321.505; E-mail: alberto.bucci@unimi.it. Financial support from the Italian Ministry for University and Scientific Research (MIUR), grant number 2005131555_003, is kindly acknowledged. The usual disclaimer applies.

1. INTRODUCTION

The neoclassical, exogenous growth literature has long ago emphasized the importance of physical capital accumulation as a factor driving economic growth (at least in the medium run). More recently the *new growth theory* has made clear that over the longer period a country's economic development is endogenous in that it is determined by a purposeful investment activity in intangible capital (mainly human/technological capital) by agents (individuals/firms) motivated by the search for future higher returns (wages/profits).

In this chapter we merge these two branches of the literature and propose the simplest model *à la* Solow (1956)-Uzawa (1965)-Lucas (1988) in order to analyze quantitatively the effects that changes in the saving rate and in income distribution (*i.e.*, in the shares of physical and human capital in income) may have on human capital investment, income growth, and the ratio of human to physical capital (all these variables being measured in *efficiency units*).

The reason that motivates the present contribution is twofold. First of all, very recently there has been a rebirth of confidence *"...that explicit neoclassical growth models in the style of Solow (1956) can be adapted to fit the observed behavior of rich and poor economies alike"* (Lucas, 1993, p.253). At the same time, it has also been recognized that *"...the main engine of growth is the accumulation of human capital"* (Lucas, 1993, p.270).[1] Together, these two facts explain our interest in using an extension of the original Solow's work in order to build a theoretical model in which equilibrium growth is sustained solely by human (rather than physical) capital investment and where real income (in efficiency units) depends positively on the stock of human capital (in efficiency units).

In an influential article Mankiw, Romer and Weil (1992) - MRW, henceforth - have already extensively analyzed the impact of human capital within an otherwise standard *Solovian* economy. Though, this chapter introduces two major differences with respect to their theoretical model. First of all, we postulate that physical and human capital are produced by different technologies, as in the model by Uzawa (1965) and later on developed by Lucas (1988). Secondly, within an aggregate model where these two forms of capital may grow at a common and constant rate in the long run (balanced-growth path equilibrium, BGPE

---

[1] Empirical research on the relationship between human capital and economic growth is almost boundless. Indeed, results on this topic still remain largely controversial depending on: 1) the methodological approach being used, whether *cross-country growth accounting* (Benhabib and Spiegel, 1994; Krueger and Lindahl, 2001; Pritchett, 2001 and Caselli, 2004, among others) or *cross-country growth regressions* (Barro, 1999; Barro and Sala-I-Martin, 1995; Easterly and Levine, 1997; Islam, 1995); 2) the measure of human capital employed. Wößmann (2003) provides a detailed survey of all the main measures of human capital used to date by empirical studies on growth (in particular adult literacy rates, school enrollment ratios and average years of schooling of the working-age population), and analyzes the pros and cons of each of them with respect to the original *theory of human capital* developed by Becker (1964), Schultz (1964) and Mincer (1974). From this point of view, while some studies use a flow measure of human capital, *i.e.* school enrollment rates (see, as an example, the works by Barro, 1991; Mankiw, Romer and Weil, 1992 and Levine and Renelt, 1992), others use the stock of human capital, *i.e.* total mean years of schooling (Barro and Sala-I-Martin, 1995; Barro, 1997 and 2001; Barro and Lee, 2001; Benhabib and Spiegel, 1994; Gundlach, 1995; Islam, 1995; Krueger and Lindahl, 2001; O'Neill, 1995; Temple, 1999); 3) the type of data utilized. Studies using cross-section data, unlike those based on panel data, generally find that human capital accumulation has a positive effect on the rate of growth of real per-capita income. Islam (1995) summarizes this finding by observing that: *"...whenever researchers have attempted to incorporate the temporal dimension of human capital variables into growth regressions, outcomes of either statistical insignificance or negative sign have surfaced"*.

hereafter), we make the distribution of individual skills across alternative uses (production of goods and education) endogenous.[2]

In more detail, our model assumes the existence of two perfectly competitive sectors. The final sector produces homogeneous consumption goods by combining physical and human capital through a constant returns to scale technology, while the education sector produces skills. As in the Solow's model (1956), physical capital is accumulated by saving in each period a positive, constant and exogenous fraction of total final output (GDP). On the other hand, the sector producing education (new human capital) is relatively intensive in human capital as an input.[3] Along the BGPE the ratio of physical to human capital is constant, so that these two production inputs grow at the same rate. This rate is a function of the economy's exogenous technological and preference parameters and depends positively on the fraction of skills devoted to human capital formation. The model allows us also to conclude that in the long run, whilst population growth is neither necessary nor conducive to economic growth, the level (in efficiency units) of real income depends positively on the level (in efficiency units) of human capital and is independent of population size. In this sense our model displays no *scale effects*.

The chapter is organized as follows. Section 2 introduces the economic environment and states the laws of physical and human capital accumulation. Section 3 analyzes the BGPE predictions of the model and determines the allocation of human capital between production of goods and education, the equilibrium growth rate, and the ratio of human to physical capital. In Section 4 we obtain the equilibrium level of real income and discuss the results of the model as far as the scale effects are concerned. Finally, section 5 concludes.

2. THE ECONOMIC ENVIRONMENT

The model we present in this section shares some of the hypotheses of the Lucas (1988) and MRW (1992) models, but with some important differences. The first difference is with the MRW's work. Following Solow (1956), we assume that there exists only one (overall) gross saving rate and that this saving rate is constant and exogenous (MRW, instead, postulates that the investment rate in physical capital is different from the one in human capital, although both are constant and exogenous).

As it is explained in Barro and Sala-I-Martin (2004, p.61), an important shortcoming of the MRW's approach is that the rates of return to physical and human capital are not equated in equilibrium. Related to this is the main difference between our model and Lucas' (1988).[4] In that approach, savings and the fraction of time devoted to human capital accumulation are both derived through maximizing (under constraints) the inter-temporal utility function of a representative agent. In our case, instead, the time allocation behavior is obtained by imposing the equalization of the rates of return on physical and human capital. In this sense,

---

[2] In MRW (1992), the allocation of the available resources (final consumption goods) between physical and human capital accumulation activities is exogenously given.

[3] In MRW's model, constant fractions of GDP are invested in physical and human capital accumulation. As it is shown in Cohen (1996), however, this formulation is not supported by data.

[4] See also Uzawa (1965) and Caballe and Santos (1993).

unlike the Lucas' model, ours is not micro-founded but allows tackling the major weakness of the MRW's paper.

The economy we consider consists of two sectors, both perfectly competitive. The final output sector produces homogeneous consumption goods combining physical and human capital as inputs via the following constant returns to scale Cobb-Douglas technology:

$$Y_t = K_t^\alpha \left(H_{Yt}\right)^{1-\alpha}, \qquad\qquad \alpha \in (0;1), \tag{1}$$

where Y_t denotes the total quantity of final goods (the numeraire goods in the model) produced at time t, and K_t and H_{Yt} represent the aggregate stocks of factor inputs used in the production of consumption goods (physical and human capital, respectively). In the above relation, α is a constant technological parameter (strictly between zero and one) that can be interpreted as the share of national income going to physical capital.[5] Population (L) consists only of educated workers, each of them being endowed at time t with a stock of human capital in *efficiency units* (h_t) defined as:

$$h_t \equiv \frac{H_t}{A_t L_t}.$$

H_t and A_t are respectively the total stock of human capital available in the economy (namely, the population's total number of years of education) and the state of the technology at time t. From the definition of h_t it follows that H_t can also be written as:

$$H_t \equiv \left(A_t h_t\right) L_t. \tag{2}$$

In (2) the term in brackets ($A_t h_t$) represents the human capital possessed by each member of the population (or *per-capita* human capital, *i.e.* the mean number of years of education).

There is full employment in this economy, and all the available human capital (H_t) can be used in two alternative activities. A fraction u_t of it (equal to H_{Yt}) is used at time t to produce homogeneous final consumption goods, while its complement to one ($1-u_t$) is used to accumulate new human capital. In other words, the human capital stock employed to produce the final good in t is $H_{Yt} = u_t H_t = u_t \left[\left(A_t h_t\right) L_t\right]$. Therefore, the aggregate production function can be recast as:

$$Y_t = K_t^\alpha \left[u_t \left(A_t h_t\right) L_t\right]^{1-\alpha}, \tag{1'}$$

and the income per efficiency unit of population is:

$$y_t \equiv \frac{Y_t}{A_t L_t} \equiv f(k_t; u_t; h_t; \alpha) = k_t^\alpha \left(u_t h_t\right)^{1-\alpha}, \qquad\qquad k_t \equiv \frac{K_t}{A_t L_t}. \tag{3}$$

---

[5] In the model, all markets are competitive and there is not any market distortion or failure.

2.1. The Laws of Physical and Human Capital Accumulation

As in the model developed by Solow (1956), we assume that the aggregate investment in physical capital is financed by devoting to this activity a positive, exogenous and constant fraction (s) of GDP (Y_t). The reason why we take s as exogenous resides in the fact that, among others, it is our interest to investigate in this chapter the effects of a change in the saving rate on such endogenous variables (in efficiency units) as investment in human capital, growth of real income, and the ratio of human to physical capital, regardless of the possible sources of that change. Moreover, we continue to follow Solow (1956) in postulating that population (L) and the state of the technology (A) grow at a rate (respectively n and g_A) which is positive, exogenous and constant ($L_t = e^{nt}$, $L_0 \equiv 1$ and $A_t = e^{g_A t}$, $A_0 \equiv 1$). We also assume that the sum of n and g_A (which we denote by δ) is a number strictly between zero and one. Finally, and only for the-sake of simplicity, we consider an economy where the aggregate stock of physical capital (K) is not subject to material depreciation. Under these assumptions, the law of motion of physical capital in efficiency units of population can be stated as:

$$\dot{k}_t = sf(k_t; u_t; h_t; \alpha) - \delta k_t \qquad 0 < s < 1 \qquad 0 < \delta \equiv g_A + n < 1 \qquad (4)$$

$$\frac{\dot{A}_t}{A_t} \equiv g_A > 0 \qquad \frac{\dot{L}_t}{L_t} \equiv n > 0.$$

Unlike Solow's (1956) model, ours also includes accumulation of human capital. In this regard, and differently from MRW (1992) where this factor is produced with the same production technology used for final output,[6] we assume that a fraction (equal to $1 - u_t$) of the aggregate human capital stock available at time t is employed to accumulate and produce new human capital (in other words, our hypothesis is that the education sector is skill-intensive).

In more detail, we postulate that in the time unit $\dot{H}_t$ units of new skills are obtained with the following production function:

$$\dot{H}_t = (1 - u_t) H_t = (1 - u_t)[(A_t h_t) L_t]. \qquad (5)$$

Hence, our model explicitly incorporates the same technology of human capital formation used by Uzawa (1965) and Lucas (1988). It is evident from equation (5) that we are assuming that the production of human capital occurs at constant returns to scale. This assumption, which is shared by many other models, can be justified by referring either to the existence of external effects in education (such that the decreasing returns to this activity at the individual level are converted into constant returns at the aggregate one) or to the fact that the production of new human capital involves not only the time spent on pure educational activity

---

[6] "...We are assuming that the same production function applies to human capital, physical capital and consumption. ...Lucas (1988) models the production function for human capital as fundamentally different from that for other goods", MRW (1992).

but also other production factors (in this case, human capital should be considered in a broad sense).

Equation (5) and the definition of h can be used to find the law of (gross) accumulation of human capital in efficiency units:

$$\dot{h}_t + \delta h_t = (1 - u_t)h_t, \qquad\qquad h_0 \text{ given;} \qquad\qquad (6)$$
$$0 < u_t < 1, \qquad \forall t.^7$$

Note from (6) that, like the stock of physical capital, the stock of human capital is also subject to a process of (effective) obsolescence in the production of new human capital (the term δ). The reason for this is simple: if the rate of investment in human capital $(1-u_t)$ were equal to zero, then the human capital stock in efficiency units of population would tend to diminish over time, partly because of population growth (at rate n) and partly because of technological progress (g_A). This amounts to saying that the faster technological progress and population growth and the more rapidly the available stock of knowledge (h_t) depreciates over time.

Equations (1) through (6) are the basic equations of the model. In the next section we characterize the balanced-growth path equilibrium (BGPE) of this economy.

3. THE BALANCED-GROWTH PATH EQUILIBRIUM (BGPE)

In this section we determine the equilibrium value of the three endogenous unknowns of the model, that is the ratio h/k, the sectoral distribution of human capital (u) and the growth rate of income in efficiency units. However, before doing that, we start by providing a formal definition of BGPE.

Definition: **Balanced-Growth Path Equilibrium (BGPE)**
A BGPE is a long run equilibrium where the endogenous state variables of the model grow at constant rates.

In the model the endogenous state variables are physical and human capital (both measured in efficiency units, respectively k and h). On applying the definition of BGPE to equation (6), we find that in the long run, with $\delta \equiv g_A + n$ constant and exogenous, the shares of human capital devoted respectively to production of consumption goods (u) and new human capital $(1-u)$ are constant. Moreover, from equations (3) and (4), we obtain (in order to ease the notation, and unless necessary, from now on we shall omit the subscript t near the time-dependent variables):

---

[7] We take u to be strictly between zero and one because we are interested in an equilibrium solution in which human capital is always used simultaneously in the sector producing final goods and the education sector.

$$\frac{\dot{k}}{k} = \frac{sk^{\alpha}(uh)^{1-\alpha}}{k} - \delta = \gamma_{bg} \equiv \gamma \Rightarrow s \cdot u^{1-\alpha}\left(\frac{h}{k}\right)^{1-\alpha} = \gamma + \delta, \tag{7}$$

where $\gamma_{bg} \equiv \gamma$ is a constant to be determined.

With s and δ constant and exogenously given, and with u and γ also constant but endogenous, two fundamental conclusions can be drawn from equation (7). Indeed, along the BGPE:

h and k must grow at the same constant rate, given by $\gamma_{bg} \equiv \gamma = (1-u) - \delta$;   (7a)

$$\frac{uh}{k} = f(\gamma; \delta; s; \alpha) = \left(\frac{\gamma + \delta}{s}\right)^{\frac{1}{1-\alpha}} = \left(\frac{1-u}{s}\right)^{\frac{1}{1-\alpha}} \text{ is also constant.} \tag{7b}$$

The fact that h and k grow at the same common rate implies that in equilibrium their ratio is constant (this is stated in equation 7b).

From equation (3), and recalling that $\dfrac{\dot{h}}{h} = \dfrac{\dot{k}}{k} = \gamma_{bg} \equiv \gamma$ and that u is constant, one obtains:

$$\frac{\dot{y}}{y} = \frac{\dot{k}}{k} = \frac{\dot{h}}{h} \equiv \gamma = (1-u) - \delta. \tag{8}$$

Equation (8) suggests that, under the hypotheses of our model, there exists a BGPE along which income, physical capital and human capital (all measured in efficiency units) grow at a common and constant rate being a linear function of u, still to be determined.

In order to characterize the level of income per efficiency units in the BGPE (y_{bg}), we must first find out k_{bg}. At this aim, we reconsider equation (7) above and obtain:

$$k_{bg} = \left(\frac{s}{\gamma + \delta}\right)^{\frac{1}{1-\alpha}} \cdot \left(u_{bg} h_{bg}\right), \tag{9}$$

where x_{bg} represents the value of variable x along the BGPE.

Given k_{bg}, y_{bg} can be immediately obtained from equation (3) as follows:

$$y_{bg} = \left(k_{bg}\right)^{\alpha} \left(u_{bg} h_{bg}\right)^{1-\alpha} = \left(\frac{s}{\gamma + \delta}\right)^{\frac{\alpha}{1-\alpha}} \cdot \left(u_{bg} h_{bg}\right). \tag{3'}$$

3.1. General Equilibrium and the Endogenous Distribution of Human Capital across Production of Goods and Education

In the model described above the sector producing consumption goods and the one that produces new human capital are both competitive. In order to determine the endogenous allocation of skills across these two sectors we use the following condition:

$$P_h = (1-\alpha)\left(\frac{k}{uh}\right)^{\alpha} \equiv w. \tag{10}$$

This equation states that the (shadow) price of human capital in units of goods (P_h) must be equal to the ratio between the marginal product of human capital employed in the production of goods (the wage rate, w) and the (gross) marginal product of human capital employed in the education sector (equal to one). In other words, the productivity (in value) of the human capital employed in the education sector (the left-hand side of equation 10) must be equal to the productivity (in value) of the human capital employed in the production of consumption goods (the right-hand side of the same equation). Accordingly, equation (10) can be interpreted as an arbitrage condition for the allocation of the available human capital between the two sectors demanding this resource as an input. Compliance with this condition ensures that in equilibrium both activities in which human capital is utilized as a production factor are undertaken and can therefore co-exist.

Moreover, in the presence of a perfectly competitive capital market, from the point of view of the returns on the two kinds of asset it should make no difference to an economic agent to hold capital in the form of physical or human capital. Because the return (in terms of goods) from possessing one unit of human capital coincides with the wage rate (w), while that from possessing one unit of physical capital coincides with the real interest rate (r, i.e. with the productivity of physical capital in the goods sector), the second condition that we impose is the following:

$$r = (1-\alpha)\left(\frac{k}{uh}\right)^{\alpha}, \qquad \text{with } r = \alpha\left(\frac{uh}{k}\right)^{1-\alpha}. \tag{11}$$

Solving this equation in (uh/k) yields:

$$\frac{uh}{k} = \left(\frac{1-\alpha}{\alpha}\right). \tag{12}$$

Equation (12) states that in equilibrium the ratio of human (uh) to physical (k) capital employed in the production of goods must be equal to the ratio of their respective distributive shares ($1-\alpha$ and α). The same equation gives us another expression for the ratio of uh to k. Equalizing this equation to equation (7b) yields a closed form solution for u_{bg} and ($1-u_{bg}$). Respectively, the share of human capital employed along the BGPE by each agent to produce consumption goods and skills is:

$$u_{bg} = 1 - s \left(\frac{1-\alpha}{\alpha} \right)^{1-\alpha} ; \tag{13}$$

$$\left(1 - u_{bg}\right) = s \left(\frac{1-\alpha}{\alpha} \right)^{1-\alpha} . \tag{14}$$

Given u_{bg}, it follows from equation (7a) that the common, balanced-growth rate of this economy is:

$$\gamma_{bg} \equiv \gamma = s \left(\frac{1-\alpha}{\alpha} \right)^{1-\alpha} - \delta . \tag{15}$$

Finally, given u_{bg}, it follows from equation (7b) -or alternatively from equation (12)- that:

$$\left(\frac{h}{k} \right)_{bg} = \frac{(1-\alpha)}{\alpha - s\alpha^{\alpha}(1-\alpha)^{1-\alpha}} . \tag{16}$$

Along the BGPE, u, γ and h/k depend solely on the model's exogenous variables (g_A and n) and its technological (or distributive, α) and preference (s) parameters. However, the growth rate (γ) is endogenous because it depends on u (that we have determined inside the model by equalizing the returns to human and physical capital). Moreover, unlike the model with physical capital accumulation alone (Solow, 1956), the possibility for agents to invest also in human capital gives rise to a balanced-growth rate (γ) that is constant and positive even in the absence of exogenous technical progress and demographic dynamics (*i.e.*, when $g_A = n = 0$). Finally, it is immediate to notice that this growth rate is a positive function of the overall (exogenous) saving rate, s.

After describing the model, we are now able to state the following:

Proposition 1

The relation between the model's exogenous parameters for it to be simultaneously the case that:

$$\gamma_{bg} \equiv \gamma > 0, \qquad\qquad 0 < u_{bg} < 1 \qquad and \qquad \left(\frac{h}{k} \right)_{bg} > 0,$$

is:

$$0 < \delta \left(\frac{\alpha}{1-\alpha} \right)^{1-\alpha} < s < \left(\frac{\alpha}{1-\alpha} \right)^{1-\alpha} < 1 .$$

Proof:

The proof of this proposition follows immediately from equations (13), (15) and (16). ■

In words, the proposition suggests that when the saving rate (s) is strictly comprised between the two extremes written above the equilibrium that arises (equations 13 through 16) ensures:

- The existence of a positive balanced-growth rate;
- The existence of a decentralized distribution of human capital across the two sectors of the economy such that each of them can simultaneously employ this factor input.

Notice that when $\alpha < 1/2$, then the restriction $\left(\dfrac{\alpha}{1-\alpha}\right)^{1-\alpha} < 1$ is surely checked. This hypothesis ($\alpha < 1/2$) is in line with the evidence that the physical capital share of income is approximately equal to 1/3 (and, thus, less than ½).

In order to convey the intuition behind the above proposition, let us see what would happen in equilibrium if the saving rate were instead 'too' low ($s \to 0$) or 'too' high ($s \to 1$). If the saving rate were 'too' low, in the long run there would be, *ceteris paribus*, a low level of physical capital ($k \to 0$), and most of human capital would be used to produce final goods ($u \to 1$). This would naturally subtract resources from investment in education (which is a skill-intensive activity, $1 - u \to 0$), and the growth rate of the economy would gradually diminish until it ultimately becomes negative ($\gamma \to -\delta$). This possibility is explicitly ruled out by our proposition. By contrast, if the saving rate were 'too' high, the reverse situation would obtain. In fact, under the hypothesis that the share of income going to physical capital is less than ½ ($\alpha < $ ½), if s tended to one then u would tend to zero (from below). This implies that, unlike the previous case, now most of human capital is employed in the education sector, to the obvious benefit of economic growth. Yet, also this second extreme possibility, like the previous one, is excluded by the above proposition.

The next proposition analyzes the relationship between the endogenous variables of the model, income distribution and the saving rate.

Proposition 2

The relation between the model's endogenous variables, the saving rate and income distribution is summarized by Table 1.

Proof:
See equations (13), (14), (15) and (16). ■

Results v), vi) and vii) in Table 1 take explicitly into account the fact that $\alpha < 1/2$, while all the other results hold for each $\alpha \in (0,1)$ and $s \in (0,1)$.

Table 1. The BGPE relationship between the share of human capital employed to produce goods (u_{bg}) and skills ($1-u_{bg}$), the common growth rate of the economy ($\gamma_{bg} \equiv \gamma$), the ratio of human to physical capital, $(h/k)_{bg}$, the saving rate (s) and the share of income going to physical capital (α)

i) $\dfrac{\partial u_{bg}}{\partial s} < 0$	v) $\dfrac{\partial u_{bg}}{\partial \alpha} > 0$
ii) $\dfrac{\partial\left(1 - u_{bg}\right)}{\partial s} > 0$	vi) $\dfrac{\partial\left(1 - u_{bg}\right)}{\partial \alpha} < 0$
iii) $\dfrac{\partial \gamma}{\partial s} > 0$	vii) $\dfrac{\partial \gamma}{\partial \alpha} < 0$
iv) $\dfrac{\partial\left(h/k\right)_{bg}}{\partial s} > 0$	viii) $\dfrac{\partial\left(h/k\right)_{bg}}{\partial \alpha} < 0$

The comparative statics results set out in the table have a clear economic intuition. For example, an increase in s will increase in equilibrium the stock of available physical capital (k). The larger availability of k, combined with the fact that physical capital is used solely for the production of goods, will have two effects: human capital employed in the manufacturing sector will be substituted by physical capital (u will diminish) and the shadow-price of human capital will increase (P_h rises both because k is now larger and u is smaller, *ceteris paribus*). The increase in P_h will stimulate investment in education ($1-u$ will increase), making human capital relatively more abundant than physical capital (h/k will increase, too). Vice versa, an increase in the share of income spent on physical capital (α) in equilibrium will reduce (with u remaining equal, see equation 12) the h/k ratio (the available physical capital will be relatively more abundant than human capital), and this will ultimately increase the productivity of human capital in the goods sector and the share of skills used in that sector (u increases). In turn, the increase in u will reduce the investment in new human capital ($1-u$) and, thus, will drive the balanced rate of growth (γ) down.

4. SCALE EFFECTS

Using equations (3'), (13) and (15) we can now obtain the BGPE level of real income in efficiency units of population (y_{bg}):

$$y_{bg} = \psi \zeta h_{bg}, \qquad \psi \equiv \left(\frac{\alpha}{1-\alpha}\right)^{\alpha}, \qquad \zeta \equiv \left[1 - s\left(\frac{1-\alpha}{\alpha}\right)^{1-\alpha}\right], \qquad (17)$$

where h_{bg} is the BGPE level of human capital in efficiency units.

From (15) the equilibrium growth rate of this economy ($\gamma_{bg} \equiv \gamma$) can also be recast as:

$$\gamma_{bg} \equiv \gamma = (1-\zeta)-\delta = (1-\zeta)-(n+g_A)=(\vartheta+\eta)+\sigma n,$$

$$\vartheta \equiv 1-\zeta, \qquad \sigma = -1, \qquad \eta = -g_A. \qquad (15')$$

Putting together (17) and (15'), we get:

$$y_{bg} = \psi \zeta h_{bg} = \psi \zeta h_0 e^n = \frac{\alpha^{2\alpha-1}}{(1-\alpha)^\alpha}\left[\alpha^{1-\alpha} - s(1-\alpha)^{1-\alpha}\right]h_0 e^{[(\vartheta+\eta)+\sigma n]t}, \qquad (17')$$

h_0 being the given, initial (*i.e.*, at time t=0) level of human capital in efficiency units.

Equations (15') and (17') allow us setting the last result of this chapter:

Proposition 3

For given h_0, the equilibrium level of real income in efficiency units (y_{bg}) is independent of the size of population (L).

Population growth (n) is neither conducive nor necessary to long run growth since, when

$$g_A < s\left(\frac{1-\alpha}{\alpha}\right)^{1-\alpha}, positive growth (\gamma > 0) occurs even in the presence of no demographic$$

change ($n = 0$).

Proof:

The proof of this proposition follows immediately from equations (15') and (17') above.

∎

In our model population growth has an unambiguous negative effect on economic growth. However, unlike the *semi-endogenous growth* literature (see, among others, Jones, 1995 and Jones, 1999; Dinopoulos and Thompson, 1999 and Jones, 2005 for surveys), economic growth is feasible even in the absence of demographic change, as long as the exogenous saving rate is sufficiently large. Still, the model displays no scale effect in that along the equilibrium path the level of real income is proportional to the level of human capital (both measured in efficiency units).

5. CONCLUSION

Using a model in which agents may accumulate both physical and human capital, this chapter has studied the long run effects of changes in the overall saving rate of an economy and in income distribution (*i.e.*, in the shares of human and physical capital in income) on such variables as the allocation of skills across production of goods and formation of new human capital, growth of income and the ratio of human to physical capital (all measured in efficiency units).

Compared to the existing literature (most notably Mankiw, Romer and Weil, 1992), in our balanced-growth model the distribution of human capital between alternative uses (production and education) has been endogenously determined through the equalization of the rates of return to physical and human capital.

Our results suggest that over the long run the saving rate is positively related to economic growth and the ratio of human to physical capital and negatively related to the fraction of skills employed in the manufacturing sector. On the other hand, an increase in the share of physical capital in income leads in equilibrium to a reduction in economic growth, in the ratio of human to physical capital and in the fraction of skills employed in the education sector. Moreover, we found that population growth is neither necessary nor conducive to long run growth and that the elasticity of real income to human capital (both in efficiency units) is unitary, meaning that along the balanced-growth path equilibrium the level of real income is linearly proportional to the level of human capital and independent of the size of population. The absence of scale effects in the level of income is in line with empirical evidence and represents a property that, according to Jones (2005), each growth model must possess. The empirical test of the results of this chapter is left to future research.

REFERENCES

Barro, R.J. (1991), "Economic Growth in a Cross Section of Countries", *Quarterly Journal of Economics*, 106(2), pp. 407-43.

Barro, R.J. (1997), *Determinants of Economic Growth: A Cross-Country Empirical Study*, Cambridge, MA: MIT Press.

Barro, R.J. (1999), "Human Capital and Growth in Cross-Country Regressions", *Swedish Economic Policy Review*, 6(2), pp. 237-77.

Barro, R.J. (2001), "Human Capital and Growth", *American Economic Review, Papers and Proceedings*, 91(2), pp. 12-17.

Barro, R.J. and Lee, J.W. (2001), "International Data on Educational Attainment: Updates and Implications", *Oxford Economic Papers*, 53(3), pp. 541-63.

Barro, R.J. and Sala-i-Martin, X. (1995), *Economic Growth*, New York: McGraw Hill.

Barro, R.J. and Sala-i-Martin, X. (2004), *Economic Growth*, Second Edition, Cambridge, MA: MIT Press.

Becker, G.S. (1964), *Human Capital*, New York: Columbia University Press.

Benhabib, J. and Spiegel, M.M. (1994), "The Role of Human Capital in Economic Development: Evidence from Aggregate Cross-Country Data", *Journal of Monetary Economics*, 34(2), pp. 143-73.

Caballe, J. and Santos, M.S. (1993), "On Endogenous Growth with Physical and Human Capital", *Journal of Political Economy*, 101(6), 1042-67.

Caselli, F. (2004), "Accounting for Cross-Country Income Differences", NBER Working Paper Series, WP No. 10828.

Cohen, D. (1996), "Tests of the "Convergence Hypothesis": Some Further Results", *Journal of Economic Growth*, 1(3), pp. 351-61.

Dinopoulos, E. and Thompson, P. (1999), "Scale Effects in Schumpeterian Models of Economic Growth", *Journal of Evolutionary Economics*, 9(2), pp. 157-85.

Easterly, W. and Levine, R. (1997), "Africa's Growth Tragedy: Policies and Ethnic Divisions", *Quarterly Journal of Economics*, 112(4), pp. 1203-50.

Gundlach, E. (1995), "The Role of Human Capital in Economic Growth: New Results and Alternative Interpretations", *Weltwirtschaftliches Archiv*, 131(2), pp. 383-402.

Islam, N. (1995), "Growth Empirics: A Panel Data Approach", *Quarterly Journal of Economics*, 110(4), pp. 1127-70.

Jones, C.I. (1995), "R&D-Based Models of Economic Growth", *Journal of Political Economy*,103(4), pp. 759-84.

Jones, C.I. (1999), "Growth: With or Without Scale Effects?", *American Economic Review, Papers and Proceedings*, 89(2), pp.139-44.

Jones, C.I. (2005), "Growth and Ideas", in P. Aghion and S. Durlauf, eds., *Handbook of Economic Growth*, Volume 1, Part 2, Chapter 16, pp. 1063-111, Amsterdam: Elsevier Science, North Holland.

Krueger, A.B. and Lindahl, M. (2001), "Education for Growth: Why and For Whom?", *Journal of Economic Literature*, 39(4), pp. 1101-36.

Levine, R.E. and Renelt, D. (1992), "A Sensitivity Analysis of Cross-Country Growth Regressions", *American Economic Review*, 82(4), pp. 942-63.

Lucas, R.E. (1988), "On the Mechanics of Economic Development", *Journal of Monetary Economics*, 22(1), pp. 3-42.

Lucas, R.E. (1993), "Making a Miracle", *Econometrica*, 61(2), pp. 251-72.

Mankiw, N.G., Romer, D. and Weil, D.N. (1992), "A Contribution to the Empirics of Economic Growth", *Quarterly Journal of Economics*, 107(2), pp. 407-37.

Mincer, J. (1974), *Schooling, Experience, and Earnings*, New York: National Bureau of Economic Research.

O'Neill, D. (1995), "Education and Income Growth: Implications for Cross-Country Inequality", *Journal of Political Economy*, 103(6), pp. 1289-1301.

Pritchett, L. (2001), "Where Has All the Education Gone?", *World Bank Economic Review*, 15(3), pp. 367-91.

Schultz, T. (1964), *The Economic Value of Education*, New York: Columbia University Press.

Solow, R. (1956), "A Contribution to the Theory of Economic Growth", *Quarterly Journal of Economics*, 70(1), pp. 65-94.

Temple, J. (1999), "A Positive Effect of Human Capital on Growth", *Economics Letters*, 65(1), pp. 131-34.

Uzawa, H. (1965), "Optimum Technical Change in an Aggregative Model of Economic Growth", *International Economic Review*, 6, pp. 18-31.

Wößmann, L. (2003), "Specifying Human Capital", *Journal of Economic Surveys*, 17(3), pp. 239-70.

In: Political Economy Research Focus
Editor: Walter R. Levin, pp. 135-148

ISBN: 978-1-60456-154-8
© 2008 Nova Science Publishers, Inc.

Chapter 7

THE POLITICAL ECONOMY OF RENT SEEKING IN A CONCENTRATED MARKET

Gil S. Epstein
Bar-Ilan University Ramat-Gan Israel, IZA Bonn and CReAM London
Renana Pomerantz
Bar-Ilan University Ramat-Gan Israel

ABSTRACT

This chapter considers the political economy of rent-seeking under the circumstances of concentrated markets. In concentrated markets there exist an "economic elite" whose members control the major companies of the market. The major companies, accompanied by their shareholders, participate in several rent-seeking contests, and as a result, one shareholder may co-operate with player A against player B in one contest, while the same shareholder may co-operate with player B against player A in a different contest. We consider the implications of this concentrated situation over the rent dissipation and the expenditures of the different participants in the contests and compare these results to those established in the traditional rent-seeking literature. We find that mutual interests among shareholders reduce the rent dissipation in the concentrated market. We also examine the behaviors of participants when the value of the rent changes in our model compared to the traditional model presented in the literature.

Keywords: Concentrated market, mutual interests, rent-seeking, rent dissipation

1. INTRODUCTION

In this chapter we consider the effects of a concentrated market on the rent-seeking expenditures of contestants.

In a concentrated market single groups control a large part of the economic activity and participate in most of the significant contests existing in this market, thus increasing their political involvement. The economic incentives for corporations to become politically connected have been recognized among economists for many years. The source of such values can be from preferential treatment by government-owned enterprises[1].

The structure of ownership and control in corporations is a major concern in many political and economic studies. For example, Gugler (1998), Yurtoglu (2000) and Kang (2003) examine the ownership and control structure in corporations and firms in certain countries, and, inter alia, distinguish between firms that are being controlled by families, governmental firms, firms controlled by banks, etc.

The literature also deals with the relationship between corporations and politicians. According to Shleifer and Vishny (1994), politicians themselves will extract at least some of the rents generated by such connections. Fisman (2001) concludes that in Indonesia a sizeable percentage of well-connected firms' values, come from political connections. In a study based on Canada, Morck, Stangeland, and Yeung (2000) discuss the political influence of dominant business families. Faccio (2006) provides a comprehensive look at corporate political connections around the globe and addresses three questions: Are corporate connections with political officials common worldwide? Are there similarities among countries where corporate political connections are more common? And do such connections add to the company values?

The literature is concerned with the control and ownership structures in companies and refers to the implications of a concentrated market on the decision-making process in a country. For example, Claessens, Djankov and Lang (2000) find that a significant corporate wealth in East Asia is concentrated among a few families and that this concentration creates powerful incentives and abilities to lobby government agencies, which leads to crony capitalism. Faccio (2006) also notes that these "connected firms" enjoy an easy access to debt financing, tax benefits and market power.

In spite of the important consequences of this concentration on both economic and political activity in markets, as widely described in the above mentioned papers, the rent seeking literature does not deal with the issue of the concentration of different groups and with the rent-seeking competition between them (see Nitzan (1994)).

The purpose of this chapter is to integrate the rent-seeking literature and the concentration of power in the market and to examine possible implications of the political situation on rent-seeking theories. The basic question we pose is how this concentration affects the rent-seeking efforts of the contestants.

---

[1] If we take the Israeli market for example, about 20 major groups/families control the most important and influential companies in Israel, and take part in its main transactions and contests. Examples of these families are Dankner, Arison, Fishman, Strauss, and others. Evidence for this concentration can be found in the researches published by the Israeli leading research company "BDI - Business Data Israel Ltd.". Its researches are based on several quantitative and qualitative indexes which measure the level of influence of individuals and groups over the Israeli market, and it actually confirms what we mentioned above, and determines that the Israeli market is highly concentrated in the hands of 20 wealthy families who control the most influential companies in Israel. We can find these groups and families in most of the important tenders and transactions taking place in Israel, in several different industries, such as communication, banking, food manufacturing, etc.

The underlying assumption of the chapter, and what distinguishes it from the standard rent-seeking papers, is that an individual's political influence is determined according to the amount of resources spent by him in *all* the contests in which he participates.

In this chapter we distinguish between a non-concentrated market, where there are no connections between the participants in the different contests, and a concentrated one, where the players have mutual interests such that one individual may co-operate with player A against player B in one contest, while he may co-operate with player B against player A in a different contest. We show that in a concentrated market the level of rent dissipation is lower compared to the non-concentrated market. This derives from the fact that in a concentrated market when assuming mutual interests between the individuals, we allow them to engage together in contests and reduce their costs in the different contests. The mutual interests decrease the amount of resources they spend.

We also show that in the concentrated market, in a similar way to the literature (Nitzan (1991) and Ursprung (1990)), increasing any of the rents in the contests will increase the rent dissipation. In the rent-seeking literature, it is also known that there is an ambiguity in the response of a contestant to a change in the valuation of the rent by one of his opponents (see for example Nti (1999), Epstein and Nitzan (2002, 2007)). Our results also show an ambiguity in the response to a change in the value of the rent, but the nature and reasons for the ambiguity are different. In our modified model, the ambiguity's source is the fact that each individual relates to a specific contest as part of a broader system of contests and interactions between members of the "economic elite". Therefore, under certain circumstances, it is better to let his opponent get stronger in one contest and by doing so improve his own probability of winning in other contests which are more important for him.

Our results proved new insights into the rent-seeking activities in markets with high concentrations where individuals participate in different contests in which one individual competes against another, while in a different contest these two individuals compete against a third.

We continue by presenting the formal model and results.

2. THE MODEL

We consider a concentrated market that consists of three major companies and three controlling shareholders. Each of the shareholders has interests in two of the three companies, as follows:

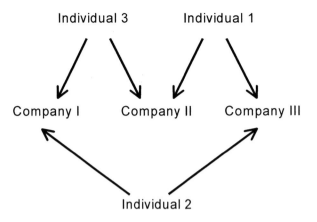

Figure 1.

This situation is suitable for a concentrated market where a small group of "economic elite" controls most of the major companies of a market. We assume three contests take place over three non-related and separate rents. In every contest one of the three companies in the market tries to achieve a specific benefit (rent) from the government and the other two companies try to prevent it. Again, we believe that attendance of the same companies in all the contests is a realistic assumption, and major companies, being controlled by the "economic elite" in a concentrated market, can find themselves on the same side during one contest and on two opposite sides in another contest. In order to determine whether to grant a benefit to a company or not, the government considers who controls this company and his political power. The political power of an individual is measured according to the aggregate amount of resources he invests in the three different contests that take place. We denote by x_i the amount of resources invested by individual i which represent this individual's political power.

A few points should be emphasized and clarified:

1. Basically, the contests are between the companies and not between the individuals. Only the government, when making its decision regarding the allocation of the rents, considers the abilities and the power of the individuals controlling the companies.

2. As explained above, an important assumption which distinguishes our model from the existing literature is that the government determines the political influence and power of an individual according to his aggregate efforts and contributions as a shareholder in all the companies he holds. We find this assumption realistic in concentrated markets where the government decides whether to benefit a company according to the power of this company's shareholders in the market, and where the power of the members of the "economic elite" is being determined according to their contributions to the market as a whole and not according to their behavior in one specific contest. This assumption does not mean that each individual has to make only one decision in order to determine his political power, but it *does* mean that the government will consider this individual's political power according to total investment in all the contests in which he participates.

3. The three contests which are taking place are non-related contests. The reason that each individual participates in more than one contest is that this is a concentrated market and thus an individual, belonging to the economic elite of that market, usually chooses to participate in most of its main contests, although no one is forced to participate in more than one contest.

In the following sections, we distinguish between a non-concentrated market and a concentrated one. When talking about a concentrated market, we assume mutual interests, as widely described above. The mutual interests change from one contest to another, such that one player may co-operate with player A against player B in one contest, while he will co-operate with player B against player A in a different contest. When talking about a non-concentrated market, we release the main character of the concentrated market - the existence of mutual interests among the participants.

2.1. A Concentrated Market

We now assume that the market is a concentrated one, which means that several individuals are the controlling shareholders of the most important and influential companies in the market, and as such these shareholders usually participate in the important contests and tenders taking place in this market. Under the current assumption, we consider three individuals (shareholders), each of whom controls two companies. Mutual interest exists between the shareholders, such that two shareholders control each company (see Figure 1 above).

Three contests take place, where the ith contest describes a situation in which the ith company tries to win a specific rent, and the other two companies try to prevent it.

The expected payoff of all three shareholders is given by,

$$E(U_1) = P_2 R_2 + P_3 R_3 + (1 - P_1)R_1 - x_1$$
$$E(U_2) = P_1 R_1 + P_3 R_3 + (1 - P_2)R_2 - x_2 \qquad (1)$$
$$E(U_3) = P_1 R_1 + P_2 R_2 + (1 - P_3)R_3 - x_3$$

Where R_i represents the rent that is being contested by company i in contest i and P_i represents the winning probability of this company in the contest.

Our contests require a contest-success function (see Hirshleifer (1989)). We opt to use the Tullock (1980) (see also Hillman and Riley (1989)) contest success function:

Contest 1: $P_1 = \dfrac{x_2 + x_3}{x_1 + x_2 + x_3}$; $1 - P_1 = \dfrac{x_1}{x_1 + x_2 + x_3}$

Contest 2: $P_2 = \dfrac{x_1 + x_3}{x_1 + x_2 + x_3}$; $1 - P_2 = \dfrac{x_2}{x_1 + x_2 + x_3}$ (2)

Contest 3: $P_3 = \dfrac{x_1 + x_2}{x_1 + x_2 + x_3}$; $1 - P_3 = \dfrac{x_3}{x_1 + x_2 + x_3}$

We would like to emphasize again the first clarification written above. The winning probabilities in (2) do not describe a situation of a contest between individuals or a contest between a company and an individual. If we consider the first contest, for example, we do not mean that individuals 2 and 3 fight against individual 1. What we *do* mean, is that the government compares the political strength of individuals 2 and 3 who control company 1 with the political strength of individual 1. If company 1 wins the contest, the individuals benefiting from it would be 2 and 3, and the individual who would lose would be individual 1. Thus the government has to decide if she prefers hurting individuals 2 and 3 or individual 1^2. In addition, the winning probabilities in (2) describe our unique assumption regarding the political power of the individuals. We did not differentiate between the amount of resources that each individual invested in one specific contest, but rather treated his total investment in the three contests together as the measurement for his political strength.

As can be seen, it is assumed that the three shareholders (individuals) value the rent in every contest equally. The simplest example is when the contest is over a public entitlement, such as the right to build a park or a highway. However symmetric valuations can also be the case in private commodities.

Each of the contestants maximizes his/her expected payoff by determining its optimal aggregate level of investment in the contests, $\dfrac{\partial E(U_i)}{\partial x_i} = 0$ $\forall i = 1,2,3$. Solving the first order conditions of all three shareholders together, we obtain the Nash equilibrium resources invested by them as follows:

$$x_1 = \frac{R_1(R_1 + R_2)(R_1 + R_3)(R_2 + R_3)^2}{4(R_1 R_2 + R_1 R_3 + R_2 R_3)^2}$$

$$x_2 = \frac{R_2(R_1 + R_2)(R_1 + R_3)^2(R_2 + R_3)}{4(R_1 R_2 + R_1 R_3 + R_2 R_3)^2}$$ (3)

$$x_3 = \frac{R_3(R_1 + R_2)^2(R_1 + R_3)(R_2 + R_3)}{4(R_1 R_2 + R_1 R_3 + R_2 R_3)^2}$$

The rent dissipation of the contests is given by:

---

[2] It should be noted, that individuals 2 and 3 have interests not only in company 1 but also in companies 3 and 2, respectively. Nonetheless, if company 1 wins they will be satisfied because they care about this company, and the only individual that will not be satisfied at all is individual 1.

$$X = \sum_{i=1}^{3} x_i = \frac{(R_1 + R_2)(R_1 + R_3)(R_2 + R_3)}{2(R_1 R_2 + R_1 R_3 + R_2 R_3)} \tag{4}$$

And the relative rent dissipation in all of the contests is:

$$RRD = \frac{(R_1 + R_2)(R_1 + R_3)(R_2 + R_3)}{2(R_1 R_2 + R_1 R_3 + R_2 R_3)(R_1 + R_2 + R_3)} \tag{5}$$

2.1.1. Comparative Statics

It is clear that increasing any of the rents, R_i, will increase the total expenditure of the contestants.

Let us now consider the effect of a change in the different rents on the expenditure of each shareholder. Since the functions in (3) are symmetric with relation to the different players, we consider the case of individual number 1:

$$\frac{\partial x_1}{\partial R_1} = \frac{(R_2 + R_3)^2 [(R_1)^3 (R_2 + R_3) + 3(R_1)^2 R_2 R_3 + R_2 R_3 (R_1 R_2 + R_1 R_3 + R_2 R_3)]}{4(R_1 R_2 + R_1 R_3 + R_2 R_3)^3} \tag{6}$$

$$\frac{\partial x_1}{\partial R_2} = \frac{R_1 (R_1 + R_3)(R_2 + R_3)[R_1 (R_2)^2 + 2R_1 R_2 R_3 + (R_2)^2 R_3 - R_1 (R_3)^2 - R_2 (R_3)^2]}{4(R_1 R_2 + R_1 R_3 + R_2 R_3)^3} \tag{7}$$

$$\frac{\partial x_1}{\partial R_3} = \frac{R_1 (R_1 + R_2)(R_2 + R_3)[-R_1 (R_2)^2 + 2R_1 R_2 R_3 - (R_2)^2 R_3 + R_1 (R_3)^2 + R_2 (R_3)^2]}{4(R_1 R_2 + R_1 R_3 + R_2 R_3)^3} \tag{8}$$

The sign of (6) is clearly positive. Let us now look at the sign of the derivatives in (7) and (8). Since (7) and (8) are symmetric we consider the derivative in (7). From (7) we obtain that,

$$\frac{\partial x_1}{\partial R_2} \overset{>}{\underset{<}{=}} 0 \text{ iff } R_1 (R_2)^2 + 2R_1 R_2 R_3 + (R_2)^2 R_3 - R_1 (R_3)^2 - R_2 (R_3)^2 \overset{>}{\underset{<}{=}} 0. \tag{9}$$

If $(R_2)^2 + 2R_2 R_3 - (R_3)^2 > 0$ the condition in (9) is equivalent to

$R_1 \overset{>}{\underset{<}{=}} \dfrac{R_2 R_3 (R_3 - R_2)}{(R_2)^2 + 2R_2 R_3 - (R_3)^2}$ and if $(R_2)^2 + 2R_2 R_3 - (R_3)^2 < 0$ the condition in (9) is

equivalent to $R_1 \overset{<}{\underset{>}{=}} \dfrac{R_2 R_3 (R_3 - R_2)}{(R_2)^2 + 2R_2 R_3 - (R_3)^2}$. Let us now analyze two different cases:

a. If $R_2 \geq R_3$, $(R_2)^2 + 2R_2R_3 - (R_3)^2 > 0$ thus the condition in (9) is equivalent to

$$R_1 \underset{<}{\overset{>}{=}} \frac{R_2R_3(R_3 - R_2)}{(R_2)^2 + 2R_2R_3 - (R_3)^2}$$. It can be shown that the numerator of the fraction is

negative while the denominator is positive, which means that the fraction itself is

negative. R_1 is greater than the fraction and hence $\dfrac{\partial x_1}{\partial R_2} > 0$. Namely if R_2 is greater

or equal to R_3 an increase in the rent R_2 will increase shareholder 1's resources
invested in the contests.

b. If $R_3 > R_2$ the sign of $(R_2)^2 + 2R_2R_3 - (R_3)^2$ is not clear, and consequently we

cannot determine if the sign of the inequality in (9) changes when dividing (9)

by $(R_2)^2 + 2R_2R_3 - (R_3)^2$.   However,   if $R_3 > \left(1 + \sqrt{2}\right)R_2$ then

$(R_2)^2 + 2R_2R_3 - (R_3)^2 < 0$ and consequently, in this situation, the condition for

$$\frac{\partial x_1}{\partial R_2} \underset{<}{\overset{>}{=}} 0 \ \text{ rests on } \ R_1 \underset{>}{\overset{<}{=}} \frac{R_2R_3(R_3 - R_2)}{(R_2)^2 + 2R_2R_3 - (R_3)^2}$$. It can be seen that when this is

the case, the nominator of the fraction is positive, the denominator, as mentioned, is

negative, and thus the fraction itself is negative, R_1 is greater and $\dfrac{\partial x_1}{\partial R_2} < 0$.

As a result of the symmetry between the different groups we conclude that,

Proposition 1:

a. $\dfrac{\partial X}{\partial R_i} > 0 \ \forall i = 1, 2, 3$;

b. $\dfrac{\partial x_i}{\partial R_i} > 0$;

c. $\dfrac{\partial x_i}{\partial R_j} \underset{<}{\overset{>}{=}} 0 \ \text{ iff } \ R_i(R_j)^2 + 2R_iR_jR_k + (R_j)^2R_k - R_i(R_k)^2 - R_j(R_k)^2 \underset{<}{\overset{>}{=}} 0$

$$\forall \ i, j, k = 1, 2, 3 \ and \ i \neq j \neq k$$

The proposition states that increasing any of the rents will increase the rent dissipation in
the contests. In addition, it states that the increase in the rent will always increase the
investment of the "single" player in the contest and has an ambiguous effect on the two other
individuals. This ambiguity is somewhat similar to the results presented in the literature (see

for example Nti (1999), Epstein and Nitzan (2002, 2006[3])) [4]. However, there is an important difference between the results in our modified model and the results in the literature. The literature deals with a situation where only one contest takes place. As such, a change in R_i means a change in the valuation of the rent by player i though the valuations of the other players remain the same. In our modified model there are *three* different contests, and when we talk about a change in R_i it means that the three contestants changed there valuation of the rent in the *i*th contest (which as we mentioned above is the same valuation). We would expect that such a symmetric change will cause the three individuals to react in the same way, however we find that the response is again ambiguous.

Let us analyze this ambiguity in the following corollary:

Corollary:

a. If $R_2 \geq R_j \; \forall j = 1,3$ then $\dfrac{\partial x_i}{\partial R_2} > 0 \; \forall i = 1,2,3$.

b. If $R_j > \left(1 + \sqrt{2}\right) R_2 \; \forall j = 1,3$ then $\dfrac{\partial x_i}{\partial R_2} < 0 \; \forall i \neq 2$.

c. If $\dfrac{\partial x_i}{\partial R_j} < 0$ then

$$\frac{\partial x_k}{\partial R_j} + \frac{\partial x_j}{\partial R_j} > - \frac{\partial x_i}{\partial R_j} \quad \forall i,j,k = 1,2,3 \; and \; i \neq j, \; j \neq k, i \neq k$$

In light of the difference between our modified model and the literature, as detailed above, let us try to explain the above corollary. In our game, the utility of every individual is

---

[3] Epstein and Nitzan (2006) developed a framework to study a *general* class of two-player public-policy contests and examined the effect of a change in the proposed policy, a change that may affect the payoffs of one or both contestants, on their effort and performance. In this chapter Epstein generalizes the comparative statics results presented in the literature that focus on the effect of changes either in the value of a contest prize in symmetric contests or in one of the contestants' valuation of the prize in asymmetric contests, assuming special forms of our general CSF.

[4] Supposing there is a contest between three individuals. The expected payoff of each of the individuals is given by

$$E(U_i) = P_i \, R_i - x_i \quad \text{with a contest success function determined by} \quad P_i = \frac{x_i}{x_1 + x_2 + x_3} \quad i = 1,2,3.$$

In equilibrium $\dfrac{\partial x_i^*}{\partial R_i} \begin{smallmatrix} > \\ = \\ < \end{smallmatrix} 0$ iff $R_i \begin{smallmatrix} > \\ = \\ < \end{smallmatrix} \dfrac{R_j R_k}{3(R_j + R_k)}$ and $\dfrac{\partial x_j^*}{\partial R_i} \begin{smallmatrix} > \\ = \\ < \end{smallmatrix} 0$ iff

$R_j \begin{smallmatrix} > \\ = \\ < \end{smallmatrix} \dfrac{3 R_i R_k}{(R_i + R_k)} \quad \forall i,j,k = 1,2,3 \; i \neq j \neq k.$

influenced by three separate rents – not only one. Let us focus on individual 1. Individual 1, like the two other shareholders, participates in all the three contests. In the first contest, individual 1 tries to achieve a rent by himself. This is a "regular" rent seeking situation, with the small difference that individual 1 fights against two opponents and not only one. Therefore, and unsurprisingly, when the size of the rent in the first contest changes, individual 1 changes the amount of resources he invests in the same direction. For example, when there is an increase in R_1, individual 1 has a higher benefit from winning the contest and thus will increase his efforts in equilibrium. Now let's analyze the effect of an increase in one of the other rents, say R_2. Individual 1 knows, that an increase in R_2 will cause *individual 2* to increase his investment in the contest. That is because individual 2 is the "single" player in the second contest. Now individual 1 has to decide whether he should react by increasing his investment this time also, thus trying to prevent individual 2 getting stronger. Individual 1 knows that now he and individual 2 are acting as opponents, but in the third contest they are going to co-operate against individual 3. Thus, individual 1 actually considers which of the two contests is more important to him: the second contest or the third one. In case the second contest is the more important one (which means $R_2 > R_3$) individual 1 increases the amount of resources he invests as a response to the increase of individual 2's efforts. In this case the contest becomes a more intensive one. However, in case the third one is much more important (when $R_3 > \left(1 + \sqrt{2}\right)R_2$), individual 1 lets individual 2 get stronger in the second contest, and even decreases his own efforts which by itself strengthens individual 2 even more, because he knows that this will help him win the third and much more important contest.

In light of the above explanation, let us analyze another interesting possibility. As we can see from the Corollary (a) if $R_2 \geq R_3$ and $R_2 \geq R_1$ namely R$_2$ is the largest rents out of the three contests, so increasing this rent increases the variance between the largest rent and that of the rest. In this case, not only does individual 2 increases his expenditure but also that of individuals 1 and 3. If, on the other hand, R$_2$ is the smallest rent in the contests, namely it is the underdog of the three contests, and not only that but it is sufficiently small, $R_j > \left(1 + \sqrt{2}\right)R_2 \;\forall j = 1,3$, then increasing this rent will only increase the expenditure of individual 2 while decreasing the expenditure of the other two individuals. This will happen because both individual 1 and individual 3 know that letting individual 2 getting stronger would help them in their more important contests.

An interesting point relates to the magnitude of the increase of the expenditure of individual number 2. From proposition (a) it is clear that increasing R$_2$ will increase the total rent dissipation. Therefore, since individual 1 and 3 have decreased their expenditure and individual 2 increases expenditure, we learn that the increase in the expenditure of individual 2 is greater than the decrease of both the other individuals.

The main difference between this result and the common result in the rent-seeking literature, is that when making decisions, each individual takes into account not only considerations relating to one specific contest, but also considerations that relate to other interactions between him and the other participants. Before letting a contest between himself and someone else who belongs to the "economic elite" to become more intensive, he considers whether it is better letting his opponent getting stronger in one contest and by doing so improve his own probability of winning in other contests which are more important for him. We believe that this behavior is realistic in concentrated markets, where both the government and the "economic elite" itself relate to any single contest as one of a broader system of contests and interactions, and thus do not treat one contest only at its own narrow aspects.

2.2. Non-concentrated Market

We now turn to look at the comparable non-concentrated market contests. Under the assumption of this stage, no mutual interests exist between the individuals. Again, three contests take place, but now each of the individuals participates in all three contests on his own and no co-operations exist. Each of the participants invests resources in order to win and obtain rents for himself. The probability of a participant winning a contest is determined again according to his relative political influence compared to that of the other two participants, and as mentioned many times above, what distinguishes this model from the standard rent-seeking literature is that a participant's political influence is determined according to the amount of resources spent by him in *all* the contests in which he participates. We actually still assume that the government takes into account one's investment in all the contests he participates in, but we change the main character of concentrated markets – the mutual interest character.

Based on Tullock (1980), the contest success function of participant i in all of the three contests is: $\dfrac{x_i}{\sum x_i}$. Consequently, the parallel contest to that presented in the concentrated market will therefore be as follows:

$$E(U_i) = \frac{x_i}{x_1 + x_2 + x_3} R_1 + \frac{x_i}{x_1 + x_2 + x_3} R_2 + \frac{x_i}{x_1 + x_2 + x_3} R_3 - x_i = \frac{x_i}{x_1 + x_2 + x_3} \sum R_j - x_i \qquad (10)$$

Again, it is assumed that the three individuals value the rent in every contest equally. Each of the contestants maximizes his/her expected payoff by determining its optimal level of investment in the three contests, $\dfrac{\partial E(U_i)}{\partial x_i} = 0 \ \forall i = 1,2,3$. Solving the first order conditions of all three shareholders together, we obtain the Nash equilibrium resources invested by them as follows:

$$x_i = 2/9 * \sum R_j \qquad (11)$$

The rent dissipation of the contests is given by:

$$X = \sum x_i = 2/3 * \sum R_j \qquad (12)$$

The relative rent dissipation in all contests is:

$$RRD = 2/3 \tag{13}$$

And the expected utility equals:

$$E(U_i) = 1/9 * \sum R_j \tag{14}$$

Let us now compare the concentrated market where individuals have mutual interests with the non-concentrated market, where individuals do not have mutual interests. In order to simplify the comparison between the results obtained in the concentrated and non-concentrated markets, we turn to a specific example, according to which the three rents in the contests are equal: $R_1 = R_2 = R_3 = R$ (similar results can be obtained in the general case).

Non-concentrated market: *Concentrated market:*

$$
\begin{array}{lcl}
x_i = 2/3 * R & > & x_i = 4/9 * R \\[2em]
X = \sum x_i = 2R & > & X = \sum x_i = 4/3 * R \\[2em]
E(U_i) = 1/3 * R & < & E(U_i) = 11/9 * R \\[2em]
RRD = 2/3 & > & RRD = 4/9
\end{array}
\tag{15}
$$

While in a non-concentrated market each of the contestants spends 2/3 of R, in a concentrated market each of them spends 4/9 of it. Regarding the rent dissipation, the aggregate amount of resources being spent by the individuals in all the three contests is $2R$ in a non-concentrated market and 4/3 *R in a concentrated one. The aggregate amount of rents in the contests is $3R$, which means that in a non-concentrated market the contestants spend 2/3 of this amount, and in a concentrated market they spend only 4/9 of it. Therefore the concentrated market has decreased the rent dissipation and increased the expected payoffs of the contestants.

Proposition 2:

In a concentrated market where individuals have mutual interests, the outlay of the contestants will decrease, rent dissipation will decrease and the expected payoff will increase.

Proposition 2 is a direct outcome of the mutual interests that exist under the concentrated market circumstances. In the non-concentrated market, each of the individuals participates in the contests by investing his own resources in order to win the rents. However, in the concentrated market where the individuals co-operate and have mutual interests, the winning probability of an individual is determined not only by his own efforts and resources but also by the resources of his partner with whom he has mutual interests in that specific contest. As a result, individuals reduce the amount of resources they spend compared to the non-concentrated market contests. Thus the rent dissipation in the contests is reduced.

3. CONCLUSION

In a concentrated market, where individuals have mutual interests, several single groups control many companies and participate in rent-seeking contests. The traditional rent-seeking theory does not examine possible implications of this concentrated situation on the common rent-seeking model[5]. We assumed three shareholders controlling three companies. Three contests take place while in every contest each company tries to achieve a certain rent and the other two companies try to prevent this. The CSFs were formulated based on the assumption that the winning probability of a company, participating in a contest, is proportional to the relative amount of resources spent by its controlling shareholders in comparison to the amount of resources being spent by all the participants in the contest. Differing from traditional rent-seeking theory, we do not take the amount of resources that were spent in the framework of a specific contest, but the total amount of resources each shareholder spends throughout all the contests in which he participates. The main difference between our results and the common results in the rent-seeking literature is that when making decisions, each individual takes into account not only considerations which relate to one specific contest, but also to those that relate to other interactions between him and the other participants. Thus when the rent in one of the contests increases, an individual takes into account other interactions between him and his opponent in this specific contest, before letting the contest become more intensive. We believe that this behavior is realistic in concentrated markets, where both the government and the "economic elite" itself relate to any single contest as one of a broader system of contests and interactions.

Finally, we compared the outcome of the concentrated market where individuals have mutual interests with the non-concentrated market where individuals have no mutual interests at all. It is shown in the case of equal rents, that the resources being spent by each individual and the rent-dissipation are lower in the concentrated market, while the expected payoff of the participants is higher.

We are aware of the fact that there are many other differences between concentrated and non-concentrated markets. In this chapter we examined mainly the differences which relate to the mutual interests aspect, but for example, it is also reasonable to assume, that in non-concentrated markets, one's winning probability in every separate contest is determined according to his investment in this contest alone. We plan to further investigate this and other differences between concentrated and non-concentrated markets in future research.

---

[5] For example, the 20 major groups in the Israeli Economic Elite have holdings in the most significant and influential companies in Israel and are involved in the main Israeli transactions and tenders.

ACKNOWLEDGEMENTS

Financial support from the Adar Foundation of the Economics Department of Bar-Ilan University is gratefully acknowledged.

REFERENCES

Claessens, S., Djankov, S., & Lang, L.H.P. (2000). The Separation of Ownership and Control in East Asian Corporations. *Journal of Financial Economics, 58,* 81-112

Epstein, G.S., & Nitzan, S. (2002). Endogenous Public Policy, Politicization and Welfare. *Journal of Public Economic Theory, 4,* 661-677.

Epstein, G.S., & Nitzan, S. (2006). Effort and Performance in Public Policy Contests. *Journal of Public Economic Theory,* 8(2), 265-282.

Epstein, G.S. & Nitzan, S. (2007). *Endogenous Public Policy and Contests.* Springer.

Faccio, M. (2006). Politically Connected Firms. *American Economic Review, 96,* 369-386.

Fisman, R., (2001). Estimating the Value of Political Connections. *American Economic Review, 91,* 1095-1102.

Gugler, K. (1998). Corporate Ownership Structure in Austria. *Empirica, 25,* 285-307.

Hillman, A.L., & Riley, J.G. (1989). Politically Contestable Rents and Transfers. *Economics and Politics, 1,* 17-39.

Hirshleifer, J., (1989). Conflict and Rent Seeking Success Functions: Ratio vs. Difference Models of Relative Success. *Public Choice, 63,* 101-112.

Kang, D.C. (2003). Transaction Costs and Crony Capitalism in East Asia. *Comparative Politics, 35,* 439-458.

Morck, R.K., Stangeland, D.A., & Yeung, B. (2000). Inherited wealth, corporate control, and economic growth: The Canadian Disease?. In R.K. Morck. (Ed.), *Concentrated corporate ownership.* University of Chicago Press: Chicago.

Nitzan, S. (1991). Collective Rent Dissipation. *The Economic Journal, 101,* 1522-1534.

Nitzan, S. (1994). Modelling Rent Seeking Contests. *European Journal of Political Economy, 10,* 41-60.

Nti, K.O. (1999). Rent Seeking with Asymmetric Valuations. *Public Choice, 98,* 415-430.

Shleifer, A., & Vishny, R.W. (1994). Politicians and firms. *Quarterly Journal of Economics, 109,* 995-1025.

Tullock, G. (1980). Efficient Rent Seeking. In J. Buchanan, R. Tollison, & G. Tullock (Eds.), *Toward a Theory of the Rent Seeking Society,* (pp. 97-112). College Station: Texas A&M University Press.

Ursprung, H.W. (1990). Public Goods, Rent Dissipation and Candidate Competition. *Economics and Politics, 2,* 115-32.

Yurtoglu, B.B. (2000). Ownership, Control and Performance of Turkish Listed Firms. *Empirica, 27,* 193-222.

In: Political Economy Research Focus
Editor: Walter R. Levin, pp. 149-169

ISBN: 978-1-60456-154-8
© 2008 Nova Science Publishers, Inc.

Chapter 8

OPTIMUM CURRENCY AREA AND POLITICAL ECONOMY APPROACHES TO EXCHANGE RATE REGIMES: TOWARDS AN ANALYTICAL SYNTHESIS

Thomas D. Willett[*]

The Claremont Colleges

ABSTRACT

My goal in this paper is not so much to present a case for the right answer for Canada or the UK as to try to lay out the beginnings of a framework for analyzing both the normative economic issue of what countries should do and the positive political issue of what they are likely to do. A key theme is that the simple choices involving monetary integration involve a complex range of issues, some of which are still only dimly understood. Fortunately, however, we do have considerable analysis, both political and economic, on which we can draw.

INTRODUCTION

Should medium size countries such as Canada and the UK maintain their monetary independence or should they join the fashionable trend toward tying their monetary fates to larger currency areas? Unlike New Zealand, whose international exchange is widely diversified, it's clear that if Canada and the UK were to retire their dollar and pound respectively, Canada should choose the American dollar or some new North American monetary unit and the UK should choose the euro. Having a large monetary area next door

---

[*] Horton Professor of Economics, The Claremont Colleges, 160 East 10th Street, Claremont, CA 91711, Phone: 909-621-8787, E-mail: Thomas.willett@cgu.edu. Presented at the University of Victoria Conference on "Britain and Canada and their Large Neighbouring Monetary Unions" held 17-18 October 2003. Comments from the conference participants and two anonymous reviewers, research assistance from Lukas Loncko, and financial assistance from the national Science Foundation are gratefully acknowledged.

makes that part of the debate easier to answer. The much harder question is whether the domestic currency should be abandoned in the first place. There is considerable dispute in both countries on this fundamental question, as there is in similarly placed countries such as Mexico and Sweden. The immediate seriousness of the debate is much stronger for the UK than for perhaps any other country at present (since Sweden recently voted against entry at this time) and the new EU entrants do not enjoy the opt out clauses of Sweden and the UK. In Canada, however, there has been a vocal minority of experts calling for monetary integration that has attracted considerable public attention.

A striking feature of these debates is how hard it is for non-experts to gain an understanding of the key issues on which such choices should be made. Media coverage, of course, focuses on sound bites, and in this arena exaggerated claims generally drive out reasoned analysis in a sort of Gresham's law process. Thus the public is frequently told (by different people of course) that either choice would be an economic and/or political disaster.

My goal in this paper is not so much to present a case for the right answer for Canada or the UK as to try to lay out the beginnings of a framework for analyzing both the normative economic issue of what countries should do and the positive political issue of what they are likely to do. A key theme is that the simple choices involving monetary integration involve a complex range of issues, some of which are still only dimly understood. Fortunately, however, we do have considerable analysis, both political and economic, on which we can draw.

For most serious international monetary economists, the starting point for the analysis of such currency issues is the optimum currency area (OCA) approach, pioneered by Robert Mundell (1961), Ronald McKinnon (1963) and Peter Kenen (1969). It highlights the crucial point that no one exchange rate is best for all countries. There are both costs and benefits to all exchange rate regimes and their ratios will vary systematically across countries based on factors identified in the OCA literature.[1]

While the development of the OCA approach has done much to raise the quality of the analysis of exchange rate regimes, it has made much less progress in reducing the amount and volume of the debate about exchange rate issues. A major reason for this is the number of different considerations that have been shown to be relevant for the determination of (economically) optimal exchange rate regimes. These have risen well into double figures, and there is considerable disagreement about their relative importance and how to operationalize them.

Given the time required to master the full technical literature on OCA analysis, and the often inconclusive results of doing so, it is not surprising that a substantial proportion of the policy literature by economists takes just a few of the considerations from OCA analysis to emphasize. The problem is that authors often give the impression that these few are the only important considerations. Nor should we be surprised that by some mysterious process, economists who are strong advocates of fixed exchange rates tend to emphasize criteria on

---

[1] For recent discussions of OCA analysis see de Grauwe (1997), Krugman (1995), Masson and Taylor (1993), Tavlas (1993), (1994), Wihlborg and Willett (1999), and Willett (2003b). Of course, there have been many criticisms of specific aspects of OCA theory and in some cases these have escalated to criticisms of the whole framework. Perhaps the most common example of the later came from new classical economists who argued that traditional OCA analysis was based on outmoded Keynesian ideas. It is true that OCA theory was initially developed within a simple Keynesian framework, but most of its key insights continue to hold in all but he most extreme new classical versions of modern macroeconomic analysis.

which fixed rates look good, while advocates of floating rates tend to focus on other criteria that support flexible rates. This tendency for advocacy pieces is not limited to full time popularizers. Sadly, examples can be found from some of our most distinguished economists.[2] Thus, it is not difficult for a policy maker to find economists to support almost any position on exchange rate policy they would like.

While one may debate whether or not exchange rate policy is too important to be left to the economists, there's little question that it seldom is. This helps explain the less than perfect success with which the normative theory of OCA predicts actual exchange rate policies. Indeed, Charles Goodhart (1995) has rightly pointed out that OCA theory has little explanatory power when it comes to the formation of currency unions. Here political considerations dominate. Despite the amount of rhetoric about economic considerations, the creation of the euro does little to contradict Goodhart's argument. OCA theory does have a good deal greater power to explain countries' choices with respect to the degree of exchange rate flexibility, but for the development of a satisfactory positive theory of the choice of exchange rate regimes additional considerations must be added.

A BRIEF OVERVIEW OF A
POLITICAL ECONOMY FRAMEWORK

The obvious place to look is in the political realm. It is virtually meaningless to talk simply about the relative importance of economic versus political considerations for policy relevance since the salience of economic effects is determined through the political process. Thus, a good theory of the political economy of the choice of exchange rate regimes should include the basic elements of the standard economy theory of OCA's and expand and modify these to take into account political objectives and recognition that economic policies are normally determined through a political process.

Traditional OCA theory focuses on aggregate economic efficiency. An obvious step to make the theory more politically relevant is to look at the distributional issues of who gains and who loses. Gainers and losers would then in turn be weighted by their influence in the political process. As we know from public choice theory, it is not just numbers that matter. Small well-organized groups are often much more influential than large groups with little organization, such as consumers, in large part because of free rider problems.

What motivates choices, however, is perceptions of gains and losses and for relevant analysis we must consider the possibility of systematic biases of perception. The new field of behavioral economics and finance is showing that systematic misperceptions are important for some areas of economics and finance.[3] The public choice concept of rational ignorance suggests that such biases may be even greater in the political sphere.[4] Thus, in looking at the political economy of currency choices, we need to take seriously issues of biases due to short time horizons and imperfect information flows. The conceptual schemes or mental models that actors adopt can also be of major importance. For example, a Keynesian who believes

---

[2] See Willett (2001a).
[3] For references and an application to international finance see Willett (2000a).
[4] This idea is that it does not pay to invest in acquiring information in areas where you are unlikely to be able to influence outcomes.

that discretionary domestic macroeconomic policy can have substantial effects on unemployment will be more concerned about adopting a fixed exchange rate than a new classical macro economist who believes that discretionary macro policy can do little good.

For the political economy of exchange rate regimes, time horizons and the operation of time asymmetries can also be quite important. A good deal of international macroeconomic literature has focused on the possible beneficial role that the discipline effects of fixed exchange rates can play in overcoming domestic time inconsistency problems. Less well understood is that pegged exchange rates can generate time inconsistency problems of their own. Because the benefits of pegging exchange rates are often heavily skewed toward the beginning, while many of the costs tend to be delayed, pegged rates will tend to have more favorable benefit-cost ratios in the short run that in the long run. Combined with short time horizons for political actors, these time asymmetries can help explain the popularity of adopting pegged rates regimes that fail in the longer run.[5]

Finally, we need to include pure political considerations such as foreign policy and desires for political integration that have been so important in the formation of the Euro areas. It will be argued that the euro case is quite unusual. Normally the major non-economic political considerations will operate against, rather than in favor of, the formation of fixed rate areas.

Of course, a full integration of the OCA and political economy approaches lies outside the scope of any one paper (or even one lifetime), but there is a substantial literature on which we can draw to begin to sketch out some key elements of such an analytic synthesis.

We begin in section 3 with a brief review of some of the major considerations emphasized in the literature on OCA theory. We interpret this literature as implying that for most countries, it is economically optimal to have neither of the extremes of genuinely fixed or completely free floats in which exchange rate developments have no influence on domestic monetary policy.[6] Intermediate exchange rate regimes have been prone to considerable instability in a world of substantial capital mobility. Section 4 argues that this problem is due as much to political economy as to technical economic considerations. The role of time asymmetries in the effects of exchange rate changes and the resulting creation of time inconsistency problems where policy makers have short time horizons is emphasized.

Section 4 turns to a broader range of political considerations that are relevant to the choice of currency regimes. It stresses that just as there are a number of economic considerations relevant for OCA theory, there are also many different types of political considerations that may be relevant for the actual choice of currency regimes. Section 5 offers a brief application to the UK Treasury's five economic tests for euro entry. Section 6 concludes with an emphasis on the need to take uncertainty explicitly into account when choosing a currency regime.

---

[5] See Willett (1998) and (2001b).

[6] A free float is typically defined as having no official intervention in the foreign exchange market. Some use the term more loosely to include regimes where intervention is used to smooth fluctuations but not the trend of the exchange rate. Even under a completely free flat a government could use exchange rate movements as a partial guide for monetary policy. This could be accomplished by varying domestic open market operations in light of exchange market developments. More commonly, however, a country following such an intermediate approach would practice unsterilized intervention in the foreign exchange market. Where there is no sterilization, intervention to support a falling currency would automatically lead to a tightening of domestic monetary policy while intervention to hold down the currency would generate expansionary monetary policy.

AN OVERVIEW OF THE BASIC ECONOMICS OF OCA THEORY

The basic idea of OCA theory is that there are both costs and benefits to any monetary regime. The benefits of a single currency include reduced transactions costs and the removal of uncertainty about the future relative values of different currencies. Individual currency areas should continue to be expanded as long as the marginal benefits exceed the costs, which are associated primarily with the loss of the exchange rate as a policy tool and the connected loss of the ability to follow an independent monetary policy. In general the expansion of a currency's domain will have diminishing marginal benefits and increasing marginal costs. Their intersection would delineate the boundary of an optimal currency area. Of course the early OCA theorists recognized that the globe was already divided up into nations so these were typically taken as the unit of analysis. The OCA question was thus typically posed as whether a country should maintain an independent currency or join with others in a broader currency area.

While the initial contribution by Mundell (1961) argued that the liquidity value of money was less, the smaller its domain and this was developed into a major focus of McKinnon's (1963) following contribution, the vase majority of OCA analysis has focused on the evaluation of the costs of given up an independent currency and how these vary based on structural characteristics and patterns of disturbances. The European Commission: "One Market, One Money" (1990) reflected a major effort to focus attention on the magnitude of possible benefits from currency union.[7]

A key focus of OCA analysis has been on alternative methods of adjusting to disequilibrium. When the domestic and international sectors of an economy become misaligned with one another, which should be adjusted to the other? Under fixed exchange rates the domestic sectors will be forced to adjust to the international sectors as under the classical gold standard mechanism. Under a pure floating rate system, it is the international sectors that must largely adjust to the domestic sectors. Which mode of accommodation is preferable will depend on the relative importance of the sectors and the relative costs and effectiveness of the adjustment mechanisms available.

Under ideal systems of fixed and flexible rates, there would be little difference. With highly flexible domestic economies, the cost of adjustment would be low and the issue will essentially come down to the relative importance of domestic versus external price stability. This would in turn normally depend on the relative size of the domestic versus external sectors. Thus the more open is the economy, i.e. the larger is the external sector relative to the internal sector, the greater would be the case for fixed exchange rates.

In such analysis it is openness with respect to prospective currency partner that is relevant. Thus while not emphasized until OCA analysis, the pattern of one's trade can be as important as the overall level of openness of an economy. For example, while New Zealand's overall level of openness to trade is relatively high, its pattern of trade is quite diversified so it does not have an obvious partner for a currency union. The Baltic States are all small, highly open economies but initial proposals for a Baltic currency area actually made little sense

---

Thus sterilized intervention is much more likely to contribute to the buildup of disequilibrium than unsterilized intervention. See Willett (2003b).

[7] The imbalance in technical analysis was due primarily to the dearth of costs versus benefits of attractive analytical approaches to dealing with the latter. See Krugman (1969).

because they had little trade with one another. On this criteria while the UK does trade heavily with the euro economies, this represents a far lower percent of its overall trade than for Canada with respect to the United States.

Such multi-country analysis raises an issue of path dependence in the formation of currency areas. A pattern of trade could easily be such that it could make sense for a group of countries to collectively agree to form a currency area that would not have formed through independent decision making based on OCA criteria. While not the driving force for the creation of the euro, such prospective path dependence likely did play some role in the success of the negotiations for EMU.

To this point we have implicitly assumed that exchange rate adjustments are an effective mechanism for adjusting external imbalances. In fact, however, this will depend on the openness of the economy. For a tiny highly open economy such as, say Luxembourg, there is little pure internal sector and a change in the exchange rate would bring about little change in relative prices. Most domestic wages and prices would rise in step with a devaluation. In effect, the internal sector would be so heavily influenced by the external sector that there would be little effective independence between them.

For these purposes the external sector includes not only exports but also domestic sales of goods and services that are close substitutes. Thus, we again reach the conclusion that the higher the degree of openness, the greater is the case for fixed over flexible exchange rates. Recent literature has shown that international currency substitution and the denomination of debt and other contracts in foreign currency are additional important aspects of openness for this purpose.[8]

Where currency substitution is high, exchange rates are likely to be more volatile with the possibility of small shocks generating changes in exchange rates. Where there are substantial unhedged foreign currency positions, large exchange rate changes can in turn have large wealth effects. In such circumstances large currency depreciations can be a major cause of bankruptcies. This mechanism was a major cause of the severity of the Asian crisis. To date such considerations have been primarily relevant to developing rather than industrial countries.

Note that these effects are distinct from capital mobility per se. The latter is often mentioned as a criterion for OCA analysis, but the effects on the choice of optimal exchange rate regimes is not clear cut. Assuming that speculation is stabilizing, high capital mobility can make either regime work better on some criteria. It lessens effective monetary autonomy under both regimes but also helps spread out the effects of shocks. Whether the latter is desirable depends in large part on whether the shocks are domestic or foreign. In general high capital mobility reduces the differences between fixed versus flexible rates and does not generate a clear comparative advantage for one regime or the other.[9] It does, however, clearly make the operation of intermediate regimes more difficult. This holds especially for the narrow band, adjustable peg type of regime adopted at Bretton Woods.

On the openness score, both Britain and Canada fall in an intermediate category between tiny countries such as Estonia where a fixed rate seems clearly optimal and a giant like the US where some form of flexibility is clearly best. There is as yet little consensus among

---

[8] While there is considerable use of the US dollar in Canada, there is little evidence that this is so high that it is a major source of exchange rate instability or that it undercuts the effectiveness of exchange rate adjustments. Currency substitution is even less of a problem for Britain.

[9] See Tower and Willett (1976).

economists about boundary levels of openness. Countries much smaller and more open than Britain and Canada have had experiences with flexible rates that many economists have judged to be quite successful, but not all share this assessment. We see the scope for controversy highlighted by the papers on Canada in this volume. My own reading of the evidence is more in line with the generally positive analysis of the success of Canada's floating presented by Laidler and by Schembri than with the negative views of Grubel and of Harris, but collectively these papers give the reader a good basis for making their own judgments. What we can clearly say on the openness criteria is that both Britain and Canada are large enough to have viable independent currencies. Thus the decision to pursue monetary integration is one of choice, not necessity.

Where internal adjustment is costly because of sticky wages and prices and low factor mobility, deflationary policies will generate recessions and high unemployment[10]. The openness criteria still applies, but the threshold of openness at which fixed rates should be preferred is raised. In effect exchange rate adjustments then provide a second best method of generating effective real wage and price flexibility and thus lower the costs of adjustment.[11] Again neither Britain nor Canada appears to have sufficient labor market flexibility to make the openness criteria irrelevant.

So far we have discussed the OCA criteria of labor market flexibility and openness that were stressed in the initial OCA contributions and the subsequent expansion of the concept of openness to include international currency- and asset substitution. Much of the more recent literature has focused on the influence of patterns of shocks and efforts to measure these. As Masson and Taylor argue "The cost of monetary union for a given country involve the loss of exchange rate flexibility, which can be seen as an instrument to cushion 'shocks' to the economy" (1993: 381). As Bayoumi and Eichengreen put it "only if disturbances are asymmetrically distributed across countries or if speeds of adjustment are markedly different will distinctive national macroeconomic policies be needed and the constraints of monetary union be a hindrance" (1994: 1). As they go on to note "subsequent to Mundell, the [OCA] literature has followed Kenen in linking structural characteristics of economies, as in particular, the sectoral composition of production, to the characteristics of chocks" (1969: 4).

The analysis of patterns of shocks and subsequent covariations in national price, output, and consumption levels, often using quite sophisticated econometric techniques, has become a major industry. This has been encouraged both by statistical technology and recognition that, as Masson and Taylor put it "It is clear that there Is no single over riding criterion [for OCA's]...Increasingly analytical attentions has therefore turned to analysis of shocks affecting economies since shock absorption combines the net influence of several of the traditional criteria" (1994: 35). While certainly contributing a great deal to our knowledge there are also some major problems with the literature in this area. The biggest problem is that it is not always clear just how the effects of shocks relate to the traditional criteria, but that researchers often do not always stress this sufficiently. Thus the results of statistical exercises that should be viewed as contributing to our knowledge of a subset of criteria are sometimes offered or interpreted as offering a more complete answer. For example, some economists have agreed that there is a strong case for a common currency in Asia because on some

---

[10] In his initial contribution to OCA analysis Mundell (1960) took the Keynesian assumption of sticky wages and focused on the role of factor mobility.

[11] Conversely, new classical macro economists who assume highly flexible economics see much lower threshold levels of openness.

measures of patterns of shocks these countries score as well as pre EMU Europe.[12] This overlooks the many criteria on which many Asian countries score quite low, as well as assuming that Europe is a good benchmark.

Furthermore, the various major ways in which patterns of shocks are relevant for the choice of exchange rate regimes are often not made clear. At least three ways have been stressed in the literature. One is the cost of balance of payments adjustment. A second is the ability to use discretionary monetary policy for short and medium term macroeconomic stabilization and a third, stressed especially heavily in the theoretical literature, is effects as automatic stabilizers. These criteria will sometimes conflict with and other times reinforce one another just as the objectives of price and output stabilization can conflict or be complements depending upon the shock in question. Added to all this is the question of how reliable as guides to the future are past patterns of shocks. None of these concerns argues that we should pay no attention to the studies in this area, but they do suggest that careful attention needs to be given to the design and interpretation of such work.

Formal analysis of the effects of shocks generally assumes either that speculation is efficiently stabilizing or, as in the traditional Mundell-Fleming analysis, that it is effectively absent through the assumption of static expectations. Without at least some stabilizing speculation, however, freely floating rates would likely be highly volatile. It is well known that trade elasticities tend to rather low in the short run and that the resulting J curve effects would make flexible rates unstable in the short run in the absence of speculative smoothing. Thus a reasonable degree of financial market development is an essential prerequisite for a free float. Its absence would call for managed flexibility rather than fixed rates. To shift the case to favoring fixed rates what is needed is not just the absence of stabilizing speculation but the existence of actively destabilizing speculation that cannot be effectively offset through official management.

Critics of flexible rates often argue that they will be unstable and generate additional disequilibrium that would not occur under fixed rates. Likewise they assume that a country will be able to credibly fix against a stable country or groups of countries. Advocates of flexible rates tend to make opposite assumptions, stressing the role of flexible rates in helping to insulate countries from the effects of disturbances abroad. Critics of Britain's flexible rate such as Buiter (2000) argue that a large part of the movements in the pound have been due to destabilizing speculation. As Artis discusses in this volume, the HM Treasury's recent report pays considerable attention to challenging this view.

Similarly in Canada, critics of Canada's floating rate such as Grubel and Harris argue that much of the decline of the Canadian dollar has been due to unjustified speculation while the Bank of Canada and academic economists favorable to flexible rates such as David Laidler argue that most of the decline was due to fundamentals. This issue prompted heated debate at the conference on which this volume is based. The technical research on this issue makes it clear that neither of the extreme views of fully efficient speculation at all times nor of persistent wildly destabilizing speculation are supported by the evidence, but this leaves a wide gray area within which analysts may reasonably disagree.

In the case of Canada, it seems highly unlikely that all of the decline of the Canadian dollar over the past decade was due to destabilizing speculation. If even half of the decline

---

[12] See, for example Kwack, Lee, and Ahn (2003). For more detailed critiques of examples of such analyses see Willett and Maskay (2003).

were due to fundamentals, then this would have required an enormous amount of adjustment to have been carried out domestically. It is difficult to believe that the required deflation could have been managed without substantial unemployment and lost growth. It has proven difficult, however, to get advocates for fixed exchange rates for Canada to take this counter factual scenario seriously. While the advocates of fixed exchange rates for Canada include some distinguished economists who have made important contributions to the analysis of exchange rate issues, on this topic they have generally acted more like debaters than open-minded researchers.

There is also much debate about the extent to which patterns of disturbances are exogenous or endogenous to the choice of exchange rate regimes. For example, while it has been traditionally argued that countries with substantial differences in inflation rates make poor candidates for a common currency, advocates of fixed rates often argue that countries with high inflation rates should see this as a golden opportunity to use fixed exchange rates to import discipline from the low inflation country. Sometimes authors even list the seemingly contradictory conditions of high inflation (need for discipline) and stable relative prices with the anchor as criteria in the some papers.[13] The key making these two criteria consistent, of course, is that fixing the exchange rate be capable of bringing inflation down to the anchor country's level.[14]

Exchange rate based stabilization or the use of the exchange rate as a nominal anchor may favorably influence expectation and establish credibility more quickly. The development of emphasis on problems of time inconsistency in the macroeconomic literature established in a rational expectations framework an analog to Keynesian type analysis of the incentives for political business cycles and stimulated a search for "commitment technologies" to help overcome resulting inflationary basis. Exchange rate pegging became the instrument of choice for many economists and officials. The successful disinflations of the members of the European Monetary System in the late 1970s and early 1980s were widely cited as examples of the benefits of such exchange rate discipline by European and IMF officials, despite subsequent research that questioned whether the EMS countries did in fact disinflate at lower cost than the industrial countries with flexible exchange rates.[15] For the developing countries, experience shows that this sometimes works and that more often it does not, but there are enough examples on each side to keep the debate going.[16]

Advocates of fixed rates also often argue that because labor market rigidities are more costly under fixed rates, their adoption will for greater labor market flexibility. Both of these types of strategies, which go under the label of endogenous OCA theory, in effect commit the economy to a game of chicken. For Argentina, the balance worked well in the short run, but not in the longer-run.[17] This is likely not an atypical experience. Fortunately, the euro zone didn't start from such a situation of large initial disequilibrium, but the process to date of increasing labor market flexibility to deal with emerging imbalances has not been promising. Howarth notes in his contribution to this volume that perceptions that the euro countries have made little progress on this score have reinforced views in Britain that the British economy is

---

[13] See Gale and Vines (2002).

[14] Actually the requirement is even stronger than this since a price level differential will have accumulated during the process of disinflation.

[15] See Westbrook and Willett (1999).

[16] See Edwards (2003), Martin, Westbrook, and Willett (1999), and Willett (1998).

[17] See Willett (2002).

doing better than the euro economies and has contributed to the predominantly negative attitude of the British public toward joining the euro. (Elite opinion in Britain is much more positive.)

Another method of offsetting or reducing the need for undesirable adjustments is through fiscal transfer. Thus starting with Peter Kenen a number of economists have stressed that high levels of fiscal integration across countries can contribute importantly to the smooth operation of common currencies. On the other hand, highly divergent fiscal policies can be a major source of pressure on currency areas. There has been considerable debate over the degree to which the adoption of fixed exchange rates will automatically discipline fiscal policies. The evidence from Italy and Argentina suggests that rather than providing discipline, fixed rates may in the short run make it easier to finance budget deficits and hence reduce discipline.[18] Recent OCA analysis has also emphasized the political cost of fixed rates in allowing inflation taxes, i.e. seigniorage, to be set independently. This has replaced the initial Keynesian Phillips curve arguments for why countries might prefer different rates of inflation. From the standpoint of optimal policy, this should make little to industrial countries whose economically optimal rates of inflation are low.[19] Politically optimal rates may be much higher, however, and with weak governments inflation is often a residual method of finance.[20]

This again illustrates the importance of the political assumptions underlying economic analysis. While there is still a long way to go, recent OCA analysis by economists has been paying greatly increased attention to political considerations. While such political attention has often involved highly questionable ad hoc assumptions, there is also a healthy trend toward more systematic political economy analysis. Many economists involving in international monetary economics now recognize that some of the most important requirements for a currency area to function well are political. Where there is a substantial political desire for a currency area, not all of the OCA criteria need to be met for the currency regime to be workable. The less the criteria are met, however, the greater will be the economic costs. As was sadly illustrated by the recent case of Argentina, if a number of important economic criteria are not met, the costs can be considerable. Argentina scored high on the currency substitution and need for discipline criteria, but it was a relatively closed economy with only a small proportion of its trade with its anchor country, the United States. Its labor markets were fairly rigid. While the adoption of Argentina's fixed rate system does appear to have contributed to an increase in flexibility, it did so by far less than enough to avoid high unemployment when adverse shocks occurred. Furthermore, while the fixed rate was quite successful in imposing monetary discipline, this was not duplicated with fiscal policy. Thus Argentina stands as a vivid example of the costs of not taking seriously the importance of all of the major OCA criteria reviewed above.[21]

Indeed the number of these criteria suggest that relatively hew countries are likely to meet the criteria for either extreme of fully fixed or completely free floating to be optimal. The implications of this are explored in the next sections.

---

[18] See Willett (2000a) and (2001b).
[19] See Banaian, McClure, and Willett (1994).
[20] See Willett and Banaian (1996).
[21] See Willett (2002).

THE PROBLEM OF UNSTABLE INTERMEDIATE REGIMES

The review in the preceding section indicated that there are a number of important OCA. Many, if not most, countries will not fit well all of the criteria for making fixed rate optimal. The same can be said with respect to pure float, however. For most countries, the relative weights given to external versus internal considerations in setting domestic macroeconomic policy should be neither zero nor one hundred percent. In other words, most countries should have intermediate exchange rate regimes, or as I have put it elsewhere, "Fear of floating needn't imply fixed exchange rates" (Willett 2003b). This conclusion, however, is in sharp conflict with the bi-polar view of exchange rate regimes that has gained great popularity in recent years as a result of the rash of international currency crises. There is general agreement among international monetary experts about the validity of the weaker forms of the unstable middle hypothesis. In a world of substantial capital mobility, the traditional narrow band adjustable peg regime of the Bretton Woods variety is clearly inherently unstable. It is less clear, however, that therefore to avoid currency crises one must go all the way to one corner solution or the other, i.e. fully fixed or freely floating exchange rates. The track record of managed floats and crawling band regimes does not yield to easy interpretation. Some have worked well and others badly.

The reasons why some have worked well and others poorly seems likely to have at least as much to do with political economy considerations as with purely economic reasons. In short, while OCA analysis suggests that most countries should adopt some form of intermediate regimes, experience shows that such regimes have a tendency toward instability.

My recent research suggests that there are powerful political economy incentives for governments to operate intermediate regimes with insufficient flexibility to avoid the buildup of disequilibrium that leads to currency crisis.[22] Consequently in the design of intermediate regimes, careful attention needs to be given to political economy as well as technical economic considerations.

One important implication of my research is that rather than viewing crawling band regimes as a source of domestic discipline, as has been done in a lot of the literature advocating exchange rate based stabilization, regimes of limited exchange rate flexibility may be subject to the same types of time asymmetry pressures that generate incentives for political business cycles.[23] Thus to help avoid crises there is a strong case for insulating both exchange rate and monetary policy makers from short-run political pressures.

This potential instability of intermediate regimes was a major factor in promoting the creation of the euro. While the exchange rate mechanism of the European Monetary System was designed to be considerably more flexible than the narrow band adjustable peg adopted at Bretton Woods, over time it developed similar rigidities. This in turn, was a major contributing factor to the currency crises of the early 1990s. The failure of this intermediate option generated a move toward greater flexibility in the short run, but acceleration toward monetary union over the longer run. On the other hand, the collapse of Mexico's crawling band regime at the end of 1994 resulted in a move toward greater flexibility that has been sustained, albeit not without considerable debate.[24]

---

[22] See Willett (2004).
[23] See Willett (1998) and (2001b).
[24] See Auerbach and Flores (2003).

Some regimes of crawling bands have worked well (Chile, Poland and Hungary provide examples), but the overall record is far from stellar. In general, managed flexibility appears to provide a more stable alternative, although the Asian crisis shows that many regimes officially listed as managed floats have considerable de facto rigidity.[25] Britain and Canada have both suffered periods of poor discretionary exchange rate management. Examples are Britain's shadowing of the DM under Chancellor Lawson and Canada's disruptive end to its floating regime of the 1950s. Over all, however, intervention has generally been light and management sensible in both countries. Thus the danger of political manipulation leading to currency crisis looks low well below average for both countries.

THE POLITICS OF CURRENCY UNIONS

The natural transition from OCA to political economy considerations is to focus on distributional effects. Since fixed rates give more primacy to the international sectors and flexible rates to the internal sectors, we would expect distribution considerations to generally reinforce the conclusions of the OCA efficiency analysis that the relative size of the internal and external sectors will be an important factor in the choice of exchange rate regimes.[26] On both grounds, we would expect to find currency boards to be adopted primarily by small open economies and this is indeed generally the case. Argentina was an important exception, but this was not an experiment that ended well.

The politics of the formation of the euro zone were much more complicated than for unilateral adoption of currency boards, but even in the euro case the leading economy advocates of EMU were the large multinational businesses and financial institutions that stood to gain particularly from a fixed rate system, while workers, owners, and managers of smaller, more domestically oriented firms have tended to be skeptical.[27] Of course, as we know from the political economy of trade policy,[28] we cannot always predict political outcomes just from counting the number of gainers and losers. Rational ignorance and free rider problems explain why small groups are often much more politically influenced than large but poorly informed and organized groups.

Given the relatively modest levels of international economic cooperation that one generally observes, we would expect that both governments and the public have a bias in favor of preserving national autonomy. Thus, we would expect a bias against fixed exchange rates. Running counter to this could be informational and analytical biases that would lead to under-appreciation of the implied constraints that fixed exchange rates would place on domestic policy. This appears to be the case even among many of the relatively well-informed advocates of fixed exchange rates among multinational corporations. There is likely

---

[25] See Willett et al (2003).

[26] Such distributional considerations have been especially emphasized by Jeffrey Frieden. See for example, Frieden and Stein (2001). As a reviewer noted, the economic gainers and losers from a currency union due not translate perfectly into the international and domestic sectors. While for analytic tractability our theoretical models usually make a sharp distinction between traded and nontraded goods, in reality there is a continuum of degrees of trade versus non tradeness. Furthermore, even firms that have no direct international connections can be influenced by the behavior of firms that do.

[27] See for example, Eichengreen and Frieden (1994), Hefeker (1997), and the papers by Helleiner and Howarth in this volume.

[28] See the analysis and references in Kaempfer, Tower, and Willett (2003).

a bias toward a better understanding of the direct gains from fixed rates in making international business easier than of the indirect constraints that this will imply for national macroeconomic policies. Of course as these constraints become visible in practice, as in the case of the recent German recession, greater recognition should result. There is little question that perceptions that their economies are doing better than the major euro economies substantially increased opposition in Britain and Sweden to joining the euro zone.

Because of the likely relatively low levels of relevant information and high uncertainty about the most relevant analytic models, we would expect nationalists to exaggerate the costs of giving up the home currency while those associated with multinational institutions would tend to exaggerate the benefits.[29] This has indeed typically been the case. What was unusual in the case of the creation of the euro was the success of political leaders in linking monetary union to the broader objectives of the European Union.[30] A small euro area may well have made sense on OCA grounds, but few experts in OCA analysis believe that the broad euro area that has emerged has much to do with OCA criteria.[31] (Both large and small countries entered and both large and small stayed out; there is little correlation between OCA criteria and the composition of the ins and outs.)

Several types of groups have been especially active in generating discussions of currency unions. One group consists of political leaders who seek to gain credit for farsighted statesman like actions and/or the benefits of a quick fix. In both Latin America and Asia there - have been calls for regional monetary integration to avoid the effects of currency fluctuations and to provide a stronger basis for regional integration. For a long time to come, however, such talk is likely to remain just talk. For most of the regions, the political pre-conditions for monetary union more closely approximate the Europe of a century ago than the Europe of the post war period.

More relevant for non-European regions is that many of the benefits of adopting fixed exchange rates tend to show up more quickly, than the costs. Favorable effects on confidence and inflationary expectations tend to occur quickly while the costs of recessions due to the development of overvalued currencies tend to not begin for several years. Such considerations are likely to weigh particularly heavily in cases of high inflation and domestic political instability. This helps explain the adoption of currency boards by both Argentina and Ecuador. Such conditions clearly do not apply to the countries that are the focus for this conference, Canada and the United Kingdom. However, some advocates of fixed rates for Canada have attempted to argue that flexible rates have been the cause of unsatisfactory rates of productivity growth.[32] While a good bit less potent than the economic distress of Argentina and Ecuador, this quick fix argument for fixed rates has enjoyed some currency in Canada.

It is an interesting question whether such time asymmetry considerations were important for the development of the EMS and the euro. Economists have frequently ascribed the desire to generate credibility to the formation of the EMS, but this was a rationale that was developed primarily after the EMS was already in operation. The initial focus was more on limiting the size of exchange-rate fluctuations.

---

[29] As Helleiner discusses, this latter effect has been muted in Canada.
[30] See, for example, Pauly (forthcoming) and Willett (2000b).
[31] See, for example, De Grauwe (1997).
[32] For examples of the debate in Canada, see the contributions in this volume and in Salvatore, Dean, and Willett (2003).

A reviewer rightly suggested that my statements about time asymmetries in an initial draft seemed too sweeping. Noting the importance of whether countries peg at the 'right' rate and adopt appropriate policies; the reviewer pointed out that some EMS participants found membership a struggle at first and doubted whether many EU states, with the possible exception of Italy, were allocated to the EMU by thoughts of quick fixes and early benefits. With respect to the EMU I believe that these doubts are well taken. With Europe the most relevant time asymmetries were political not economic. The primary motivations for EMU in the first place were political and desire to be in the inner club was a major motivation for some countries. Furthermore, the Maastricht entry requirements nullified much of the time asymmetry of unilateral fixes from a disequilibrium position by requiring substantial adjustment for most countries before entry.

A second group of advocates for currency union or dollarization are academics who can attract public (and sometimes also academic) attention by promulgating highly imbalanced treatments of the costs and benefits of adopting fixed exchange rates. I have analyzed several examples of such highly misleading policy advocacy pieces in my recent paper on "Truth in Advertising and the Great Dollarization Scam" (2001a). A third group is multinational enterprises that stand to gain particularly from the adoption of fixed exchange rates. Not surprisingly we find that in Europe large multinational corporations have been much stronger supporters of monetary union than small, domestically oriented firms.[33] An interested point noted by Helleiner is that while this argument does fit well with the lobbying of the city in London, it fits much less well for Canada. For example, most of the major banks in Canada favor maintaining a flexible rate, understanding that this is necessary to preserve domestic monetary autonomy. A second reason is fear that under a currency union they would face more competition from US banks.

With respect to the potential entrants into the euro zone itself, we would have a fourth class of advocates who see euro membership primarily in terms of broader political objectives. Consider, for example, the fear that EU member states that do not adopt the euro will have less political influence in Europe and will be thought of as second-class citizens. This is likely to be a much more important consideration to the political leaders who will see themselves exerting the increased leverage and avoiding stigma than there are for the public at large. Thus it is not surprising that European political leaders have tended to be stronger supporters for the euro than their publics. The median voter model does have a good deal of explanatory power, but not for the initial decisions on membership in the euro zone; these were driven by elite opinion. For many of the latter entrants referenda were mandated, and in these cases the incidence of entry has been much lowered.[34]

We still have much to learn about the range of domestic and international political considerations that may influence national decisions on currency policies and how their relative influence varies in different situations. It is interesting that the three papers in the Salvatore, Dean, and Willett (2003) volume on dollarization that focus on political economy

---

[33] Again see the papers by Helleiner and Howarth in this volume.

[34] For the new EU entrants, eventual adoption of the euro is required so that this factor is less relevant. Most of the new accession countries have small open economies that make them strong candidates for adopting the euro on OCA grounds. (Poland is the major exception). Thus, for most accession countries the key issues involve the transition path for entry. Sadly, some in the EU establishment have failed to learn the lessons of the danger of narrow band pegs in a world of substantial capital mobility and are pushing for an exact replica of the old Maastricht entry requirements for the accession countries. Hopefully, this can be headed off by more sensible voices.

aspects of dollarization in Latin America all take different approaches. Jürgen Schuldt of the Universidad del Pacifico in Lima, Peru sees dollarization as inevitable and bases his argument heavily on his perception of how the United States sees this in its economic and political interests. Jerry Cohen offers a quite different interpretation of US interests. His analysis puts heavy emphasis on international power relationships, reflecting the realist paradigm in international relations theory. On the other hand, Nancy Auerbach and Aldo Flores-Quiroga in their analysis of Mexico place greater emphasis on the roles of domestic politics and the role of interest groups. The wide range of types of political considerations that can influence the choice of currency regimes is nicely illustrated by the papers by Helleiner and Howarth in this volume. Their careful analyses clearly demonstrate that we should be as wary of accepting political economy arguments that rest on a single factor or point of view as we should be of economic arguments for the desirability of a particular exchange rate regime based on only one or two considerations. Furthermore, as with the economic effects of exchange rate regimes, the weight of various political economy influences can vary substantially from one country to another.

THE UK'S FIVE TESTS

Chancellor Brown has promised the British government's decision on membership in the euro would be based on purely economic considerations. If true, this would make the UK unique among the countries that have considered joining the euro zone. As is discussed in the papers by Artis and by Howarth in this volume, few political commentators buy the Chancellor's assertion. Clearly influencing the Labor government's position are differences between the Prime Minister and Chancellor and concerns that a referenda on joining the euro not be lost. This does not mean, however, that the Treasury's studies are all a sham. As Artis notes, their technical quality is quite high and they have provided a great deal of useful information. As is illustrated by the number of criteria that OCA theory has developed, there are no objective statistical exercises that can give definitive answers.

The Treasury's five tests are of two types. One involves convergence of the UK and euro zone economies. It asks, if you want to go in, is this a good time? Its focus mirrors the convergence criteria of the Maastricht treaty. The much more important question, however, is whether the UK should go in at all. One can easily have cyclical convergence today and divergence tomorrow. Thus the Treasury quite wisely demands a second test: is there sufficient flexibility in the economy if problems emerge? The recent disaster in Argentina demonstrated that its economy did not have the flexibility to make a fixed exchange rate work well; and strains are already beginning to show in several continental euro-participants, notably Germany.

It is important not to take Germany, or others of the less flexible current euro-economies, as the standard. Many of the initial entrants went in with their fingers crossed, hoping membership might make it easier to push through the reforms their own countries needed to make their economies more flexible. Unfortunately this has happened only to a limited degree.[35] Where rigidities exist, it is usually not because of stupidity, but because special-

---

[35] See, for example, the UK Treasury's report on "EMU and Labour Market Flexibility" (2003). More progress appears to have been made in the smaller than in the larger euro economies.

interest groups are protected by them. The economics of creating more flexibility is simple. The politics of it is daunting.

The importance of this point has been missed by some enthusiasts for endogenous OCA theory, who argue that one shouldn't worry about the preconditions of fixed exchange rates to work well since the adoption of fixed rates will force desirable changes. It is certainly correct that the adoption of fixed rates may induce changes in trade patterns, the degree of openness, and flexibility of the economy, and in general, we would expect these changes to be in the direction of better meeting OCA criteria. However, the political influence of entrenched interests suggests that expected changes should be much less than would be implied by models of economic optimization.

Chancellor Brown's three other tests are: Would joining create better conditions for firms investing in Britain? Would the competitive position of the UK financial services industry be improved? (This is clearly a special interest consideration, but one that has long been influential.) And, most important: would joining EMU promote higher growth, stability, and a lasting increase in jobs?

This last test really subsumes the answers to the other four. It is the answer that's tricky, resting on a large body of often-conflicting evidence and dicey forecasts. Neither Britain nor Canada is so huge or so tiny that fixed or flexible exchange rates are obviously the best choice. Whether the HM Treasury's conclusions are on the firmest grounds is the emphasis on things that need to be done to make a fixed rate regime work better for the UK. By and large, these are measures that would also be desirable even if flexible rates were maintained.

CONCLUDING REMARKS I: A RECOMMENDED SEVEN STEP PROGRAM FOR POLITICAL ECONOMOY ANALYSIS

This paper has argued that OCA theory presents a valuable framework for analyzing the normative economic issues involved in currency choice, and that it is, likewise, a useful starting point for the development of a broader framework to analyze the positive political economy of currency choices.

We have seen that in contrast to many popular or advocacy pieces, numerous considerations are relevant to both OCA and political economy analysis. Single factor theories typically offer strong conclusions, but at the cost that they are often seriously deficient. A moment's reflection should make this obvious. OCA analysis subsumes most of the controversies about domestic macroeconomic policy with a number of international complications added. And then there's the politics. Here political considerations come in two forms. One is that economic policy decisions are made through the political process. The second is that non economic, i.e. political, objectives can be important.

I have suggested in this paper a framework for synthesizing such considerations. It is based on the assumption that all policy decisions are ultimately political, but that economic factors often play an important role. Thus we can start with the pure economists' focus on effects on aggregate economic efficiency. For the issue at hand, such analysis is provided by OCA theory. Concerns with political salience mean that we cannot stop here, however. How the resulting gains and losses are distributed may be as or more important than the net aggregates. Furthermore, we must recognize that actions are based on perceptions. Especially where widely distributed many effects may be little noticed while others may be wrongly interpreted. Thus it is important to look at both the pattern of information and the mental models used by actors. Where costs and benefits have different time dimensions, both issues of asymmetries of awareness and of time rates of discount become important.

Once people have formed perceptions of their economic interests, there still may be tremendous differences in whether and how politically effectively they act on these perceived interests. Here both institutional structures and the types of free rider problems emphasized in public choice analysis are important. Political aggregation mechanisms may vary substantially not only from country to country but also from issue to issue. Thus, for example, economic interest groups are likely to be much more important for trade than for monetary issues and for the latter whether decisions are made by the government or an independent central bank can be quite important, as is the actual degree of independence of the central bank.

Even after all of these considérations we must recognize that non economic objectives can also be important. Indeed for issues of monetary union they are quite often paramount. What non economic issues are important will vary from country to country and need to subject to all of levels or types of analysis just discussed for economic considerations. Just as economic treatments of currency issues have often suffered from an excessively narrow focus, so frequently have discussions of the politics of economic policy discussions. Seldom will just one political objective or group be relevant. In general, the political side-of good political economy analysis will need to be as nuanced as the economic side.

To summarize, the framework proposed here has the following key elements:

1. Start with OCA analysis.
2. Add distributional considerations and time asymmetries.
3. Recognize the possibilities of limited information and differences in mental models in influencing actors' perceptions of their interests.
4. Then consider how groups and individuals are weighted in the political process, giving attention to collective action problems and the role of institutional arrangements.
5. Add consideration of salient non economic, i.e. political, objectives.
6. Repeat the types of analysis in 3 and 4.
7. Weigh the relative importance of the economic and non economic objectives.

This recommended seven step program is certainly not the only way to go about attempting to synthesize economic and political economy considerations and may well not prove to be the best, but I believe that it offers the prospect for fruitful analysis.

CONCLUDING REMARKS II: CHOICE UNDER UNCERTAINTY

One way of describing our current state of economic knowledge relative to the currency choices of countries like Britain and Canada is that there is considerable uncertainty about how monetary union would work for them. Any sound policy analysis should explicitly take this uncertainty into account and pay attention to what is known about the potential costs of type I versus type II errors, i.e., of choosing a fixed rate when a flexible one would have been better and vice versa.

This suggests that for both Britain and Canada, their decisions should be biased toward the continuation of the status quo. We cannot be sure that the adoption of fixed exchange rates or monetary unit would not, on balance, improve the economic performance of either country. However, despite the charges of some critics, the experiences of neither currency under flexible rates have been particularly bad relative to their larger monetary neighbors.[36] Indeed, Chancellor Brown has argued that Britain's economic performance has been far superior to that of its euro neighbors. On the other hand, the potential for the adoption of fixed exchange rates to generate high domestic economic costs is considerable. The contributors to our volume differ greatly about how much of the decline in the Canadian relative to US dollar over the past decade was due to economic foundation versus destabilizing capital flow. For the sake of argument suppose we give equal weight to both views and conclude that one half of the decline was due to fundamentals. This implies that, had Canada adopted a fixed exchange rate with the US dollar, nominal income in Canada would have had to fall substantially. It seems highly unrealistic to believe that in the short run most of this decline would have been achieved by falling prices rather than rising unemployment. Hence risk aversion under uncertainty would suggest a bias toward some form of flexible rates with the weight to be given to external developments in setting domestic monetary policy-being the key issue on which economic debate should focus.

It is certainly possible that the adoption of fixed exchange rates or a common currency will create incentives for the development of more effective domestic adjustment mechanisms. However, there is good reason to question the strength of these incentives relative to the political economy pressures to maintain the status quo. We do not yet have a lot of directly relevant experience on this issue to analyze, but the current euro experiment will vastly increase our data points.

Thus most countries considering the adoption of a hard fix for their currencies would be best served by a wait and see attitude. For Britain and Canada this economic conclusion is unlikely to be offset by political considerations in the near future. Typically considerations of national sovereignty will generate a political predisposition against forming monetary unions. The European project created an important counter to this effect and was in my judgment the single most important factor leading to European monetary union. While there has been much political talk of monetary unions in other regions, I doubt that the political forces which generated the euro are likely to be duplicated elsewhere within the next few decades.[37]

As an issue of positive political economy I find it difficult to disagree with the comments of an anonymous reviewer who argued that "neither is likely to enter the respective monetary union that happens to be an offer unless a majority of voters can be persuaded that there will be large benefits from closer political union with their neighbors."

---

[36] I don't find convincing the arguments of a few Canadian economists that flexible rates have imposed a tremendous cost on Canada in terms of reduced productivity.

[37] The likelihood of the formation of a monetary union among a number of oil economies around the Persian Gulf is an exception. The political forces for monetary union are much weaker there than in Europe, but the costs of forgoing independent monetary policies are also far lower because of the much smaller role of private markets.

REFERENCES

Artis, Michael. "Evaluating Britain's Five Tests in Light of Economic Theory" in this volume.

Auerbach, Nancy and Aldo Flores-Quiroga. (2003). "The Political Economy of Dollarization in Mexico" in *The Dollarization Debate*. Edited by Dominick Salvatore, James W. Dean, and Thomas D. Willett. Oxford University Press, New York, 266-282.

Banaian, King, J. Harold McClure, Jr. and Thomas Willett. (1994). "Inflation Uncertainty and the Optimal Inflation Tax," *Kredit and Kapital*, Heftl, pp.30-42.

Bayoumi, Tamim and Barry Eichengreen (1994). *One Money or Many?* Princeton Studies in International Finance, No. 76.

Buiter, Willem H. (2000). "Optimal Currency Areas" *Scottish Journal of Political Economy*, Vol.47, No.3, August, pp. 213-250.

Cohen, Benjamin J. (2003). "Monetary Union: The Political Dimension" in *The Dollarization Debate*. Edited by Dominick Salvatore, James W. Dean, and Thomas D. Willett. Oxford University Press, New York, 221-237.

Edwards, Sebastian. (2003). "Dollarization: Myths and Realities" in *The Dollarization Debate*. Edited by Dominick Salvatore, James W. Dean, and Thomas D. Willett. Oxford University Press, New York, 111-128.

Eichengreen, Barry, and Jeffry Frieden, eds. (1994). *The Political Economy of European Monetary Unification*. Boulder, Colo.: Westview Press.

European Commission (1990). *One Money, One Market*.

Frankel, Jeffrey A. and Andrew K. Rose. (1998). "The Endogeneity of the Optimum Currency Area Criteria" *Economic Journal* Vol. 108, July: 1009-25.

Frieden, Jeffry and Ernesto Stein, eds. (2001). *The Currency Game: Exchange Rate Politics in Latin America*. Washington, D.C.: Inter-American Development Bank.

Gale, Doughlas and Xavier Vines (2002). "Dollarization, Bailouts, and the Stability of the Banking System" Quarterly *Journal of Economics*, May.

Goodhart, Charles. (1995). "The Political Economy of Monetary Union," in Peter B. Kenen, ed., *Understanding Interdependence: The Macroeconomics of the Open Economy*. Pp. 450–505. Princeton: Princeton University Press.

Grauwe, Paul de. (1997). *The Economics of Monetary Integration*. New York: Oxford University Press.

Hefeker, Carsten. (1997). *Interest Groups and Monetary Integration*. Boulder: Westview Press.

Helleiner, Eric. "The Fixation with Floating: The Political Basis of Canada's Exchange Rate Regime" this volume.

Howarth, David "Explaining British Policy on the Euro" this volume.

HM Treasury. (2003). UK Membership in the Single Currency: An Assessment of the Five Tests, June, www.hm-treasury.gov.uk.

Kaempfer, William, Ed Tower, and Thomas Willett. (2003). "Trade Protectionism" in Charles Rowley and Fredrich Schneider, eds. *Encyclopedia of Public Choice*.

Kenen, Peter. (1969). "The Theory of Optimum Currency Areas: An Eclectic View," in Robert A. Mundell and Alexander K. Swoboda (eds.) *Monetary Problems of the International Economy*. Chicago: University of Chicago, pp. 41-60.

Krugman, Paul. (1995). "What Do We Need to Know About the International Monetary System?" in Peter B. Kenen (eds.) *Understanding Interdependence*. Princeton: Princeton University Press, pp. 509 - 30.

Kwack, Sung Yeung, Choong Yong Ahn, and Young-Sun Lee. (2003). "Monetary Cooperation in East Asia: Exchange Rate, Monetary Policy and Financial Markets Issues," Korean Institute For International Economic Policy.

Martin, Pamela, Jilleen Westbrook, and Thomas D. Willett. (1999). "Exchange Rates Based Stabilization Policy in Latin America," in Richard Sweeney, Clas Wihlborg, and Thomas D. Willett, eds., *Exchange Rate Policies for Emerging Markets*. Pp.141-64. Boulder, Colo.: Westview Press.

Masson, Paul R. and Mark P. Taylor, eds. (1993). *Policy Issues in the Operation of Currency Unions*. Great Britain: Cambridge University Press.

Masson, Paul and Mark P. Taylor. (1994). "Optimal Currency Areas: A Fresh Look at the Traditional Critèria," in Pierre Siklos (eds.) *Varieties of Monetary Reform*. Boston: Kluwer, pp.23-44.

McKinnon, Ronald I. (1963). "Optimum Currency Areas," *American Economic Review, 53,* 717-25.

Mundell, Robert A. (1961). "A Theory of Optimum Currency Areas," *American Economic Review, 51,* 657-65.

Pauly, Louis W. "The Politics of EMU" in *Governance and Legitimacy in EMU*, edited by Loukas Tsoukalis, Pierre Werner Programme on Monetary Union, The Robert Schuman Centre for Advanced Studies, Fiesole, Italy: European University Institute, forthcoming.

Schuldt, Jürgen. (2003) "Latin American Official Dollarization: Political Economy Aspects" in *The Dollarization Debate*. Edited by Dominick Salvatore, James W. Dean, and Thomas D. Willett. Oxford University Press, New York, 238-265.

Tavlas, George S. (1994). "Theory of monetary integration". *Open Economies Review (Netherlands)*. March 1994, 5, 211-230.

Tavlas, George S. (1993). "The New Theory of Optimum Currency Areas." *The World Economy*.

Tower, Edward, and Thomas D. Willett. (1976). *The Theory of Optimum Currency Areas and Exchange Rate Flexibility*. (Special Papers in International Economics No. 11). International Finance Section, Department of Economics, Princeton University.

Westbrook, Jilleen and Thomas Willett. (1999). "Exchange Rates as Nominal Anchors: An Overview of the Issues," in Richard Sweeny, Clas Wihlborg, and Thomas Willett (eds.) *Exchange Rate Policies for Emerging Economies*. Boulder, Colorado: Westview Press, pp.83 – 112.

Wihlborg, Clas and Thomas Willett. (1999). "The Relevance of Optimum Currency Area Approach for Exchange Rate Policies in Emerging Market Economies," in Richard Sweeney, Clas Wihlborg, and Thomas Willett, eds. *Exchange-Rate Polices for Emerging Market Economies,* Westview Press.

Willett, Thomas D. and Nephil Matangi Maskay. (2003). "Some Conceptual Distinctions Relevant for Applied OCA Analysis," presented at the WEA Meetings in Denver, July 2003.

Willett, Thomas D. and King Banaian. (1996). "Currency Substitution and Seniorage Considerations in the Choice of Currency Policies," in Paul Mizen and Eric Pentecost (eds.) *The Macroeconomics of International Currencies*, Edward Elgar, pp.77-95.

Willett, Thomas D. (2004). "The Political Economy of Exchange Rate Regimes and Currency Crises," prepared for the Claremont Conference on the Political Economy of Exchange Rates, April 1 – 2, 2004.

_____. (2003a). "The OCA Approach to Exchange Rate Regimes: A Perspective on Recent Developments." In Dominick Salvatore, James Dean, and Thomas Willett (eds.), *The Dollarization Debate.* Oxford University Press.

_____. (2003b). "Fear of Floating Needn't Imply Fixed Rates: An OCA Approach to the Operation of Stable Intermediate Currency Regimes". *Open Economies Review.* 14, 71 – 91.

_____. (2002). "Crying for Argentina," *The Milken Institute Review* 4, 2, (Second Quarter 2002), pp. 50-59.

_____. (2001a)."Truth in Advertising and the Great Dollarization Scam," *Journal of Policy Modeling* 23, April 2001, pp. 279-289.

_____. (2001b). "The Political Economy of External Discipline." Paper prepared for the 2001 Annual Meetings of the American Political Science Association, San Francisco, August 30- September 2, 2001.

_____. (2000a). "International Financial Markets as Sources of Crisis or Discipline". *Princeton Essays in International Finance.*

_____. (2000b). "Some Political Economy Aspects of EMU". *Journal of Policy Modeling,* May 2000, pp. 379-389.

_____. (1998). "The Credibility and Discipline Effects of Exchange Rates as Nominal Anchors," *The World Economy*, (August 1998), 303-326.

Williamson, John. 1996. *The Crawling Band as an Exchange Rate Regime.* Washington, D.C.: Institute for International Economics.

Wise, Carol, and Riordan Roett, eds. 2000. *Exchange Rate Politics in Latin America.* Washington, D.C.: Brookings Institution Press.

INDEX

E

F

N

Q

R